CIA OFF CAMPUS:
Building the Movement Against Agency Recruitment and Research

CIA OFF CAMPUS:
Building the Movement Against Agency Recruitment and Research

Ami Chen Mills

Second Edition

A Bill of Rights Foundation Book

South End Press
Boston, MA

Cover design by Nancy Adams
Cover photograph © Eugene Garcia
Text design and production by the South End Press collective
Illustrations by Peggy Lipschutz
First Edition, First Printing - April 1990
Second Printing - May 1990
Third Printing - December 1990
Second Edition, First Printing - June 1991
99 98 97 96 95 94 93 92 91   1 2 3 4 5 6 7 8 9

Library of Congress Cataloging-in-Publication Data
Mills, Ami Chen.
CIA off campus: building the movement against agency recruitment
and research / Ami Chen Mills.
p. cm.
"A Bill of Rights Foundation Book."
Includes bibliographical references and index.
ISBN 0-89608-404-3 : $25.00 – ISBN 0-89608-403-5 (pbk.) : $10.00
1. United States. Central Intelligence Agency–Officials and
employees–Recruiting. 2. College graduates–United
States–Recruiting. 3. Intelligence agents–United States–Recruiting.
I. Title.
JK468.I6M53   1991
353.001'31–dc20   91-13491   CIP

South End Press, 116 Saint Botolph Street, Boston, MA 02115

® GCIU

Table of Contents

WHO WE ARE   viii
CIA Off Campus National Clearinghouse

ACKNOWLEDGMENTS   ix

PREFACE   xi

FOREWORD   xiii
by Philip Agee

CHAPTER ONE   1
Company Crimes: The Case Against the CIA

   Domestic Law and the CIA Charter   2

   International Law   4
      The UN Charter•The OAS Charter•The Geneva
      Conventions•The Universal Declaration of Human Rights
      and the Convention Against Torture•The Genocide
      Convention•Nuremberg, the Supremacy Clause and
      Individual Responsibility•What Goes Around Comes
      Around: The CIA in the Persian Gulf

CHAPTER TWO   19
CIA *On* Campus:
The Covert Hand in the Academic Cookie Jar

   Student Recruiting   20
      Robbing the Cradle: CIA High School
      Recruiting•Recruitment of Foreign Students
      •The "Whole" Officer•In the Agency's Own Words

   Institutes, Faculty Recruiting and Research   29
      Officer in Residence: Studies in Artificial Intelligence
      •Institutes•Paid Professors: Moonlighting for the
      Agency•The CIA: An Equal Opportunity Employer

   Beyond Reseach: CIA-Sponsored Experiment and
   Training Programs   37

   Conclusion: Bedfellows of the Establishment   39

CHAPTER THREE   43
CIA *Off* Campus: Learning from the '80s
and Gearing Up for the '90s

Student Activism in the '80s   43
    Givin' It to 'Em • South Africa • Latin America • Women's
    Issues • Gay and Lesbian Rights • Students of Color
    • Palestinian Rights • U.S. Students for U.S. University
    Democracy • Coalition Building

Gearing Up for the CIA Off Campus Movement
in the '90s   52
    Organization: Building a Group • Overcoming Racism,
    Sexism and Heterosexism • Strategies • Support: Moral and
    Financial • Sowing Seeds: Education • Self-Education
    • Educating Others • And Now, Will the Real History
    Please Stand Up?

CHAPTER FOUR   73
Q & A on the CIA:
Nine Infamous Questions Get Answered

Isn't the CIA Saving the World?   73
From Foreign Policy to Freedom of Speech   81

CHAPTER FIVE   85
Word and Action: Building the Most Effective
CIA Off Campus Campaign

Before You Begin: Media Relations   85

Discovering CIA Activities on Campus
Above and Below the Floorboards   86
    Recruiting • Research and CIA-Paid Professors
    • Officers in Residence • Programs and Institutes

"Consensual Strategy":
Legitimizing Before Hell Raising   91
    Legitimization: Set Your Goals and Make Them Known
    • Use Existing Guidelines • Research City, State and
    International Law • Academic Codes • Student and Faculty
    Bodies • The Administration and Boards

No More Mister Nice Guy: Agitation and
Action   103
    Consensual Strategy and Militant Action: the Story of
    Boulder

CHAPTER SIX   111
**It's a Jungle Out There: The Consequences of
Activism and How to Deal with Them**

    Counter-Demonstrators:
    Why Don't You Go Get Your Own Issue?   112

    Big Brother Has a Club:
    Police Brutality and Arrests   114
        Author's Story: Friends in Strange Places

    Look Before You Leap:
    University Disciplinary Charges and Hearings   118
        Selective Use of Student Conduct Codes

    The Criminal Justice System   121
        Arrests • Jail • Court • The Best Defense

    Big Brother is One of You: Monitoring,
    Infiltration and Disruption of Domestic
    Activists   130
        A Police State to Call Our Own: A Brief History of Covert
        Operations Against U.S. Activists • The CIA and Student
        Groups: Footing the Bill for the National Student
        Association • Today's Threat: What Do Anti-CIA Activists
        Have to Fear? • What Can We Do?

CHAPTER SEVEN   137
**Claiming Victory: Turning the Tide of CIA Presence
on Campus and Expanding the Issue**

        College Anti-CIA Actions

    U.S. Foreign Policy   141

    Economic Conversion   142

APPENDICES   145

    Appendix A: Bibliography on the CIA and
    Covert Action   145

    Appendix B: Support Organizations and
    Resources   150

    Appendix C: Educational Resources   155

    Appendix D: Avoiding Police Violence   161

NOTES   165

INDEX   185

ABOUT THE AUTHOR   199

ABOUT SOUTH END PRESS   200

Who We Are: CIA Off Campus National Clearinghouse

In the course of working on the *CIA Off Campus* book project, the Bill of Rights Foundation established a clearinghouse for CIA Off Campus networking so that activists may share information and resources in the effort to expel the CIA and other covert operations agencies from our nation's campuses.

The Clearinghouse is in touch with people who are acting on the issue: experienced anti-CIA activists at schools around the country, ex-CIA officials, veterans, debaters, speakers and progressive lawyers. We have information on past and current anti-CIA actions and their outcomes and can help strategize for actions on your campus or in your community. Educational flyers, pamphlets and books are available on order.

We are currently expanding the Clearinghouse concept to include regional planning conferences and the development of a computerized network database. If you are looking for help or can provide resources for the CIA Off Campus National Clearinghouse, we want to hear from you. Tax deductible contributions to support the Clearinghouse are always appreciated. Please contact:

The Bill of Rights Foundation
523 South Plymouth Court, Suite 800
Chicago, Illinois 60605
(312) 939-0675
CIA Off Campus 24 Hour Hotline: (312) 427-4559

Acknowledgments

Special thanks to Liane Clorfene-Casten, Deborah Crawford, Vernon Elliott, Glen Good, Loie Hayes, Walt Herrs, Cinny Poppen and Louis Wolf for their sustained contributions to the content and editorial integrity of this book.

Thanks also to Philip Agee and Phil Agee Jr., Kathleen Aiken, Brenetta Howell Barrett, Chip Berlet, Rick Bluthenthal, Tom Burke, Jonathan Feldman, John Fish, Kit Gage, Brian Glick, Don Goldhamer, Louise Golland, Kevin Harris, Mark Heimbach, Janine Hoft, Clifford Jones, Jonathan Kehew, Christine Kelly, Ken Lawrence, Chuck Lippitz, Verne Lyon, Sean Maher, Ralph McGehee, Andy Norman, Travis Parchman, John Stockwell, Jimmy Walker, Bob Witanek, Jill Zemke and dozens of others who answered my questions and submitted to interviews.

The writing and original publication of this book was assisted by grants from the Lila Brier Lederman Fund, the J. Roderick MacArthur Foundation, the Funding Exchange/National Community Funds and the Alliance to End Repression.

Preface

In the fall of 1988, 16 people, including myself, were arrested in an anti-CIA recruitment demonstration outside Northwestern University's Placement Center. The demonstration—made up of about 150 students and community members—was the largest of its kind at Northwestern in almost a decade.

Six of us went on to a trial that finally ended in a compromise with the State's Attorney. All serious charges against us were dropped with the agreement that each of the six defendants would plead guilty to disorderly conduct and submit to one month of court-supervised probation. With the case settled, the most daunting task we faced was paying our legal fees that had escalated with each court appearance we made and each day of jury selection.

Fortunately, there were others in the community who supported our actions.

After our arrests, someone had the sense to call the Chicago Committee to Defend the Bill of Rights, the midwest affiliate of the National Committee Against Repressive Legislation (NCARL). NCARL led the fight in the 1960s against the House Un-American Activities Committee (HUAC); its founder, Frank Wilkinson, spent a year in prison for refusing to testify before the Committee. Since the demise of HUAC, NCARL has evolved and pursued two primary objectives: (1) ending FBI surveillance and harassment of Constitutionally-protected political activity and (2) abolishing covert actions by U.S. government agencies.

The Chicago Committee and the Northwestern protesters made a perfect match: the protesters needed moral and financial support and the Committee needed a grassroots entry to organize against covert actions. Together, we brought former CIA officer Verne Lyon to town for a fundraising benefit. We set up interviews on local radio talk shows. We hired two innovative, progressive lawyers. *And* we were able to pay them for their work.

After the trial, the relationship developed along less "defensive" lines. The Chicago Committee saw a need for a national collaborative effort to help prevent activists from repeating other activists' mistakes— and to share their success stories. After all, the college campus is the one place where the Central Intelligence Agency actually makes a public appearance and the one place that provides the CIA with most of its new blood.

The Bill of Rights Foundation was asked to design and fund an appropriate project. The Foundation hired me to compile information on anti-CIA actions at campuses around the country, organize it into readable form and provide some analysis of what worked and didn't work at different schools.

This book is the result of the efforts of at least three generations of activists opposing the undemocratic nature of the CIA. It combines the accumulated knowledge of anti-CIA activists across the nation with recent revelations of CIA campus activity and the wisdom of ex-agents like Philip Agee, Verne Lyon and Ralph McGehee. We hope that it furthers the efforts of those brave and dedicated souls who are teaching, marching, petitioning, demonstrating, sitting in, sneaking in and even going to jail to stop the atrocities of the CIA—and who can incorporate the CIA issue into an expanding progressive agenda for the 1990s.

Keep up the good work.

—Ami Chen Mills

Foreword

by Philip Agee

It was a cold November night at the University of Rhode Island as several hundred students sat watching the debate over the Central Intelligence Agency between representatives of the CIA and the American Civil Liberties Union. The student organizers had asked me to debate the Agency man, Arthur Hulnick, but as usual he refused to share the stage with me.

The debate was a supposed compromise by the University administration to satisfy student opposition to on-campus CIA recruiting which was scheduled for the following day. Since I couldn't participate in the debate the night before, the student opposition groups had asked me to speak at an outdoor rally at noon on recruitment day, on the steps of the Student Union just in front of the building where the recruitment interviews would be held. I agreed, but I arrived on campus the night before, just in time to watch the debate from a seat in the back of the auditorium. No surprises. The ACLU man attacked the CIA for "past abuses" and for covert actions that were so often "counter-productive." Silently I noted that "abuses and excesses" are commonplace concepts—and totally false. The CIA is an instrument of the President, always has been, and has no policy of its own. If it carries out assassinations, supports murderous security services and death squads, and overthrows democratically elected civilian governments in favor of military dictatorships—then it does all this on orders from the President of the day, not on its own.

The CIA man simply wrapped himself in the flag. Congress had duly established the CIA by law, and the Congressional oversight committees know everything the CIA does. Therefore every Agency operation is an element of our country's legitimate defense in a dangerous and hostile world. Only through free access to on-campus recruiting, he said, can the CIA find the one thousand or so new people it needs every year to replace those who retire or leave the Agency for other reasons.

I noticed as the evening went on that Hulnick was emphasizing the CIA's efforts against terrorism—as if to further justify anything they do—as well as the intellectual rigor required for analysis and problem solving. Before the debate was over, I decided to challenge him.

As soon as the discussion period began, I walked down to the microphones. After introducing myself and inviting people to the rally next day, I asked Hulnick why he hadn't said a word about the Agency's "liaison" operations. I explained to the audience that these were the ways that the CIA works with the security and intelligence services of other countries, sometimes through exchange of information, sometimes through joint operations. But liaison operations also include the CIA's support for other governments' security forces through training, equipment, money, guidance and information.

"Mr. Hulnick," I said, "I ask you to describe how the CIA is working day and night with the security and intelligence services of El Salvador, the same services that either directly or through their death squads have murdered some 70,000 people during the past eight years. Tell us how the United States, through the CIA, has become a part of all that carnage. And tell us about the CIA's similar operations with the Iranian SAVAK during the time of the Shah, with the Greek K.Y.P., with the South Korean CIA, with the services of the Pinochet dictatorship in Chile, with the Philippine services under the Marcos dictatorship, with the National Guard in Nicaragua under the Somoza dynasty, with the Bureau for Anti-Communist Repression in Cuba during the Batista dictatorship, with the Guatemalan security services during the 35 years of military dictatorship since the CIA destroyed democracy in that country. And tell us about the CIA's involvement in the torture practiced by every one of those services.

"More, Mr. Hulnick, about U.S. support for democracy. How do you justify CIA organization of, or support for, the overthrow of democratically elected civilian governments and their replacement with military dictatorships? You know the list, too, and it circles the globe during the forty years of the CIA's existence. How dare you come to a university and try to entice the best of American youth into working for Murder, Incorporated?"

Applause gave Hulnick time to think, but in the end he had only two comments. At first he said he was sorry, but that he could not discuss classified information. When the roar provoked by that answer died down, he added that in any case the Congress is fully informed of everything the CIA does. That remark simply provoked more catcalls and shouts demanding that he answer the questions. He didn't, or couldn't, because the operations I mentioned cannot be justified within accepted norms of ethics in this country.

The next day hundreds of students came and went as our three-hour rally progressed. Most of the time was spent in discussion which enabled those of us at the microphone to describe the CIA's activities and the reasons why they should not be allowed to recruit on college and university campuses. And from time to time our positions were challenged by people who supported the Agency's justifications.

I left the rally wishing that we could duplicate it on hundreds of campuses across the country. Certainly there is no shortage of former CIA officers who eventually turned against that work, and who would welcome the chance to participate with concerned student groups if asked.

This book is long overdue. The challenge set out is to restore, maintain and preserve the intellectual and moral tradition of higher learning. The CIA represents the dark side of U.S. foreign policy, and all who care must oppose its activities in every possible way. Rich in experiences of those who have already taken action, *CIA Off Campus: Building the Movement Against Agency Recruitment and Research* will be invaluable for those who want to act against CIA recruiting now and in the future.

—Philip Agee

This book is dedicated to everyone who cares and is making a stand,
to Ben and to my extended family.

CHAPTER ONE

Company Crimes:
The Case Against the CIA

They [the acts of the CIA] do not reflect the ideals which have given the people of this country and of the world hope for a better, fuller, fairer life.

Senator Frank Church[1]

The CIA poses the ultimate threat to democracy, and should be dismantled for the good of the United States and the world.

Ex-agent John Stockwell, 1988.[2]

The story of Ecuador at its most elevated and most humbled moments is told in bold colors on one wall of its National Congress Building. Oswaldo Guayasamin's mural depicts various symbols with historic significance to the people of Ecuador: the Andean symbol for the sun, the collective outcry of the dominated, faces of dictators, faces of humanists, images of oppression and of freedom.

One of the faces resembles a darkly shadowed skull wearing a combat helmet like those worn by Hitler's Schutzstaffel (S.S.). Inscribed on the helmet are three letters: CIA.

This grim depiction of one of the U.S. government's best funded and best protected organizations is weighted with meaning not just for Ecuadorans, but for Guatemalans, Salvadorans, Nicaraguans, Chileans, Brazilians, Argentineans, perhaps for most Latin Americans—not to mention the Vietnamese, Indonesians, Angolans, South Africans and millions of others who have suffered as a consequence of CIA actions.

This book is not meant to be a detailed recounting of CIA actions during the last half century.[3] It is primarily for those who have learned

enough and are ready to change the all-too-familiar and ferocious forces
that guide the CIA and its actions.

This book is especially for those in university settings who are
dedicated to making the CIA an *issue* on their campuses or in their
communities, those who can no longer accept the relative silence and
accompanying complicity of their peers every time the CIA comes in to
recruit, research or sponsor programs at their schools.

This book is for those who are interested in stopping the kinds of
actions that prompted Guayasamin to paint the skull and helmet on the
wall of the Congressional hall in Ecuador, who want to stop the blood-
shed and the suffering.

As one of the largest and best-funded secret organizations in the
world, the CIA seems a mammoth obstacle. But CIA actions *can* be
curtailed by an educated, united and active citizenry.

This means you. And it means knowing who or what is on your
side. Though activists often find themselves in confrontation with the
laws in this country, there are a body of laws, humanitarian in nature,
that support the actions of anti-CIA activists in the United States. According to international law expert Francis Anthony Boyle, "civil resistance activities" based on the supremacy of international law "represent
the last constitutional avenue open to the American people to preserve
their democratic form of government [and its] commitment to the rule
of law."[4]

Some of the Agency's most "successful" actions have involved the
gross violations of domestic and international law. Not only has the CIA
broken the rules of its own charter, but it has also dragged the entire
country into transgressions against the United Nations (UN) Charter,
the Organization of American States (OAS) Charter, the Geneva Conventions, the Universal Declaration of Human Rights, the Convention
Against Torture, the Genocide Convention and the Nuremberg Tribunal
Principles—all international agreements signed by the United States,
most *initiated* by the United States.[5]

Domestic Law and the CIA Charter

The following Agency activities are either infractions against the
CIA's own charter established under the National Security Act of 1947,
which prohibits the Agency from engaging in any kind of "internal
security functions,"[6] or are breaches of regular domestic law applying
both to citizens and government bodies.

- Domestic surveillance and, in cooperation with the FBI, infiltration of dissenting political groups in the United States—including students.[7]

During the Vietnam War the "CIA...conducted probes of the anti-war movement in clear violation of prohibitions against domestic spying."[8] In some cases, the Agency employed satellites to monitor demonstrations.[9] Additionally, the CIA has provided and continues to provide covert support and funding to academic associations and individuals, including university research departments and national student organizations.[10] Chapter Two will explore CIA-supported academic projects.

- Mind-control and drug experiments on unwitting American and Canadian victims through CIA programs like MKULTRA.

Canadian victims of some of these experiments have recently sued the Agency for irreparable mental damage. They claim that during the course of CIA-funded experimentation, they were "pumped full of LSD," given "massive doses of electric shock" and forced to listen to tape-recorded character attacks.[11] In fact, the Central Intelligence Agency introduced the drug LSD to the U.S. population through universities while testing its "truth serum" potential in the early 1950s.[12]

Almost 20 years and dozens of psychological casualties later, a study by the Bureau of Narcotics and Dangerous Drugs reported that LSD's "early use was among small groups of intellectuals at large eastern and west coast universities. It spread to undergraduate students, then to other campuses. Most often, users have been introduced to the drugs by persons of higher status. Teachers have influenced students; upperclassmen have influenced lower classmen."[13] Ironically, the CIA, during MKULTRA experimentation, unwittingly initiated the 1960s' psychedelic explosion.

- Support for drug runners exporting to the United States from Latin America and Southeast Asia's Golden Triangle.

John Hull, a self-admitted CIA liaison in Costa Rica, has been accused of using his ranch as a stopover for marijuana and cocaine flights from Colombia to the United States.[14] Oliver North's diary notes that at least one contra supply plane was "probably being used for drug runs into the U.S." and Hull concedes the CIA was fully aware the contras were involved in drug smuggling.[15] Convicted drug dealers in Miami have reported working closely with the CIA, running weapons to the contras in Nicaragua in exchange for legal protection and unrestricted passage across U.S. borders.[16] While Bush and other administration heavies ushered drug dealers across the nation's borders, Ron and Nancy Reagan inaugurated the "War on Drugs," little more than a massive public relations campaign designed to maintain the illusion that Cowboy Reagan was still fighting Bad Guys despite the meltdown of the Cold War.

From the late 1940s to the early 1970s, CIA operatives both directly and indirectly assisted underworld narcotics traffickers while combatting communism, leftism and neutrality in the heat of the first stages of the Cold War.[17] After World War II, CIA operations in Europe aimed at weakening the Italian Communist Party "made it possible for the Sicilian-American Mafia and the Corsican underworld to revive the international narcotics traffic" which had fallen apart during the war.[18]

In Southeast Asia, the CIA and the U.S. Agency for International Development (AID) knowingly supported opium and heroin dealers, supplying them with arms, ammunition, transportation of food supplies, buildings and "humanitarian aid" in exchange for mercenary forces or political leverage.[19] These dealers included the Kuomintang on the Chinese border, Meo tribesmen in Laos led by narcotics trafficker Vang Pao, warring groups in Burma and various political factions in South Vietnam during the Vietnam War.[20] CIA support often went beyond a see-no-evil complicity into active participation in the collection, manufacture and transport of opium and heroin. The CIA airline company in Southeast Asia, Air America, transported opium from mountainous growing regions to distribution centers in Laos. At least one heroin production factory was based at CIA operation headquarters in Laos, and opium growers reported that during air pickups "the helicopter pilots were always Americans."[21] CIA activities in Burma "helped transform the Shan States from a relatively minor poppy-cultivating area into the largest opium-growing region in the world."[22] And the few U.S. Bureau of Narcotics investigations in the region "were blocked by...the State Department and the CIA."[23]

Thus, Agency complicity helped insure an adequate heroin supply to hook American G.I.s on the drug and open up new routes for heroin transport to addicts and future addicts in the United States.[24]

International Law

The UN Charter

Specifically, the United States, through its covert arm, the CIA, has violated Article Two, Paragraph Four of the United Nations Charter, which stipulates: "All members shall refrain in their international relations from the threat or use of force against the territorial integrity or political independence of any state..."[25] Some of the worst examples of infractions against Article Two include the following CIA-sponsored actions:

- The war in Vietnam.

CIA covert operations in that country established the base for full-scale U.S. involvement.[26] One of the CIA's counterinsurgency programs during the war, Operation Phoenix, involved the mass killing of tens of thousands of Vietnamese people suspected of collaboration with the Viet Cong. Army intelligence cooperated with the CIA in supplying names of suspected Viet Cong members to Phoenix squads. As one Army intelligence operative noted, "You did not give names to Phoenix to invite [the people] to a party."[27] General Bruce Palmer, an army commander in Vietnam, describes the Phoenix program as follows:

[O]ne had to do things one shouldn't have done. Covert things that amounted to killing [suspects]...More than once they killed some people that were innocent...You're not supposed to do those things...Old men, women and children were all your enemy.[28]

Former CIA Director and top Phoenix official William Colby has acknowledged that 20,000 Vietnamese died as a result of the program.[29] The death toll was reported as much higher (40,994) by the South Vietnamese government.[30] According to journalist Neil Sheehan, the CIA's goal was to "neutralize" 3,000 people a month.[31] Given the proportions of the slaughter and the credibility of the sources providing counts, it may be impossible to accurately tally the number of Vietnamese who lost their lives to Phoenix.

- The escalation of the civil war in Angola.

The CIA destroyed all hopes for peace in Angola by funding two of three warring factions in the Angolan liberation movement in 1974. The CIA's initial support recipient, Holden Roberto's faction, "continuously resisted a standing petition for a union of all Angolan liberation movements" and was generally considered the "more violent" of the movements.[32] CIA, South African and Chinese arms shipments to the FNLA and UNITA prompted Soviet (and later Cuban) support for the MPLA that the CIA used as justification for more U.S. support. The CIA painted a picture of the situation in red, claiming that the Soviet Union and Cuba had initiated the arms and advisor build-up. CIA propagandists asserted that the Cubans and Russians were "trying to take over the world." During Congressional oversight inquiries, William Colby "lied in 36 formal briefings" about the extent of the CIA operation and CIA involvement with the South African forces.[33]

Endless retaliations fueled the civil war for over a decade. "Hundreds of thousands have died. The cost of the war damage is estimated at $17 billion."[34] According to John Stockwell, the CIA task force commander for the Angolan operation, "The United States led the way, at every step of the escalation of the fighting...There would have been no war if we hadn't gone in first."[35]

The OAS Charter

Infractions against the Organization of American States Charter include breaches of Article 15:

> No State or group of States has the right to intervene, directly or indirectly, for any reason whatsoever, in the internal or external affairs of any other States. The foregoing principle prohibits not only armed force but also any other force of interference or attempted threat against the personality of the State or against its political, economic and cultural elements...[36]

and Article 18:

> The American States bind themselves in their international relations not to have recourse to the use of force, except in the case of self defense...[37]

The 1973 coup in Chile is perhaps the most notable, and possibly the most infamous, CIA breach of the OAS Charter. During the 1960s and '70s, the CIA interfered in all aspects of Chilean life. It offered covert support for various political organizations, produced and planted misleading propaganda, directed economic pressure and helped organize the military coup that resulted in the murder of democratically elected president Salvador Allende and the installation of dictator Augusto Pinochet Ugarte.[38] Pinochet's regime was responsible for imprisoning and torturing upwards of 80,000 Chileans and killing an estimated 10,000 to 15,000 people.[39] Under Pinochet, the government formed "a conscious, calculated plan" to destroy the Mapuche Indian culture which subsists on land coveted by Pinochet's corporate allies.[40]

The Geneva Conventions

The CIA has both organized and actively supported a motley assortment of mercenary soldiers that has earned a reputation as some of the most unprincipled and terroristic characters to carry weapons in the 20th Century.

Through its funding and organization of the Nicaraguan contras, among others, the CIA has violated the 1949 Geneva Conventions, specifically, Convention Four, Article 29, stipulating that the government responsible for establishing a band of mercenaries is also fully responsible for any atrocities committed by those mercenaries. Francis Boyle claims that during the contra war, the contras were "engaging in what we lawyers call a gross and consistent pattern of violations of fundamental human rights and particularly, the Geneva Conventions of 1949."[41] In 1987, the *New York Times* correspondent in Nicaragua observed that the contras were "essentially an instrument of American policy."[42] Thus, the United States, through the CIA, is responsible for contra breaches of Articles 146 and 147, which are designed to protect civilians from murder, mutilation, torture, rape and other atrocities which tend to accompany mercenary-type wars.[43]

Headed primarily by former dictator Anastasio Somoza's National Guard,[44] the contra war was condemned by the International Court of Justice (set up by the United States under Franklin Roosevelt's administration) as a grave breach of international law.[45] According to human rights organizations such as Amnesty International and Americas Watch, the contras waged a "terror" war against neutral and pro-Sandinista civilian populations: they systematically tortured, mutilated and killed villagers who would not cooperate with them. Their atrocities included the repeated rape of captured women and the brutalization and murder of children—sometimes while the parents looked on.[46] Given that CIA and other U.S. officials were aware of the crimes committed by the contras and "failed to take steps to stop the war crimes or punish those who committed those war crimes," they can be held guilty of those crimes.[47]

The Agency further implicated itself in breaches of the Geneva Conventions when it published and distributed a manual that directed the contras to assassinate civilian leaders in Nicaragua as a "model use of violence for propagandistic effects." [48]

All civilian officials in the Central Intelligence Agency who either knew or should have known of the existence of this manual and its provision to the contras are "war criminals," according to the [U.S.] government's own definition of that term.[49]

This furious violence was directed at a very small country: Nicaragua, a name CIA director William Casey could not even pronounce[50] and a people whose collective well-being he could hardly have cared less about.

After a decade of the contra terror war, a U.S.-sponsored trade embargo and Washington's "virtual veto" on international loans to Nicaragua,[51] Nicaragua suffers almost total economic devastation and the loss of between 30,000 and 50,000 Nicaraguans.[52]

The Universal Declaration of Human Rights and the Convention Against Torture

Further infractions of international law by the CIA involve the denial of basic human rights either by the CIA or its trained and supported subsidiaries. The Universal Declaration of Human Rights, adopted by the UN General Assembly on December 10, 1948, is "the first international Bill of Rights in human history" and includes provisions protecting all people on earth from infringements on their basic democratic freedoms and rights as well as from discrimination, slavery, cruel, inhuman or degrading punishment, arbitrary arrest, detention or exile and unequal treatment before the law.[53]

The Convention Against Torture was also adopted by the UN General Assembly 36 years later on December 10, 1984. Article Two of the Convention assigns responsibility to state parties for preventing and punishing acts of torture and forbids the creation of exceptional cases (such as states of war) in which torture may be excused. It goes on to place individual responsibility for torture, admonishing that orders from superiors or public officers may not be used to justify acts that breach the Convention.[54]

The following CIA actions are but a few of many that stand in flagrant violation of both the Universal Declaration of Human Rights and the Convention against Torture:

- Organization of coups that overthrew constitutional democracies in Guatemala, Brazil, Guyana, The Congo, Iran, Panama, Peru, Bolivia, Ecuador and Uruguay[55] followed by support for post-coup dictatorships which practiced torture, the stifling of any manner of dissent and the use of secret police forces and citizen surveillance.

- Torture training and the supply of equipment used for torture in South Vietnam, Brazil, the Dominican Republic, Uruguay and El Salvador, among other countries.[56]

Agency-trained foreign police services are reputed as the cruelest, most sadistic police that anyone could have the terrible misfortune to be arrested by.[57] Even contras who were trained by CIA-hired Argentinian police confessed to being shocked by the brutality of their teachers whose "most notable skills were torturing and murdering civilians." As one contra leader admitted, "The truth is a lot of them were Nazis."[58] After CIA training many of the police services developed their own "death squads" specifically designed to terrorize civilians out of democratic participation.

Torturers in police departments were often on the CIA payroll.[59] Many were trained at CIA camps in Texas, at Fort Bragg in North Carolina or at the Inter-American Police Academy in Panama.[60] A former Uruguayan police officer revealed to a Brazilian journalist that "U.S. advisors…had introduced scientific methods of torture" to Uruguayan policemen and that the same advisors "advocated psychological torture…to create despair" among groups of potential or actual activists.[61]

Through U.S. advisors, the Brazilian and Uruguayan police attained access to wires that were inserted into a prisoner's rectum or ears, wrapped around or inserted into his or her genitals, attached to the nipples or stuck between the teeth and then hooked to U.S. AID electrical generators or field telephones and cranked with voltage. "It was U.S. agents who informed [the police] of the permissible levels the human body could withstand."[62] The CIA supplied the Brazilian police with crowd-control equipment as well.[63]

In some cases, CIA officials and U.S. advisors were witness to the application of their own training. Torture victims have reported hearing North American voices in conversation just outside their torture rooms and certainly within hearing range of their screams.[64] Some reported that North American advisors were present while they were being tortured.[65] One woman who was tortured in South Vietnam police headquarters reported that "three Westerners in U.S. uniforms watched her being tortured, and the police told her that they were CIA officers."[66] These men watched as she was given electrical shocks and had an iron rod forced up her vagina. One of them then suggested that the police ram needles under her fingernails.

Given the history of CIA involvement in training and organizing the Latin American police/torture services, it comes as little surprise to learn that the CIA and other U.S. military groups were involved in the creation of El Salvador's notorious death squads as well.[67] Throughout

the 1960s and 1970s, "the CIA was in fact forming the police units that
are today the death squads in El Salvador, with the leaders on the CIA's
payroll, trained by the CIA in the United States."[68]

The Central Intelligence Agency has created a network of police
agencies around the world that systematically, perhaps daily, violate the
Convention Against Torture. Top officials in the Agency are fully cogni-
zant that these police services practice torture and encourage them to
do so, supplying equipment, training and direction for their work. Thus,
the CIA is a direct accomplice to egregious international crimes as
defined by the Convention Against Torture.

The Genocide Convention

The international Genocide Convention was adopted into U.S.
treaty law by Congress in 1986 and ratified with much fanfare by Ronald
Reagan in 1988. Now genocidal malfeasance is "a federal offence" in the
United States.[69] The Convention defines genocide as the purposeful
extermination of, displacement of or infliction of physical or psychological harm to a people based on race, ethnicity, nationality or religion.
Article Three of the Genocide Convention cites the varying acts of
genocide, as well as the "attempt to commit" genocide and "complicity
in" genocide as punishable crimes.[70]

The Central Intelligence Agency has, in the following examples,
either directly or indirectly participated in or initiated the conditions
culminating in acts of genocide as defined by the Genocide Convention.
While other examples exist, these cases reflect the horrifying results of
some of the most unprincipled, pugnacious and ultimately illegal CIA
actions:

- The 1954 coup in Guatemala that placed Castillo Armas and a
  military dictatorship in power.

Over 100,000 Guatemalans have been killed and 38,000 "disappeared" by the Guatemalan military since 1960.[71] The slaughter and
displacement of the Mayan Indian population—living on land desired
by U.S. and other foreign-owned corporations—aptly fulfill the definitions of genocide in the Convention. "There is massive extermination of
the population, carried out through the destruction of villages and the
razing of cultivated lands. This is genocide…"[72]

The brutality of the extermination is severe: in one of the best-doc-
umented indigenous village massacres committed by the Guatemalan
army, soldiers "cut open children's stomachs with knives…and
smashed their heads [with] heavy sticks." Most of the women were
killed with machetes, and the buildings in the village were burned.[73]

"One cannot help but wonder if the culture that the Mayans have sustained since the sixteenth century will endure even fifty more years."[74]

- The 1965 Indonesian coup that replaced a struggling but independent President Sukarno with U.S.-bred Suharto and resulted in the massacre of from 500,000 to over one million ethnic Chinese Indonesians by U.S.-funded, Muslim death squads.[75]

In May of 1990, the *San Francisco Examiner* reported that a former CIA deputy station chief and an American diplomat admitted that they and other U.S. officials were involved in "supplying the names of thousands of Communist Party leaders to the Indonesian army, which hunted down the leftists and killed them."[76] The Agency understood that people named on the lists were destined for extra-judicial firing squads: CIA officials and other Americans "later checked off the names of those who had been killed."[77] Former CIA Director William Colby compared the Indonesian program to the Phoenix program in Vietnam: "Well, you go out and get them to surrender, or you capture or you shoot them," he said in an interview.[78] The people getting killed in Indonesia, however, were not soldiers. They were not even the "enemy" in an on-going war. They were members of a popular, grassroots political party. Or they were in the way.

"They probably killed a lot of people, and I probably have a lot of blood on my hands," current State Department consultant and former member of the U.S. Embassy's Indonesian political section Robert Marten reflected pensively, "but that's not all bad. There's a time when you have to strike hard at a decisive moment."

And strike hard, they did. According to Australian journalists who were in Indonesia at the time, the massacre was hideous and enormous. Victims of firing squads were made up not just of communists, but of their families and of the ethnic Chinese who were targeted as potential communists. Northern Sumatra and eastern Java reeked with the smell of decaying flesh, and boats were immobilized on rivers choked with human corpses.[79] In a public report, the CIA described the indiscriminate killing as "one of the worst mass murders of the 20th century," then turned around in a covert study and "recommended [the operation] as a model for future operations."[80]

Nuremberg, the Supremacy Clause and Individual Responsibility

Almost all of the examples listed above also qualify as infractions against the Nuremberg Principles. For activists, these Principles are significant because their wording encompasses not only national but *individual* responsibility for violations of international law and humanitarian tenets. One of the more inspired international agreements, the Nuremberg Principles imply that the citizens of all nations have a *responsibility to act to prevent their government from committing crimes against humanity.*

In 1946, the governments of Britain, France, the Soviet Union and the United States created the International Military Tribunal (IMT) that tried Nazis for war crimes committed during World War II. In its attempts to define criminal activity on an international scale, the Tribunal established the Nuremberg Principles. According to the Principles, Nazi war criminals were held individually responsible for their actions, regardless of Germany's domestic laws and state of war.

On December 11, 1946, the United Nations General Assembly resolved to "affirm" the Nuremberg Principles, voting them into the general body of rules governing UN members.[81] This action, followed by confirmations of subsequent Declarations, Codes and Conventions which embodied the basic Principles established by the Tribunal, codified the new, universal definitions of war crimes and crimes against humanity: "It can be concluded, then, that the acts declared criminal in the Charter and Judgement of the IMT and for which individuals accused were held personally responsible, have been affirmed as valid crimes under international law in various international declarations."[82] Thus, citizens of the United States or of any nation are legally bound by the Nuremberg Principles, which state:

Article Six: The following acts...are crimes coming within the jurisdiction of the Tribunal for which there shall be *individual responsibility.* [Emphasis added.]

(a) Crimes Against Peace: namely, planning, preparation, initiation or waging of a war...in violation of international treaties, agreements, or assurances...

(b) War Crimes: namely, violations of the laws or customs of war. Such violations shall include, but not be limited to, murder, ill treatment or deportation to slave labor...of civilian population of or in occupied territory, murder or ill-treatment of prisoners of war or persons on the seas, killing of hostages, plunder of public or private property, wanton destruction of cities...or devastation not justified by military necessity.

(c) Crimes Against Humanity: namely, murder, extermination, enslavement, deportation, and other inhumane acts committed against any civilian population, before or during war or persecutions on political, racial or religious grounds...*whether or not in violation of domestic law of the country where perpetrated.* [83][Emphasis added.]

Furthermore, any and all "leaders, organizers, instigators and accomplices" that plan or participate in the listed crimes are to be held "responsible for all acts performed by any persons in execution of such plan."

Article Eight declares all defendants responsible for their crimes whether or not a defendant "acted pursuant to order of his government or of a superior." The Tribunal's chief prosecutor summed up the Judgement succinctly: "The very essence of the [Nuremberg] Charter is that individuals have international duties which transcend the national obligations of obedience imposed by the individual state."[84]

Reiterating the theme of individual responsiblity, the International Law Commission of the UN drafted a "Code of Offences against the Peace and Security of Mankind" based on the Nuremberg Principles. Article Four states: "The fact that a person charged with an offence defined in this Code acted pursuant to order of his government or of a superior does not relieve him from responsibility, provided a *moral choice* was, in fact, possible to him."[85] Finally, the Tribunal Judgement affirms that "International law, as such, binds every citizen just as does ordinary municipal law."[86] In the case of *Commonwealth v. Amy Carter, et al.,* defense counsel successfully asserted that "a person having knowledge" of international crimes committed by individuals—regardless of state complicity in such crimes—"has a legal duty to take reasonable steps to prevent such crimes and/or at least make them known to the public eye and higher authorities; given that 'international law, as such, binds every citizen just as does ordinary municipal law.'"[87]

Additionally, the Supremacy Clause in Article Six of the U.S. Constitution holds that any international treaty law signed by this country supercedes domestic state law. "The Constitution, laws and treaties of the United States are as much a part of the law of every State as its own local laws and constitution."[88]

In Supreme Court cases *United States v. Pink* and *United States v. Belmont,* precedent was established granting international agreements—even *without* "the formal advice and consent of the Senate"—supremacy over state law.[89] International treaties must be considered "the Supreme Law of the Land" by state judiciaries.[90] Therefore, informed U.S. citizens are "under a legal, positive duty requiring them to take such steps as [are] reasonable to stop, or make known, [international] crimes" or become silent accomplices to them.[91]

The Nuremberg Principles were created in an effort to prevent another holocaust, yet they have rarely been invoked, even in light of U.S. and, specifically, CIA involvement in the aforementioned international crimes—some of which constitute full-scale genocide. The CIA is responsible for a host of misdeeds that display an incredible lack of respect, if not disdain, for the self-determination of the peoples of the world and flagrant disregard for the integrity and democratic reputation of the United States. *Training torturers, arming mercenaries, overthrowing governments and participating in genocide fully qualify as "crimes against humanity."*

What Goes Around, Comes Around: The CIA in the Persian Gulf

The CIA's criminal activities and interference in the affairs of other nations has an immeasurable impact not only on the immediate generations of citizens in a given country, but on future generations as well. Ultimately, the CIA's international crimes affect us all. An Agency program that starts in a single country often spreads to surrounding countries and can build into a world crisis.

Iraq's invasion of Kuwait in August 1990 can be traced back to U.S. foreign policy in Iran and a CIA program carried out there in the early 1950s. Perhaps fittingly, it was Desert Storm Commander Norman Schwarzkopf, Jr.'s, father, Norman Schwarzkopf, *Sr.,* who helped to run the CIA's program against Iranian Prime Minister Mohammed Mossadegh in 1953.[92]

Mossadegh's policy was to nationalize Iran's oil industry, an idea that U.S. policymakers apparently found hard to accept. In 1953, CIA officer Kim Roosevelt, along with Schwarzkopf, Sr. and Iranian General Fazzolah Zahedi, organized a coup under U.S. direction to overthrow the prime minister. The program worked. Mossadegh was removed and replaced with the Shah and his secret police force, SAVAK. General Zahedi took a position beside the Shah and duly alloted 40 percent of Iranian oil ownership to U.S. companies: Standard, Gulf and Texaco.[93]

During the Shah's reign, the CIA worked with Iran to encourage a Kurdish uprising in the northeastern mountains of neighboring Iraq. The Agency spent $16 million fomenting the rebellion, which led in 1975 to Iraq's "capitulation to Iran's control of the Shatt al Arab," an area crucial to Iraq's access to the Gulf.[94]

Concurrently, the Agency was organizing SAVAK and training its members in methods of suppressing civilian dissent against the Shah, methods that included abduction, torture, terror and murder.[95] The Shah was no less a dictator than "madman" Saddam Hussein. It was, therefore, not surprising when the Ayatollah Khomeini rode to power in Iran on an anti-imperialist, anti-Western tide.

The Shah fell. Khomeini fomented and exploited the hatred of the Iranian people for the United States, and the United States got busy encouraging Iraq to attack Iran for repossession of the Shatt al Arab.[96] In 1980, Iraq did just that and began a war that would end eight years and over a million casualties later. During the war, the Reagan administration sold arms to both sides, and U.S. companies profited nicely helping Iraq develop its nuclear, chemical and biological warfare capacity.[97] Kuwait also helped finance the Iran-Iraq war by backing the Iraqi side in an effort to protect itself from Iranian aggressions.

When the war finally ended in August 1988, Iraq emerged as one of the most powerful nations in the region, though stressed by continuing border disputes and war debts to countries like Kuwait and Saudi Arabia. During the war, Kuwait had nudged its borders into disputed territories, and Hussein accused the Kuwaitis of "slant" drilling oil from Iraqi fields.[98] These and other conflicts may have been exacerbated by the Central Intelligence Agency. Top secret documents released by Iraq after the invasion of Kuwait indicate high-level meetings between Kuwaiti officials and U.S. intelligence officials, including William Webster himself. One of the documents outlines mutual goals of the U.S. and Kuwait arrived upon during meetings between Webster and the Kuwaiti Director-General of the State Security Department, Fahd Ahmad Al-Fahd. Summarizing the meetings, Al-Fahd wrote:

> ...information would be exchanged about the armaments and political structures of Iran and Iraq...We agreed with the American side that it was important to take advantage of the deteriorating economic situation in Iraq in order to put pressure on that country's government to delineate our common border. The Central Intelligence Agency gave us its view of appropriate means of pressure, saying that broad cooperation should be initiated between us...[99]

Although the CIA has denounced the document as a "crude forgery," the Agency did admit to meetings between Webster and Al-Fahd on a date indicated in the document, November 14, 1989.[100]

Kuwaiti and U.S. actions up until August 2, 1990, do suggest "broad cooperation" between the two countries to both put economic pressure on Iraq and, at least on the part of the United States, to provoke and encourage an invasion of Kuwait. In numerous meetings and Arab conferences in the spring and summer of 1990, Kuwait refused to relax the war debts owed to it by Iraq. "The Kuwaitis even went so far as to dump oil for less than the agreed-upon OPEC price,"[101] an action that would cripple Iraq's post-war economic recovery.

During meetings with Jordanian ambassadors in the weeks before the invasion, Kuwait's seemingly suicidal audacity was partially explained in Kuwaiti officials' vague references to U.S. cooperation. "If they [the Iraqis] don't like it, let them occupy our territory...we are going to bring in the Americans," said the Kuwaiti emir's brother, Sheikh Sabeh, in July of 1990. In the same week, King Hussein of Jordan learned that the Kuwaiti crown prince held a meeting of senior military officers during which the prince told them that if Iraq were to invade, "American and foreign forces would land in Kuwait and expel them."[102]

George Bush was aware of an imminent military action by Iraq against Kuwait at least five days before the invasion took place.[103] But right up until the day, representatives from the White House and the State Department assured both Congress and Saddam Hussein that the U.S. had "no defense treaty relationship with any Gulf country. That is clear...We have not historically taken a position on border disputes."[104] That statement by Assistant Secretary of State John Kelly to a worried House foreign affairs subcommittee on July 31—two days before the invasion—was preceded by a similar statement to Hussein himself in his presidential palace by U.S. ambassador April Glaspie who, responding to the many grievances of Hussein against the Kuwaitis, said this:

> We studied history at school. They taught us to say, "Free-dom or death." [Glaspie was evidently granting morality to Hussein's cause.] I have a direct instruction from the president to seek better relations with Iraq. We have no opinion on the Arab-Arab conflicts, like your border disagreement with Kuwait...[105]

Philip Agee points out that U.S. actions before Iraq's invasion "strongly suggest that U.S. policy was to have Saddam Hussein think he could invade Kuwait with impunity, and, when invasion was imminent, to do nothing to discourage him."[106] If this is the case, U.S. policy regarding the Gulf War has not even minimally departed from what U.S. policy has always been in the region: to protect multinational, corporate interests and to control the political arena regardless of the human cost. And the CIA is the agent of that policy. If the United States or the CIA makes claims to ending "lawless aggression" and stopping "madmen" like Saddam Hussein, then those claims are laid to waste by U.S. alliances with other dictators. Now the U.S. is allied with Syria's President Hafez al-Assad, whose human rights record rivals Saddam Hussein's and whose country is internationally recognized as a haven for terrorist organizations. Western corporations have already been selling Syria all the hardware necessary to create a Syrian nuclear, biological and chemical warfare capacity.[107]

No one can predict how recent U.S. policy and CIA actions in the Persian Gulf will affect the people of the world years from now. International laws were established to guide the planet's many nations toward peace and stability. If the CIA will not recognize those laws, it is easy enough to predict that the impact of CIA actions taking place today will not be a positive one.

The Central Intelligence Agency has built up a track record that tramples the principles of its own Charter, domestic laws and international accords, including the Nuremberg Tribunal Principles. According to these principles and to our own Constitution, we have a responsibility to call the Agency on its crimes. Activists should be aware of the strong legal case available for the defense of our actions—so often branded as "illegal" by authorities. There *is* a body of humanitarian laws that supports our beliefs and subsequent activities.

Clearly, we don't need a higher authority to tell us that the CIA is worth opposing. It *demands* opposition based on moral principle alone. As many activists are well aware, laws and regulations are often manipulated by governments to suit their own purposes. But the law is not entirely against us and it is, at any rate, heartening to know that you can demonstrate against the Central Intelligence Agency *in full compliance with the law,* in fact, while fulfilling your legal responsibilities as an informed citizen.

CHAPTER TWO

CIA *On* Campus: The Covert Hand in the Academic Cookie Jar

Universities are part of a complex web of intervention and militarism...the university [is a] participant in both the U.S. war system and the transnational economy.

Jonathan Feldman
Universities in the Business of Repression[1]

University administrators and presidents are not known in this country as people with great backbone in standing up to the government.

Ex-agent Philip Agee[2]

Though "higher education" has a noble ring, our nation's universities have a history of complying with, supporting and being nurtured by some less than noble federal agencies—including the National Security Agency (NSA), the Defense Department, the FBI and the CIA.

The history of the CIA on college campuses is a long one. Its activities in the world of academia stretch back to the days of the Office of Strategic Services (OSS, the World War II precursor to the CIA), when most agents were recruited through "old boy" networks at Ivy League universities. Today, the CIA has been exposed as working at every level of the university system, from undergraduate recruiting and foreign student coercion to the establishment of entire institutes, research funding and faculty recruiting.

The literature that exists on CIA campus activity is by no means complete, since it describes only those activities that have been uncovered. Most programs are conducted in secrecy. Sometimes even the university administration is unaware of CIA funding or recruiting due to the many disguises the Agency may use: front companies, State Department or Defense Department research, even purportedly independent academic institutions. In some cases, the administration may just not care to know about CIA-faculty relationships.

Although many of the ensuing examples of CIA-university ties were revealed in the 1960s and 1970s, there is good reason to believe that the number of relationships has increased rather than diminished. President Bush, "since taking office...has beefed up the secret budget for spies and for intelligence analysis and wants to do more."[3] As recently as 1986, Robert Gates, the CIA's deputy director for intelligence, told professors at a public speaking engagement: "We need your help." He indicated that the Agency wanted further access to "that vast reservoir of expertise, experience and insight in the community of university scholars."[4] And he asserted that the CIA would continue and strengthen the kinds of programs it ran in universities in the past.[5] The lesson then, in the following examples, is to be wary of any questionable campus activity. These are examples of what the CIA has done in the past and is most likely doing on a larger scale today.

Student Recruiting

> For professional success and a rewarding life, look to the Central Intelligence Agency...where your career is America's strength.
>
> CIA recruitment brochure

In June of 1986, David Wise reported in the *New York Times Magazine* that William Casey "in his classified annual report to Congress...listed personnel—the need to recruit, keep and reward high-quality people—as his No. 1 priority."[6]

The Agency has done its best to address that priority. What used to function as a shadow network that approached its recruits with a soft tap on the shoulder and an invitation to sit down and talk has become an aggressive, corporate-style campaign, complete with high-gloss, multi-colored brochures and representatives in spiffy suits at campus job fairs. The CIA's recruiting efforts—dampened by the civil rights and peace movements in the '60s and '70s—are up to full swing in the '90s. They're back. And they're thirsty for liberal to arch-conservative college grads.

In addition to going public with its recruiting process, the Agency has opened ten new recruiting centers across the country. It is actively working with university placement services and even high school guidance programs (see "Robbing the Cradle," next page) to collect resumés and set up screening interviews with prospective employees for permanent positions or temporary work programs for academic credit.

Sometimes the initial interviews are open to anyone who has even the slightest interest. At other times, the Agency picks certain students for the first meeting based on their resumés. And in some cases, the Agency recruiters have their own list of student names and will initiate contact themselves.

The sources of these lists are never publicly revealed. Most often, the Agency will establish working relationships with sympathetic professors and administrators (who may already be working with the CIA in another capacity) and ask them for student recommendations. According to a *CIA Entrance Examination* booklet written in 1988, even if the CIA does not come directly to your campus to recruit students, "almost all college facilities will have someone within the school who has the contact(s) you need."[7] The examination booklet includes a foreword by former CIA director William Colby who describes a job in the Agency as "the best possible way to serve our country and have a good time doing it."

In *Campus Watch,* a newsletter on the CIA and academia, Philip Agee asserts that some faculty members are actually paid a salary to "spot and assess" students and other faculty members for potential Agency employment. Yale's crew coach "Skip" Walz was a spotter for the Agency through the '40s and early '50s. He received $10,000 to pass the names of athletic young men on to CIA recruiters. In a record year, Skip introduced 25 such men to the Agency who went on to become paramilitary officers.[8]

"Spotters" gather as much information as they can about a given prospect and hand it over to the recruiters who begin a file that includes a background check. The *CovertAction Information Bulletin* notes that if the student fails to pass the Agency's background check, his or her dossier may become a permanent record at the CIA without the student's knowledge. A former student at the University of Wisconsin at Madison sued the CIA for keeping a file on him and eventually won in a federal appeals court.[9]

The *CIA Entrance Examination* booklet is, according to its author, the first of its kind. It marks the latest efforts of the CIA to expand its recruiting programs and gain legitimacy among its pool of potential employees. A large part of this pool consists of college students who

Robbing the cradle: CIA high school recruiting

Seventeen- and 18-year-olds are now being asked if they can "meet the challenge" of the Central Intelligence Agency. Distributed in high school guidance counseling offices, a recent CIA flyer offers high school seniors planning to enroll in a college undergraduate program "up to $10,000 per school year for tuition, fees and books. The Agency will pay the cost of transportation between school and the Agency"—where students will spend at least three summers doing CIA work.

Open to all high school seniors ("particularly minority or disabled"), the CIA "Undergraduate Scholar Program" appears to be the Agency's attempt to get 'em while they're young. In return for the CIA's favors, the college graduate must continue employment with the Agency "for a period of one-and-one-half times the length of college training," or from six to seven-and-a-half years. Whether or not the CIA's "Student Scholars" (as opposed to student non-scholars?) are required to do any digging around for the Agency while they are still in school is unmentioned. But if history can teach us anything, it is that the CIA lacks a certain amount of self-restraint.

Chicago-based CIA recruiter Jerry Crawford says that recruiting has shifted "from full-time hires to cooperative education." The CIA, he says, has 300 students currently enrolled in internship programs.[10]

In conjunction with the Undergraduate Scholar Program, the CIA offers a "Minority Undergraduate Studies Program," a "Graduate Studies Program" and a "Student Trainee Program"—all of which involve employment with the Agency prior to graduation.

have specific training in a variety of fields from agronomy and architecture to political science and sociology. For each field, the Agency produces a slick brochure enticing students to join up with "the Company" and sends memos to universities and high schools announcing its latest occupational needs. (One recent call was for "experienced editors and librarians.") The placement office along with various specific departments of your own university probably distribute these pamphlets to graduating students; they may also offer their services (resumé and transcript collection, interview set-ups and interview facilities) to the Agency for its convenience. And it's possible that your university may

The Student Trainee Program is co-sponsored by universities with "established cooperative education programs" and awards academic credit for "a minimum of three [college] periods" spent with the CIA. These are served on an alternating basis (one semester in school, one semester at CIA headquarters). The Graduate Studies Program requires graduate-level students to spend one summer in internship with the Agency. Students "must be committed to attend graduate school during the fall following the summer of the internship." The CIA has denied covert funding of graduate studies work, but Mark Heimbach, engineering graduate student at the University of Wisconsin at Madison, maintains he was offered reimbursement for secret research by an Agency recruiter.

"He said I'd train at Langley and then come back to campus to work on CIA research," Heimbach remembers. The recruiter told Heimbach that he would have to sign a statement to get classified clearance. "They admitted it was secret work. That's no secret. That's what they do," he said.[11]

The surprise was that the CIA was recruiting at Madison for covert researchers against the university's rules which ban classified research. Madison's placement office denied any knowledge of CIA-funded research offers and the CIA's recruiting "team leader" stated explicitly that Heimbach's recruiter made none of the alleged offers. Heimbach, however, stands by his story. "There is no way to tell how many students are doing this kind of work," he warns.

secretly be helping the CIA collect information on students who are of interest to the Agency.

Since 1985, the Agency has run special "seminars" for university officials on "the agency's operations and employment needs." In 1990, one such seminar included "deans from 11 law schools around the country," who were "briefed by the CIA's director, William H. Webster, and heads of each of the agency's other major components, including the clandestine operations chief, Richard F. Stolz." Hermann Viets, dean of the University of Rhode Island's School of Engineering, claims that the CIA seminar he attended "focused almost exclusively on recruiting."

Dean Edward Fagan of St. John's University School of Law also participated in a CIA recruiting seminar. The Agency will not release the
names of participating university officials who have not already admitted
to attending the seminars.[12]

Recruitment of Foreign Students

CIA-paid "spotters" train their eyes not only on promising young
American recruits but on foreign students as well. From the Agency's
perspective, young foreigners who come to study in the United States
have great leadership potential back home. According to author William
Corson in *The Armies of Ignorance,* the OSS and, later, the CIA have
examined "with varying degrees of intensity" over a million foreign
students for "mole" potential. "The foreign student recruitment program
has grown to such magnitude that it is now a going concern seemingly
beyond the ability of anyone to really control its operation or structurally
reform its overall process."[13]

Iranian students have been some of the more recent objects of the
Agency's affections. Using coercion and considerable carrot money, the
CIA has attempted to recruit Iranians to spy on their fellow students and
on their countrypeople at home. In 1976, one CIA official bragged that
"by 1985 we'll own 80 percent of the Iranian government's second and
third level of officials."[14]

The Agency's attempts to "own" foreign students are less than
aboveboard. In 1979, Iranian students were threatened by the CIA with
revelations of their use of university office phones to call their families
in Iran. The CIA told them they would be "disgraced, punished, expelled
and possibly prosecuted" for the stolen calls if they refused to spy for
the Agency.[15]

Approached by a CIA agent with an offer of cash and even U.S.
citizenship in return for information on his country, Iranian national
Ahmad Jabbari did some of his own information gathering and recorded
his meetings with the agent on a small tape recorder. Apparently the
CIA had done some preliminary checking on Jabbari's personal history
and discovered that he came from a middle-class merchant family and
had applied for jobs in Iran with the National Iranian Oil Company and
National Airlines. He was in the United States completing his Ph.D. at
Washington University in St. Louis and was introduced to CIA agent
Mark Ellerson through a colleague.

"I was being asked to choose between my government and some
foreign spy Agency, so of course there was no choice," Jabbari told the
New Times in the winter of 1976. "I was angry, but at the same time I

was intrigued…I wanted to find out more about CIA covert operations within my government."

The following is an edited version of one of his recorded conversations with recruiter Ellerson:

> J: Now, could I ask…what organization are…can you tell me that?
>
> E: I can tell you I work for the CIA.
>
> J: OK. CIA.
>
> E: And our interest in you would be to have you go back to Iran, and get a job in the government…So we would like to have you give us the information when you work. In exchange for that, why, of course…we would give you a monthly stipend to the bank of your choosing…number two, a contingency payment…a one time payment of $750 for medical expenses or whatever…We'd like to have you return for a minimum period of two years to Iran…We're willing to assist you in acquiring permanent resident alien status in the United States…The only way we wouldn't do this is if you've already applied for legal help in achieving this…[16]

Ellerson also informed Jabbari that the CIA was interested in the activities of Iranian dissidents. When Jabbari declined his invitation to spy in Iran, Ellerson offered to pay Jabbari to recruit other foreign students for the Agency, especially students from Angola, Ethiopia, Portugal and Arab countries. The CIA would pay for the cost of lunches and dinners in the recruiting process. Again Jabbari declined and the relationship finally ceased.

Compared to stories in *Ramparts* magazine of other CIA-targeted foreign nationals, Jabbari got off the hook relatively easily—perhaps because he feigned goodwill. Other foreign students have been approached by agents (under a Defense Department cover), asked to perform "some small service" and reimbursed for costs incurred. The students are asked to sign a "U.S. government receipt 'for services rendered'" and then blackmailed into spying with the threat that the CIA will turn the receipts over to the students' local embassies if they refuse to do so.[17] One Afghani student who refused to comply with the Agency was hassled by the Immigration and Naturalization Service with threats of deportation, even though he was married to a U.S. citizen.

In the early 1980s, the CIA recruited 30 Libyan students studying in the United States to return to Libya and spy for the Agency.[18] In

October of 1990, "a CIA agent showed up at the Storrs campus of the University of Connecticut asking for lists of foreign students studying on the campus, their home countries and the names of their academic advisors." Dean Richard Vengroff reported that the CIA "was apparently interested in learning about the on- and off-campus activities of the students."[19]

Tactics for foreign-student recruiting probably have changed some, given that these techniques have been published. But the use of blackmail and bribery may continue.

The coercive nature of foreign-student recruiting eventually comes back to haunt the Agency: "Once bought, foreign students only stay bought in about one out of four cases."[20] Worse still, the Agency's underhanded tactics put the potential foreign recruit in a humiliating position: betray your country or be disgraced in this one. Since 1948, more than 40 agents recruited by the CIA in U.S. universities "have committed suicide in response to the fear of exposure of their relationship with America's intelligence services."[21]

The "Whole" Officer: What Does It Take?

When students make it past the initial interviews, they are subjected to rigorous testing: analytical, medical, personal and psychological. They must undergo a number of polygraph tests and an extensive background check that reaches into their past at least as far back as grade school. Depending on prospective placement, some students may be required to submit to psychiatric testing. One ex-officer's psychiatric test included his response to the fact that his testing psychiatrist's fly was blatantly unzipped when he entered the testing room.[22] The entire recruiting process takes at least four months, sometimes longer, and polygraph tests can continue sporadically through an agent's career.

The *CIA Entrance Examination* contains a sample CIA examination ("read, reviewed and criticized by former members of the Agency"), including a number of essays written by cold warriors that would-be agents must respond to. The essays tell much about the ideological perspective the Agency is looking for in a new recruit, and the book is worth its $15 cover price for this knowledge alone.

The intellectual defense of the Agency's activities includes this bleak analysis of the world situation:

> Indeed we have to be blind after all these years of Russian intrigue and unending attack not to realize that the compulsive Russian proclivity for aggression that comes out of the

muzzle of the Marxist-Leninist dialectic has been with us and
will remain with us until either we or the Soviets collapse...

It goes on to reassert the child-like innocence of U.S. foreign policy in
the face of the "enemy," a malicious, almost inhuman molester:

> It is little wonder that the U.S. is most usually on the defen-
> sive, always having to devise a *counter* to a Soviet or Cuban
> aggressive *initiative*. In general, between the end of World
> War II and the present the Soviets and their surrogates have
> done the initiating. We have been doing the reacting or
> countering.[23]

Ironically, this excerpt rings true today, as the United States
struggles to respond to Soviet *peace* initiatives. In its original context,
the essay may not have fit the facts; still, student responses to the
passages are obviously a factor in their employment with the Agency.
Recruitment with the CIA requires a certain amount of patriotism, if not
outright fanaticism. Ex-CIA agent Ralph McGehee says that most recruits "buy the program," truly believing that the CIA does what it claims
to do.[24]

The CIA contends that work with the Clandestine Services division (covert operations, the Agency's "action arm") requires a person
with "impeccable standards of personal and professional ethics" to carry
out a job with risks "slightly higher than for police or firemen in a large
city." The recruitee's "first training assignment," according to a CIA
recruitment brochure distributed in 1989, is to "guard the secret of your
intention to try for the Clandestine Service even from your closest
friends."

Given the true nature of covert action work, the Agency's requirement of "impeccable" ethical standards rings false. More likely, the
extremity of a recruit's nationalism dictates his or her eventual placement. Those that would kill, maim and torture for their country or train
others to do so may be placed in covert operations overseas, in war zones
such as El Salvador. And those of a more benign nature may be assigned
to word processors and paper shredders at home, unwittingly supporting their more enthusiastic counterparts abroad. According to David
Wise's article in the *New York Times Magazine,* approximately 20 percent of CIA recruits from college campuses go into the clandestine
services division.[25]

A patriotic, moderately liberal agent hired to "ride the desk" for
the Agency at Washington headquarters confessed in *Ramparts* that to
him, "the actual intelligence operations were distant happenings and it

was easy to be academic and objective" while isolated in the confines of a corporate-style office. The fate of fellow agents and their contacts were no more than the fate of "pawn[s] on a great chess board."[26]

Later, transferred to the field, bribing foreign students to do work for the Agency and training new recruits in sabotage techniques, including how to blow up civilian transport buses, the agent had to question his role in promoting freedom and democracy. "The intellectual game was over. I had to leave." And he did. His belief in the CIA's fight against communism and defense of the "American way of life"—bolstered by the CIA's training program pep talks—fell short in the face of actual Agency activities. But many idealistic and patriotic college students will never learn the lessons of the field. The Agency is interested in those that possess enough of an anti-communist or pro-American ideology to keep them in their jobs, some of which are less painful to carry out than

In the Agency's Own Words

Our Challenge: Think for Yourself

CIA recruitment brochure

Can you carry out a direct personal command from your superior if you disagree with it?

CIA sample entrance examination question

More relevant, challenging and intellectually stimulating questions from the CIA's sample exam:

- Have you ever been refused a loan? If so, explain.
- Have you ever had any adult homosexual activity or contact?
- Please describe in 50 words or less your feelings toward homosexuality in society today.
- Would you like to live in a war zone?
- Explain in 50 words or less what role you feel the U.S. should play in the world.
- Discuss the differences and the likely users of the terms "Democratic Resistance" and "National Liberation."
- What is "plausible deniability" and why is it important?
- What is the "Boland Amendment?" [A sincere question?]
- What are your feelings toward the Soviet Union?
- Essay: Discuss what you know about the development of world communism.[27]

others. "The CIA wants active, charming, obedient people who can get things done in the social world but have limited perspective and understanding, who see things in black and white and don't like to think too much."[28]

Concomitant with a general zeal for this country's democratic burden, a CIA agent must possess the qualities of a "whole person," according to the sample examination booklet. Listed among many factors that would determine the "whole" intelligence officer are: "homosexual conduct and sexual perversion...cohabitation...[and] undesirable character traits." Whether or not these factors are desirable for Agency employment is left unspecified, though "frequent long trips to communist countries" and "participation in subversive groups" do not an intelligence officer make.[29]

Institutes, Faculty Recruiting and Research

> It is absolutely essential that the Agency have available to it the single greatest source of expertise: the American academic community.
>
> F.W.M. Janney, former CIA Personnel Director[30]

The CIA's interest in U.S. universities extends far beyond the search for new recruits. Not only does the Agency hunger for personnel, it also hungers for knowledge. Where else should it turn but to our bastions of education where research on foreign countries, liberation movements and social movements proceeds at a constant pace?

The Agency's close relationship with academia stems from its early intimacy with schools like Yale. George Bush, who directed the CIA during the Ford administration, is a Yale graduate. In fact, a large portion of Agency officers were recruited from Yale and formed much of the "old boy" network that was eventually dismantled by CIA Director Stansfield Turner during the Carter administration. Nonetheless, the idea of the academic community as resource for the Agency has been defended both by members of academia and Turner himself.

The CIA has both overtly and covertly established entire university institutes and research departments and recruited professors both as "spotters" for student recruiting and as CIA-funded researchers. In some cases, it is hard to distinguish the Agency and the university as two separate entities: a shared ideology, old-fashioned cronyism, and

financial and political incentives bind U.S. colleges to the CIA like
fishing line to a pole.

Officer in Residence:
Studies in Artificial Intelligence

The CIA's recently initiated "Officer in Residence" program is
another example of the Agency's attempts to re-establish its credibility
in the academic community. Through this program, "active CIA officers
teach college courses relating to their field of experience."[31] Officers are
openly identified as CIA representatives at the university.

A 1988 *Campus Watch* interview with the CIA's former Coordinator for Academic Affairs, Arthur Hulnick, revealed that the Agency has
placed officers in upwards of ten schools across the country. Though
Hulnick would not give the names of the schools, *Campus Watch* came
up with a partial list that includes Boston University (Arthur Hulnick);
University of Miami (Michael Kline); George Washington University
(formerly Laurie Kurtzweg, now Stanley S. Bedlington); Jacksonville
University (David Matthews); University of Texas at Austin (James
McInnis); Rochester Institute of Technology (Robert Merisko) and
Georgetown University (Noel Firth and Harold Bean).[32]

The Agency's public reasoning for initiating the program is to
"demonstrate the quality of CIA people," strengthen Agency ties to the
academic community and "enhance" its recruiting efforts.[33] University
administrators are encouraging professors to work with the officers, and
students seeking further information about the Agency are directed to
the officers as well.

The Officer in Residence program has met with public controversy
at many of its host schools. Actions against the program have occurred
at a few universities—notably the University of California at Santa
Barbara—and will be explored in Chapter Five.

Institutes

Journalist Ken Lawrence documents CIA involvement in the actual creation of a number of academic foreign studies institutes. In
cooperation with the American Metal Climax Corporation, a U.S.-Afri-
can mining company, the CIA established the African-American Institute in 1954 (now located in New York). According to the Africa
Research Group, the purpose of establishing the Institute was part of a
larger effort to generate academic interest in African studies that could
subsequently be tapped by the CIA and other government agencies.[34]

Unsatisfied with the creation of one think tank, the Agency began funding the joint Harvard/MIT Center for International Studies (CENIS) and developed its African Research Program through a network of academics-turned-agents and agents-turned-academics. Max Millikan, an ex-director of the CIA's Office of National Estimates, was appointed director of the Center for International Studies. He, in turn, appointed State Department official Arnold Rivkin to head the African program. "Together, the two supervised studies for the CIA's use."[35] Durwood Lockard, assistant deputy to the CIA's Near East Division, became assistant head of the Center's Middle Eastern Studies Department in 1957. From the base of these cozy, institutional relations in the early 1950s, Harvard and MIT embarked on tight working relationships with the Agency, during which "several officials and faculty members of the Harvard Business School founded and helped to administer front organizations for the CIA."[36] Both schools published a number of books in two versions: one classified for CIA reading and one unclassified and released to the general public.[37]

In 1956 the CIA established the Asia Foundation at Michigan State University, which "sponsored research, supported conferences, ran academic exchange programs, funded anti-communist academics in various Asian countries and recruited foreign agents and new case officers."[38]

As recently as 1987, Harvard University agreed to take on a $1.2 million study in conjunction with the Agency to study problems in intelligence assessment and foreign policy, using the Philippines as a model.[39] The CIA analyst in charge of that study was William Cline.[40]

While not all university foreign studies programs are CIA-inspired, a number have worked in close cooperation with the Agency. Spinoffs of the CIA-founded African-American Institute include Boston University's African Studies program, created in the same year and headed by William O. Brown, a member of the State Department's Office of Intelligence.[41] The now defunct Africa Research Group detailed numerous examples of the inbred nature of the Agency and its academic bedfellows.[42] Ex-agents are frequently recruited by universities, and scholars are often recruited by the CIA. The relationship is especially productive for the Agency if someone is on both the university and the CIA payroll at once, with access to university facilities and resources.

Furthermore, military intelligence and domestic intelligence agencies work together. According to ex-agent Ralph McGehee, "intelligence is widely distributed" among the many branches of the government.[43] Information collected through research sponsored by the State Department, Defense Department, FBI, NSA and CIA is often used for the same purposes. A research project funded by the Department of Defense may end up being used in a CIA covert operation. Even information gathered from those projects not sponsored by the Agency can wind up in its hands.

Paid Professors: Moonlighting for the Agency

In 1986, professor Nadav Safran left his director's position at Harvard's Center for Middle Eastern Affairs when it was revealed that he was on the CIA's payroll.[44] Safran's experience parallels that of professors across the nation who are working secretly for the CIA: he received over $100,000 from the Agency to write a book on Saudi Arabia and almost $50,000 to organize a university conference on Islam. The contract Safran signed with the CIA required that he conceal the source of his funding and submit his book to the Agency for censorship.

Just a year earlier, the former director of Harvard's Center for International Affairs, Samuel P. Huntington, "was also uncloaked as a CIA 'asset,'" working secretly with a CIA consultant and publishing documents that were both paid for and censored by the Agency.[45] Andrew Kopkind notes that the "F" in the Center's acronym CFIA is given capital status for obvious reasons.[46]

The rule is that for every uncloaked professor, there exist a dozen others in hiding. "It is safe to assume that only a small amount of CIA academics are ever exposed while the great majority remain secret."[47]

It is difficult to typecast the CIA scholar. One Agency academic who held posts at Harvard and Johns Hopkins University, Gustav Hilger, was a former member of the Nazi Foreign Office.[48] But even liberal or left-leaning professors have been inducted into the CIA's intelligentsia. James R. Hooker of Michigan State's African Studies Center was regarded as at least left-leaning. He spoke publicly against the Vietnam War and was friendly with leaders of liberation movements in Africa and the Caribbean. However, as CIA researcher, Hooker traveled to Africa in the late 1960s to document the support of various political parties and eventually gave his personal support to UNITA and the FNLA in Angola. He attempted to recruit fellow academic George Rawick of the sociology department in 1968 and was turned down. According to Ken Lawrence, Hooker was probably working for the CIA well into the 1970s when the CIA's public image was suffering badly.[49]

Why would a liberal volunteer for the CIA? Hooker's wife claimed the Agency approached her husband with the argument that if liberal intellectuals got involved with the CIA, perhaps the quality of the organization would improve. Revelations of recent CIA activities strain the validity of that theory. Hooker's story says more about liberal intellectuals than the CIA. Almost anyone in academia who supports the general motives (if not the tactics) of the Agency is a potential recruit to do the Agency's bidding.

Scholars who do secret CIA work, whether it be research or wiretapping, compromise their positions as independent intellectuals and jeopardize their relationships with the universities by using their positions to gather information for the CIA. Research assistants or students involved in a professor's research without knowledge of CIA funding become pawns in a game they may not want to play.

In 1984, Professor Richard Mansbach, head of the political science department at Rutgers, assigned an undergraduate class to do data-intensive research on Western European political culture. The studies that the students carried out on Western Europe's disarmament, labor, women's and environmental movements were secretly passed on to the CIA. Mansbach had been hired by the Agency to participate in its "European Non-State Actors Project," a moonlighting job that his students knew nothing about and were assisting without their consent.[50] As of 1989, Mansbach was heading the political science department at the University of Iowa at Ames.

The stories of professors who were approached by the Agency, turned their offers down and then reported the experience to journalists give a good deal of insight into the CIA's recruiting tactics and university compliance with those tactics.

In a letter to journalist Ken Lawrence, Rene Lemarchand, professor of political science at the University of Florida in the '60s and '70s, describes a CIA attempt to glean information on Burundi politics from him just after he returned from Burundi in 1965. Lemarchand had not yet received tenure from the university and was asked by his department chair, Manning Dauer, to "display maximum cooperation" with the Miami-based CIA representative. Lemarchand refused to comply and was highly resentful of the internal pressure placed on him to do so.[51]

In 1979, Howard University psychology professor Kemba Maish was offered a research grant from the CIA. According to Maish, the Agency offered her a "fantastic salary," fully paid trips to Africa and "all kinds of very enticing programs." Her job would have been to develop profiles on foreign nationals in Africa, specifically, "communists that were in Africa." The CIA official who talked to Maish on the phone assured her that she would not be spying on her "own people."[52]

Maish turned the Agency down, but not before she found out where the CIA had gotten her name as a potential faculty recruit: a fellow

professor in the psychology department. Maish learned that the CIA
also received names from the director of one of the black studies
programs at the University of Maryland. Conversations with these
"contacts" revealed that they understood little about what the CIA was
doing. Maish described them as "unwitting agents" who passed names
along because they felt the CIA would get them somehow anyway. Her
co-worker in the psychology department said that a number of government agencies came to him for names. The CIA was one of many. Maish
was concerned.

> A lot of people don't realize what they are doing and they are
> getting a lot of other people involved in something they have
> no idea about. Or they are closing their eyes to it; they don't
> want to face the fact that if they turn down the CIA, they
> might jeopardize some funding or grants. Perhaps they want
> to cooperate so it won't interfere with the development of
> their careers.[53]

The one thing Maish couldn't fathom was why the CIA was
interested in her. She was well known by the university community as
a black activist who supported the liberation struggles of the African
people. The CIA was probably speculating that they could buy her out,
she thought. "They've obviously bought other people. This was just one
more person."

As Maish began to tell her story, other members of the Howard
community came out with theirs. A number of professors had been
contacted by the CIA; students had been contacted as well. Many people
were angry that their names were given to the Agency. And many had
been afraid to tell their stories until Maish had taken the first step. Those
who had been approached by the CIA were living with the fear that even
minimal contact with the Agency would somehow shed bad light on
their reputations as scholars.

The CIA banks on this paranoia to keep their presence a secret.
However, Maish was adamant in her opposition to the Agency and used
her discussions with administrators and other professors to relate the
CIA's activities around the world and emphasize "how organized this
recruiting effort really is, and how dangerous it can be, not just to African
people, but also to all people of the 'Third World.'"[54]

Even professors like Maish who condemn the actions and motives
of the CIA may be contributing to CIA-backed research unwittingly.
John Marks's book on the CIA's mind-control experiments, *The Search
for the Manchurian Candidate,* details examples of socialist professors
who lent their expertise to co-workers who were secretly doing research

for the Agency. "If I had known that this study was sponsored by the CIA, there is really, obviously, no way that I would have been associated with it," remarked one of the professors who was unwillingly involved in CIA research.[55] Other professors have had their mail opened, read and filed by the Agency without their consent.[56] In 1982, the CIA brazenly proposed that *all* scientific research papers written in the United States by U.S. academics be submitted to the Agency for "prior review." Fortunately, the proposal was repudiated by scientists before it could gain much ground.[57]

CIA-funded research, whether overt or covert, is underway in North American universities in epidemic proportions. In the '60s Georgetown University participated in the creation of the International Police Academy (a CIA police training headquarters) and provided Latin American CIA-trainees with English lessons, through its American Language Institute.[58] With the financial support of the Agency, the Fund for International Social and Economic Education, headed by Harvard's assistant dean of the graduate school of arts and sciences, underwrote a series of labor- and union-related projects geared toward developing nations.[59] CIA research monies have surfaced at Cornell's School of Industrial and Labor Relations, in Stanford's engineering department, at Harvard in prodigious amounts and at Michigan's Institute for Social Research.[60] The CIA has contracted projects at Berkeley, Columbia, Princeton, the University of Denver and Yale; and a number of academics have used their fieldwork to collect information for the Agency.[61] The list goes on and on and includes almost every well-recognized higher education institution in the nation.

Recently disclosed cases of CIA research funding indicate a sustained trend. As of the spring of 1990, University of Illinois political science professor Steven Seitz was under a $1 million contract with the CIA to develop "a computer model to forecast the spread of AIDS" and its impact in Africa.[62] Seitz, who criticizes the government's general failure to fund AIDS research, believes the CIA is financing his project to "contribute toward a better understanding of the AIDS pandemic." He asserts his contract with the CIA "is a noble effort to bring science to the service of mankind in an hour of deep human crisis." A liberal in the same tradition as James Hooker, Seitz fails to put the products of CIA research into the context of CIA activity and rationalizes his participation with the Agency the same way Hooker did: "I'd prefer the CIA to recruit from among our well-trained, intelligent students than for it to seek its applicants from among misanthropic McCarthyites who lack both talent and training."[63]

As of the late 1970s, approximately 5,000 professors were doing CIA work in some capacity, either "spotting" U.S. or foreign recruitment candidates, participating in research and grant work or carrying out more active programs like foreign police training. It is estimated that about 60 percent of these academics were aware of the nature of their employment, while another 40 percent did the CIA's bidding in the dark—through front companies or foundations.[64] In the 1990s, the number of academics on the CIA payroll has undoubtedly increased.

University of Missouri at Columbia chancellor Haskell Monroe says that CIA agents contacted him in the fall of 1988 to announce their

The CIA: An Equal Opportunity Employer

Congressional critics of the CIA have bemoaned the fact that women and minorities have historically been "vastly underrepresented throughout the professional grade structure" of the Agency.[65] Under fire from Congress and probably feeling a real need to "attract women and minorities with skills critical to the performances of [its] mission" (how is a white agent going to infiltrate an African liberation movement?), the CIA took steps to improve its image. Ensuring that U.S. minority groups and women have the same opportunity as the average white (heterosexual) male to subvert sovereign nations around the world, the CIA established its very own "Office of Equal Opportunity Employment."

The Equal Opportunity Office's "Black Affairs" division offers a "Summer Fellowship Program" for the faculties and administrations of historically black colleges and universities (HBCU). Now ten years old, the Summer Fellowship Program has recruited "75 faculty members and administrators from 32 HBCUs" who have both gained "access to [CIA] resources" and "shared information which gives our Agency the opportunity to strengthen relationships between the Agency and HBCUs."

More specifically, the CIA provides program participants with "new data for use in curriculum development and student counseling...research grants...[and] initiation of student intern and co-op programs." The CIA, in return, is provided with "insights into the role, problems, and programs of black colleges...[and] increased Agency recruitment."

Black colleges and universities beware. As Howard University's Kemba Maish warned in 1979: "We must not become the enemies of our people...We must fight the CIA."[66]

presence and their intentions to approach professors at the school. In the past, agents had also visited him "shortly after he took over top posts at Texas A & M University and the University of Texas at El Paso."[67]

CIA representatives also show up at academic conferences. According to Louis Wolf, co-editor of the *CovertAction Information Bulletin,* the CIA has been present at Latin American and African Studies Association and Association of Asian Studies conferences, "as well as all, and I repeat, *all* the professional organizations such as the [organizations] of librarians, geographers, anthropologists, mathematicians, statisticians, etc."[68]

CIA spokesperson Sharon Foster said in 1988 that the CIA has enough professors under Agency contract "to staff a large university."[69] Our universities are crawling with covert scholars-turned-agents and our independent academic foundations are being seriously undermined.

Beyond Research: CIA-Sponsored Experiment and Training Programs

With ample facilities for experimentation and an abundance of physical sites, college campuses are ideal for carrying out much larger and more insidious CIA programs. U.S. universities have housed some CIA activities that go beyond research and into active covert operations.

Michigan State University was under a $25 million contract with the CIA from 1955 to 1959 to provide academic cover to five CIA agents stationed in South Vietnam. MSU professors also helped draft the South Vietnamese government's Constitution and provided police training and weapons to the repressive Diem regime.[70]

During the same years, professors from Cornell and MIT's Center for International Studies were training an elite group of Indonesian military and economic leaders at the Center for South and Southeast Asian Studies at UC Berkeley; they would later be christened "the Berkeley Mafia." These trainees went back to Indonesia and "became the impetus behind the coup that brought Suharto to power."[71] The result was the massacre of from 500,000 to over one million Indonesians, mostly ethnic Chinese.

The University of Michigan developed infrared surveillance and reconnaisance technology that was used in Southeast Asia to track guerrillas and in Bolivia to track Che Guevara. According to *Counterspy* magazine, the university personnel who worked on the project were fully aware of its intended use.[72]

Universities also made up a network of bases for the CIA's MKULTRA mind-control experiments in the mid-'50s. Research for MKULTRA was conducted at 44 colleges and universities in the United States. At the Georgetown University Hospital, Professor Charles Geschickter lent his name to a CIA research front foundation, the "Geschickter Fund for Medical Research," and tested mind-control drugs on pyschiatric and terminally ill cancer patients.[73] Students from Harvard and other Boston area universities were among those who were given doses of LSD through the MKULTRA program at the Boston Psychopathic Hospital, now the Massachusetts Mental Health Center.[74]

According to Ken Lawrence's testimony to a University of Wisconsin at Madison faculty committee in 1985 on the issue of CIA campus activity, Madison professor Carl Rogers participated in MKULTRA through the CIA's academic front organization, the Human Ecology Fund. Madison alumnus Frank Olson, an MKULTRA guinea pig, committed suicide after drinking Cointreau that had been laced with LSD. Lawrence believes that a revival of the MKULTRA program exists at the University of Florida, where CIA-funded researchers have been doing "truth detector" experiments using a computer to read brain waves.[75]

In the summer of 1986, Northwestern University's Traffic Institute, a police training facility, began participation in the State Department's "Anti-Terrorism Assistance Program." The program at the Traffic Institute was scheduled to run for ten months and involved the training of Salvadoran police force members who were connected with the Salvadoran death squads. Media coverage and protests from campus and community groups eventually forced Northwestern to pull out of the program but State Department spokesman Michael Kraft said that "schools in the New England area" had already participated in the program.[76]

CIA involvement in the training of Salvadoran military forces was documented in the *New York Times* of March 22, 1984, which reported that the "head of Salvador's Treasury Police [had] been a paid [CIA] informant since the late 1970s." The Treasury Police are known as "major organizers" of the death squads.[77] Further evidence not only of CIA connections to the death squads but of the Agency's creation, support and training of the Salvadoran death squads was revealed in *The Progressive* in May 1984. The CIA, along with State Department and military personnel "conceived and organized ORDEN, the rural paramilitary intelligence network" that initiated the use of terrorism against government opponents. ORDEN became Mano Blanca, the

"White Hand," and developed into a network of death squads whose members received direct training from U.S. officials.[78]

Though a CIA connection to the Traffic Institute's program has not been found, Northwestern's cooperation with the State Department program is typical of schools across the country who seek working relationships with government agencies and the funding that comes with them—regardless of the moral implications.

Conclusion:
Bedfellows of the Establishment

Many U.S. universities carry on an intimate relationship with the CIA. The fledgling OSS was made up of academics from the Ivy League and, like twins connected in the womb, the CIA and academia have grown up together. Universities allow the CIA to recruit from their pools of qualified students, sometimes doing the Agency's screening work themselves. They open their doors to CIA recruiters who bribe and intimidate foreign students to become U.S. agents. They accept CIA monies and leadership to establish entire university departments or initiate special programs and allow their workforce to moonlight for the Agency and submit to censorship while keeping up a front of academic integrity. In extreme cases, our universities provide cover for and carry on covert operations that have a direct effect on the peoples of other countries as well as on the people of the United States. The CIA and academia have an almost fully cooperative relationship: trading information and resources and supporting each other in the face of hostility.

Very rarely do university administrators and professors resist working with government agencies like the CIA, and when they do the Agency takes great offense. The case of Harvard in the late '70s is one of the few examples of even token resistance to the Agency.

After the 1975 Church Committee revelations of illegal CIA activities—including secret contracts with university employees and students—Harvard President Derek Bok issued a set of guidelines restricting CIA activity at the university. The regulations did not go as far as banning the Agency from Harvard; they merely required any university employee under contract with the CIA to reveal that contract to the Harvard administration. Bok requested a similar regulation from the CIA: that undisclosed relationships with Harvard be forbidden.

Stansfield Turner, then director of the Agency, refused to issue a regulation and refused to comply with the Harvard ruling. Turner admitted quite honestly to being relieved that "very few other universities followed Harvard's example and this did not become a continuing problem." His reason for not respecting Harvard's authority over its own affairs: the CIA was unfairly being singled out for treatment when "any relationship can compromise a professor's objectivity."[79] Turner conceded only to "reminding" professors of their responsibilities to their universities before entering into a contract with the Agency—rather like reminding Oliver North that he's under oath—and stated that the CIA "would not be the university's policeman."[80]

The Agency vehemently objects to any attempt to block its efforts to "tap the wisdom of academia." If restrictions are placed on its activities, the CIA finds some way to work around them. Ironically, Turner could not understand why the Church Report raised such a stir among academics when similar revelations of the on-going relationship between the CIA and the business community elicited minimal reaction. According to Turner, businessmen were just more pragmatic and realized that "most relationships have benefits that go two ways."[81]

Although Harvard and a few other universities have expressed some resistance to the academic arm of the Agency (Harvard is still one of the CIA's most loyal and active academic supporters), most university administrators have no problems with the CIA.

> Certainly, the failure of academic leaders to act is not based on a lack of information...In the spring of 1976, at a secret meeting...eight presidents of America's most prestigious universities were given information describing the full extent of the CIA's foreign student recruiting and its special relationships with faculty members at their institutions...none of the university presidents wanted to know anything more, vouchsafing contentment with the status quo.82

Even if they question some Agency activities, administrators are reluctant to give up the grant money offered by the CIA or to imperil government funding in general. Philip Agee notes that "any president who refuses CIA access for recruiting jeopardizes millions upon millions of dollars in government money—I don't mean CIA money, but U.S. government [money] in general."[83] Jonathan Feldman, former program director at the National Commission for Economic Conversion and Disarmament (NCECD), describes "the desperation of universities for Pentagon money." Due to the "incentives of money and power which Pentagon largesse brings," many universities have become so dependent on defense research and development contracts that they will bend over backwards to win them. "Senator Stennis put the matter bluntly in 1969: 'at some of our Appropriations Committee hearings, we see...universities come down here fighting tooth and nail to get that money.'"[84] How can university administrators justify decisions which ban the CIA from their universities to the Defense Department and related military agencies—which are, in some cases, supporting more than 50 percent of their schools' research projects?

Consequently, university administrators do more than watch helplessly as the CIA runs rampant through their halls of education. Many university presidents are particularly skilled at *defending* the Agency's presence on campus. In 1968, a University of California administrator, Berkeley vice president Earl Bolton, prepared a lengthy, secret memorandum for the Agency advising it on how to improve its academic relations. Candidly blunt and cynical in tone, the memo instructs the Agency to manipulate university and academic "credos" to justify CIA activities. He suggests "full use of the jargon of the academy" in defending the CIA and notes encouragingly: "There is sufficient vagueness in the total traditions of the profession to provide a skillful polemicist with formidable ammunition for defense."

Better, however, to avoid being on the defensive. Hide the Agency, Bolton writes, behind a front entity, preferably one with "a ringing name" like the "Institute for a Free Society."[85] Further, increase carrot money, avoid involving the administration with individual grants—and how about changing the words "classified" and "secret" to "limited access research" or something a little less intimidating? Bolton hurls integrity straight out the window and even advances the use of Orwellianisms to obscure the truth about CIA campus activity. According to the *CovertAction Information Bulletin,* Bolton's memo was widely circulated among the leaders of other universities in the late '60s.[86]

Bolton's advice for the Agency also covered dealing with student unrest and furthering student recruiting. In both areas, administrators have been known to actively participate with the Agency. CIA documents released under the Freedom of Information Act describe college administrators monitoring student dissent and acting as informants for the Agency.[87]

Our university administrators, in most cases, are either financially bound to welcome all government organizations, or they support the CIA's existence and actions on college campuses for ideological reasons. They are usually incapable or unwilling to shut the door on the Agency. The struggle against the Central Intelligence Agency and university militarism in general will *not* be carried out by those who run our universities. It will be carried out by the students, faculty and community members who are not entrenched in CIA business and who *do* care about the truth and about acting on it.

CHAPTER THREE

CIA *Off* Campus:
Learning from the '80s and
Gearing Up for the '90s

In the last three and a half years 102 universities have been forced
to join the divestment movement...That is not because they have
come to their moral senses...it's because of organized pressure by
students.

Abbie Hoffman, 1988[1]

We live in an environment which is—supposedly—based on
intellectual inquiry...and we are not hampered by the institutional
pressures that affect the rest of society. The university is a
concentrated community where it's easy to communicate. That's
hard to do elsewhere in our atomized suburban culture. And I think
there are really a lot of idealistic people here. With the time, energy
and motivation, students can have a tremendous influence on
society and politics.

Sean Maher, Peace Project, Northwestern University[2]

Student Activism in the 1980s

As scholars enrolled in institutions of "higher learning," students
are exposed to the many noble and ignoble achievements of their
predecessors: brilliant physicists, gifted writers, renowned historians,
journalists, psychologists, philosophers, physicians and politicians.

As citizens of a planet in decay—a planet threatened by nuclear
weapons and ecological destruction and cursed with rampant starvation,
illiteracy, racism, sexism and violence—today's students are charged

43

with the daunting task of doing their part to save the earth. Fortunately, they are in the unique position to utilize the wisdom of the ages for the benefit of humanity. As students, they have an opportunity to learn. As humans, they have a responsibility to act. Most university brochures insist that knowledge carries with it a moral imperative. Most college classes, however, teach that people rarely act solely on moral imperative. History describes a human race that is too often caught in a destructive course of economic or political gain.

But empathy with the basic human needs for food, shelter, dignity and freedom have combined with the basic human impulse for peace and justice to create social and spiritual movements that penetrate a bleak global history of destruction and repression with, if you will, "a thousand points of light." Forces of progressive change spring from an inexhaustible source to counteract the fear, corruption and greed that become the status quo.

University students are in a unique position to take on the responsibilities of democracy and promote change. Their position in institutes of education gives them access to huge resources of knowledge and at least a little time to explore this knowledge and apply it to what they see happening around them. Their mandate is to *learn,* not yet to climb the corporate ladder or run for office. All young people, students and non-students alike, face an increasingly immediate task. This earth, replete with its afflictions, is theirs to inherit, to care for, to love and, therefore, to change. Each generation can make a contribution if it has the will to give. Today's student generation *must* give, if only to assure that future generations will survive.

Givin' It to 'Em

The history of student activism in the United States is one that we can rightly be proud of. The 1930s witnessed a surge of student participation in national politics as labor movements and the spread of socialist ideology challenged the structure of American capitalism. The radicalization of students in the '60s and early '70s was one of the most democratic developments in our history. After the Vietnam War and the well-publicized anti-war movement, "progressive student political activism never really stopped."[3] Unfortunately, the struggle for change that has taken place across the country on college campuses in the 1980s—that will undoubtedly strengthen in the 1990s—has been all but completely ignored by the mass media and, hence, by most of the U.S. population. But the struggle has, at its finest moments, been as dedicated and as effective as its predecessors.

Just for example:

South Africa

Over 14,000 students and faculty members at U.S. universities were arrested in divestment actions in the 1980s.[4] Together, they pressured over 155 universities—including the entire University of California system—to pull investments from corporations doing business in South Africa.[5] At Johns Hopkins University, students identified seven trustees who served as directors for the Maryland National Bank "which had extensive financial ties to South Africa." In a "serious, longterm effort," the activists blocked an effort by the bank to merge with another, pressured it to withdraw all of its investments in South Africa, obtained the bank's agreement to "commit $50 million over a five year period to low-income Baltimore neighborhood development" and persuaded it to offer free checking accounts to low-income customers.[6]

Students moved beyond the boundaries of their universities to picket companies that were uninvolved with their schools, but heavily involved with South Africa. An estimated 20,000 students marched on Washington in April 1987 as part of a "Mobilization for Justice and Peace in Central America and Southern Africa." Activists targeted the federal government as well, including "more stringent and more inclusive sanctions...[and] a total ban on trade" among their just concerns. These actions—bolstered by educational efforts—have expanded the limits of the divestment debate, not only on college campuses, but in the national media as well. Today, "campaigns continue at schools where divestment has not been achieved."[7]

Latin America

Students brought Latin American issues to university forums and helped lead the fight against contra aid. Combatting the State Department's Office of Public Diplomacy and its propaganda flow, students worked with Nicaraguan solidarity organizations to help prevent an outright invasion of Nicaragua.

Student to Student International Solidarity programs with El Salvador began in 1980 and include hundreds of campus Latin American solidarity groups. Support for the struggle in El Salvador led to the initiation of "rapid response" networks to call international attention to the abductions of Salvadoran students and increased the visibility of Latin American issues in general. These efforts were punctuated by the Committee in Solidarity with the People of El Salvador (CISPES) and Pledge of Resistance "Steps to Freedom" demonstration at the Pentagon in the fall of 1988. Of the 1,800 demonstrators, over 600 were students.

According to CISPES national student organizer Doug Calvin, "Students have been there all the way."[8]

At Illinois State, Wesleyan and schools across the country, students have dressed in fatigues, kidnapped and held each other at gunpoint in guerrilla theater acts aimed at bringing Washington's war in El Salvador a little closer to home. In support of the victims of that war and in opposition to U.S. neo-colonialism in all of Latin America, at least three California universities and the University of Colorado at Boulder brought the sanctuary issue to their student governments and formed the beginnings of the Campus Sanctuary Network. Many student groups organized to collect material aid, including clothing and medical supplies, to send to the displaced and needy in El Salvador and Nicaragua. And at the University of Wisconsin at Madison, women's groups are forming relationships with Latin American women's groups like the Movement for the Emancipation of Women in Chile (MEMCHA). As one Madison woman explained, "We're going to start talking about what's happening with them, because we're sick of it just being the guerrillas and warfare. We're going to talk about the women's issues."[9]

Women's Issues

Through the 1980s, the women's movement struggled to keep its issues on the national agenda. As new generations of women shunned the stereotyped "feminist" tag, women's groups had to work even harder to win the interest and support of their constituency. Despite a national trend against the active promotion of feminism, university women's groups survived and even thrived in the Reagan-Rambo era. On campus, women students developed popular programs that "can be divided into six loose categories: (1) personal safety; (2) reproductive rights; (3) women's studies; (4) economic equality; (5) administration policies, and (6) empowerment and leadership."[10]

In October 1989, 800 students at the University of Wisconsin at Madison united in a "Take Back the Night" march through the streets and to the student union. Similar marches have become annual events at universities around the country. At Boulder "a workshop for men has been conducted while the march takes place and at some schools, fraternity members have shown support by standing along the parade route with lighted candles."[11] At other universities, however, fraternity men have thrown bottles and screamed obscenities at marchers. When this happened at Northwestern University, march organizers demanded formal apologies from the fraternities in question, which were published in the school newspaper. The hostility shown against organized women by male fraternities also manifests in date rape, "gang" rape and "black-out" rape in which men have sex with unconscious women. University feminist groups provide support for rape victims and educate about what are commonplace incidents at college campuses.

University women's groups have also contributed to expanding the feminist agenda by joining forces with other progressive groups on broader issues. For the November 12, 1989, National Organization for Women (NOW) march on Washington, regional student networks turned out tens of thousands of students united under the slogan, "Abortion is not a single issue," and stressed the race and class concerns that are integral to abortion rights. Altogether, students made up approximately a third of major reproductive rights demonstrations in Washington, D.C., and other cities.

Gay and Lesbian Rights

"Students who are gay, lesbian or bisexual have emerged in the last few years with a strong political consciousness and a fierce determination to end the discrimination and homophobia that has often turned to violence."[12]

In the 1980s, gay and lesbian students got together and organized as part of a nationwide "emergence of recognized [gay and lesbian] campus organizations."[13] Gay and lesbian groups at Georgetown University and the University of Arkansas challenged administrative discrimination by taking their schools to court over refusals to allocate student government funding to their organizations, ultimately winning precedent-setting victories for gay rights.[14] Gay and lesbian groups and gay-straight alliances rallied to increase AIDS awareness and dispel the homophobic slander of the gay community by the religious right. The Rutgers University Lesbian/Gay Alliance issued a two-page pamphlet to the student body entitled: "What Jesus Christ said about homosexuality." The pages inside were blank.[15] United lesbians and gays pressured many universities—including the mythically "conservative" Northwestern University—to adopt sexual orientation non-discrimination clauses.

These clauses are in direct contradiction with university ROTC programs, and at least a dozen schools have inititated anti-ROTC campaigns based on the army's sexual preference discrimination. As MIT provost John Deutch wrote in a letter to Secretary of Defense Richard Cheney: "The contradiction between [the schools'] principle of nondiscrimination...and the presence of an ROTC that does discriminate cannot exist on campuses indefinitely. Many universities will withdraw."[16]

Gay Awareness Week has become an annual event on many campuses. At the University of Wisconsin at Madison, the gay and lesbian Ten Percent Society joins Madison feminists once a year by contributing funds to the Take Back the Night march.[17] By speaking out and taking charge, organized gay rights activists create more tolerant atmospheres on campuses that encourage gay students to come out and affirm their sexual preference. At Northwestern University, the Gay and Lesbian Alliance held a standing-room-only workshop within a larger "Progressive Students Conference" in which gay students described the kinds of subtle harassment and discrimination they were subjected to on a daily basis, even from self-described progressives. Straight students who attended the workshop left with a sharpened awareness of gay and lesbian concerns and pledges to examine their own homophobia.

Students of Color

"Minority" students, who together comprise the majority of the student populations at most U.S. universities, continue to fight for recognition, respect, academic programs that address their specific needs and structural reforms within society that address the problems of economic exploitation and inequality.

African-American students have championed civil rights issues despite almost a decade of Reagan administration backsliding. Sometimes allied with other progressive organizations on campus, students of color have protested racist incidents on college campuses and pushed for more demographically representative student recruiting and faculty hiring, as well as ethnic studies programs and mandatory racism courses. "Demonstrations against racial harassment and for greater diversity hit at least twenty-five schools [in the spring of 1990], including Harvard, Oberlin, and the University of California, Santa Barbara."[18]

Anti-racist protests in the 1980s "were almost always intitiated and defined by students of color, though most of these struggles did make alliances with and gain support from progressive whites."[19]

The Movimiento Estudiantil Chicano de Aztlan (MECHA), or the Chicano Student Movement of Aztlan, which started in the late 1960s at the University of California at Santa Barbara has spread to campuses across the country. Today, at the University of New Mexico, MECHA works in rural communities to encourage teenagers to pursue their educational dreams. The Movement there has also worked with "a minority coalition that includes blacks, Native Americans and Arab students" and addresses Central American as well as domestic issues.[20]

Organizations of students of color have found that coalitions are instrumental in bringing reforms to the university. Coalition work compelled University of California at Berkeley's Academic Senate to adopt an "American Cultures" course as a graduation requirement in the spring of 1989. On April 19 and 20 of 1990, a coalition of student groups calling themselves the "United Front" organized a "Strike for Diversity" to protest the university's affirmative action record in faculty hiring and tenure granting. The strike was observed by about 75 percent of Berkeley students and included demands for a bisexual, lesbian and gay studies center, a multicultural community center and a staff union call for an end to sexism, racism and homophobia in the workplace.[21]

In the '88-'89 school year at Detroit's Wayne State University, 200 students moved into the administration building for a 12-day "study-in" protesting campus racist incidents that were ignored by the administration. In the same year, demonstrations by African-American activists at Howard University kept right-wing Republican Lee Atwater off the board of trustees.[22] Very effective and wide-reaching anti-racist campaigns were also launched at the University of Michigan and Columbia University.[23]

"Finally...student activists understood that institutional racism was the crux of the problem in higher education."[24] Students of color have not rested with the "feel good," superficial reforms (such as race relations classes) that universities like Michigan State proposed in response to their activism. They continue their campaign for more meaningful changes such as "abolishing racist and sexist criteria such as the SAT and making more financial resources available to students that may otherwise not have an opportunity to go to college," as well as allying with community struggles.[25]

Palestinian Rights

"Palestinian rights may be the newest issue to hit campuses in the name of fighting racism."[26] In response to Israel's continuing occupation of the Occupied Territories, the negative stereotype of Arabs in the mass media and sometimes violent racist incidents against Arab students, Arab student groups and Palestinian Solidarity Committees were formed at over 200 universities in the 1980s. Regional progressive student networks and unions took up Palestine and Palestinian rights as issues and began campaigns at affiliated universities, inviting speakers and sponsoring debates on their campuses. Two national organizations, the November 29th Committee for Palestine (N29) and the Association of Arab-American University Graduates (AAUG), helped coordinate student activities across the country.[27]

The Palestine Solidarity Committee at the University of Michigan initiated a series of educational events on racism against Arabs, Israeli human rights abuses and life in the Occupied Territories that provoked an almost violent response from right-wing Zionist groups. After exhaustive debate, the UM Student Assembly resolved to send a delegation of students to the West Bank and Gaza to observe living conditions there and further resolved to study the feasibility of a sister university program with Bir Zeit University. On April 22 of 1990, the City University of New York system did adopt Bir Zeit as a sister school through a resolution in the student senate. The adoption was part of a general protest against Israel's shutdown of Palestinian universities. "Similar sister-university relationships have been adopted by the University of Wisconsin, Madison with An-Najah University in Nablus; [UC] Berkeley, with Bethlehem; and Columbia College with Bir Zeit. Draft resolutions are pending at many other colleges."[28]

U.S. Students for U.S. University Democracy

The fight for democracy continues right here at home, where students have voiced their demands for democratic educational rights—and won. Strikes at the City University of New York (CUNY) in the spring of 1989 shut down 17 campuses and put a halt to a proposed tuition increase in the state budget. Chanting "Fight, fight, fight. Education is our right!" over 15,000 students took over the streets of New York in a show of force that apparently convinced New York Governor Mario Cuomo to veto the legislation. The CUNY actions represent an inspirational, racially-integrated majority student movement "rooted in the working class and communities of color."[29]

The general lack of democratic process at most universities becomes apparent to activists the first time their respective governing boards refuse either to hear student concerns or fail to respond to them. At many schools, students have struggled long and hard to win seats on Boards of Regents, Governors or Trustees. In April of 1990, over 100 Rutgers students occupied an administration building for ten days to demonstrate the determination of their call for three voting representatives on the Board of Governors. United under "The Campaign for an Affordable Rutgers Education," the occupying students also demanded a tuition increase freeze, tenure for radical black professor Amiri Baraka and immediate negotiation of fair contracts with labor unions at the university.[30]

Through groups like the United States Student Association, students are campaigning for their right to vote in the districts where they attend school. They are also getting involved in the national political process. At Fairfield College in Connecticut, students initiated a letter-writing campaign to members of Congress when funds for educational loans were being threatened.[31] Students also volunteered time to work for Jesse Jackson's presidential campaign in the '87-'88 school year and lobbied specific congresspeople to stop aid to the contras and to El Salvador.

Coalition Building

As the student movement grows in the 1990s, activists face the challenging task of building effective coalitions composed of whites and students of all races. Progressive, multiracial coalitions have formed at different universities through the Atlanta and D.C. Student Coalitions Against Apartheid and Racism (A-and DC-SCAR), the Northeast Student Action Network (NSAN), the Progressive Student Network (PSN), the Student Action Union (SAU) and the United Coalition Against Racism (UCAR), among others.

These affiliations are attempting to create agendas that include the concerns of all ethnicities—from African- and Asian-American to Filipino, from Latino to Palestinian.

National progressive and racially diverse conferences at Rutgers and in Washington, D.C., have formed networks between schools that provide much needed communication and support for student activists. In a relatively apathetic era, the concerned minority is laying the groundwork that will prove invaluable to the future active majority that is waiting to get involved just beyond the next bend in the road.

The examples listed are a few of many and hardly represent the full spectrum of issues students are currently working on. Again and again, students have come together and proven their strength, courage and determination to influence the course of university and world events. Undaunted by indifferent and sometimes hostile administrations, students have faced uninformed or complacent student bodies, an unfriendly media, aggressive conservatives, arrests, university penalties, trials and even jail to show that students have always been and will continue to be a force for change and a force to reckon with.

No one knows this better than the friendly folks at the Central Intelligence Agency.

Throughout the 1980s, student activism against CIA presence in U.S. univerisities has accelerated and intensified. At the end of the decade, CIA recruiters met with increasingly militant demonstrations at almost a third of the schools they visited. The current decade portends only more difficulties for the Agency as it attempts to further its academic activities.

Gearing up for the CIA Off Campus Movement in the 1990s

Through their actions, the students, faculty and staff of U.S. universities raise the issues, bring them front and center and can eventually create learning environments based on democratic principles and progressive change. It is their imperative to help create universities that contribute to society, that influence the course of world events in a positive way for the protection and sane development of the planet and its people. After all, isn't that why students go to college and professors choose to teach in the first place?

Given that the CIA is antithetical to democratic principles, progressive change and academic integrity, the university community is ultimately responsible for the struggle against the Central Intelligence Agency's campus presence.

Ousting the CIA is a small step in a stairwell where each step builds upon the other. The CIA issue readily lends itself to other issues: U.S. foreign policy, neo-colonialism, racism, civil liberties, monopoly capitalism and media manipulation. Obviously, if we achieve our goal of banning the CIA from the schools, the Agency and its foundation in the U.S. power structure will continue to exist: "U.S. foreign and domestic policy has roots in institutional structures."[32] U.S. policy also has roots in greed and the attitudes and perspectives that perpetuate greed. There will always be more work to do and issues to explore.

But because the CIA encompasses so many issues and because its activities reflect the most horrifying results of unbridled Western capitalism, the CIA Off Campus issue is a potent and radical educational tool. As a base for expansion into a broad progressive program, the call for CIA Off Campus is a solid foundation, a foundation well worth building.

Organization: Building a Group[33]

When you say, "What can I do? Nothing!" I agree with you. But when you ask another: "What can *we* do?" I would say: "Everything."

Nicaraguan campesino[34]

If you are not already part of a group of students and/or faculty organized against the CIA, there are a number of ways to get involved. First, find out if there are any existing organizations that are already doing this kind of work. At many universities, affiliates of the Northeast Student Action Network (NSAN), the Progressive Student Network (PSN), the Student Action Union (SAU) and other progressive student networks have already been through various stages of struggle with the CIA at their schools. Anti-CIA work has gone on even at notoriously conservative campuses like Georgetown, Harvard, Northwestern, Penn State and Princeton University. Check for posters, students handing out flyers, meetings listed in the school newspaper, booths at activities fairs and other subversive behavior.

If no such organization exists, you may want to consider forming your own. However, a lasting student group organized along political lines needs a clear agenda and a dedicated membership. Begin your organizing in campus groups that already oppose U.S. imperialism. Work with experienced activists to create an agenda that covers a spectrum of issues and includes the call for CIA Off Campus. Students from Latin American, Filipino, Palestinian, African-American, South African (divestment) and other organizations can band together and form an ad hoc committee against CIA recruitment. Gay and lesbian rights groups may want to get involved because of the CIA's policy of sexual preference discrimination. At Princeton, the CIA was completely banned from recruiting because of its discrimination against gays and lesbians, a struggle carried out mainly by Princeton's Coalition Against Homophobia.

The CIA Off Campus struggle is part of a larger struggle against a range of ills that include but are certainly not limited to: domestic and Thirld World poverty; a profit-oriented, neo-colonial foreign policy; militarism; racism; bigotry; secrecy and the national security state. As noted in the student activism issue of *The Nation*: "It is a measure of the potency of the demand to end university-CIA ties that those organizers who have stressed coalition building have been able to enter into effective relationships with Latino groups, gay and lesbian rights advocates, solidarity workers, black activists and religious people."[35] Though the variety of reasons to oppose the Agency may initially seem overwhelming, it is this variety that makes the CIA issue key in building an all-inclusive progressive student movement. The diversity of potential participants in a CIA Off Campus campaign makes the unification of single-issue campus groups a realistic possibility. Until those people working on single issues cooperate, combine and form a common agenda that addresses all human needs, *freedom and justice for all,* their total potential for change will never be realized.

At Penn State, African-American activists joined forces with anti-intervention activists in the struggle against the CIA and the racist underpinnings of its activity. They issued a flyer comparing the CIA to the Ku Klux Klan on the grounds that the CIA has undermined the sovereignty of independent black nations, assisted the South African government in its arrest of Nelson Mandela and participated in the assassination of Patrice Lumumba. According to the flyer's author, white Student Action Union member Travis Parchman, "the CIA is one of the strongest issues" his group can work on, "because of its all-encompassing nature that encourages the group to "connect with the black groups on campus" as well as other ethnic and foreign student groups.[36]

At Northwestern University, white anti-CIA and divestment activists wanted to join a black student march for increased ethnic studies funds and more black faculty. Initially, this participation was controversial within the black student group, but the decision was made to allow non-black students to join the march and the effort turned out to be a success.

Overcoming Racism, Sexism and Heterosexism

While some schools have made great progress uniting disparate groups, most CIA Off Campus campaigns are initiated by predominantly white student groups. "When the 15 members of Madison's PSN congregate…in the back room of the Black Bear Tavern, there are no black faces, and all the "CIA On Trial" defendants in Massachusetts [were] white."[37]

Black student groups often see the CIA issue as less of a priority than the domestic repression they deal with on a daily basis. Similarly, gay, lesbian and bisexual rights groups are organized primarily to deal with gay, lesbian and bisexual rights. Feminist organizations also face more immediate tasks that directly address the concerns of their members. Yet there is common ground on which students working on different issues can come together. The route to that common ground, however, is blocked by a number of obstacles which need to be faced and overcome.

Oppressed groups often resist working with male, white and/or more privileged activists because they don't see these activists confronting oppression at home, nor do they see a willingness on the part of white activists to give up leadership or establish a multicultural or tolerant atmosphere within their organizations.

Tracye Matthews, a graduate student at Michigan State and a board member of the Ella Baker-Nelson Mandela Center for Anti-Racist Education, offers some views on the reluctance of black activists to work with mostly white leftist groups:

> Activism tends to be very segregated for a variety of reasons. There's an historical distrust [on the part of black students] of working with white students—and it's due to racism within white leftist groups. There are also differing levels of politicization within the students of color community...But [for politicized black students to be able to work with whites,] whites have to be willing to accept leadership from people of color and work with us *from the beginning,* not as an afterthought. Also, white activists sometimes fail to frame the issue in terms of its impact on people of color; they fail to put the issue into a framework of racism...It's always a tough question; people of color have so much else to do within the community. At the same time, we want to address the racism within white activist groups and the racism [inherent in] the CIA issue.[38]

Students of color are "increasingly unable to work with 'militant' white activists," and have become "frustrated with white activists' apparent indifference toward the problems of racism in the university," according to black activist Matthew Countryman.[39] Lack of understanding within student groups also impedes activists' attempts to work together. "Whites are unfamiliar with and insensitive to the alienation minority students feel."[40]

According to Tony Vellela, journalist and author of *New Voices: Student Political Activism in the '80s and '90s,* "racism is the single greatest threat to the emergence of a progressive student movement in the United States."[41] Domestic racism, sexism and heterosexism are certainly not limited to the non-academic world. It is in university settings that some of the most violent racist, sexist and homophobic attacks of recent years have occurred. Nor are these problems limited to students outside of progressive organizations.

Members of mostly straight and white anti-CIA groups should take stock of their personal politics as well as the politics of the group as a whole. What are the members' underlying attitudes toward gays, lesbians and people of color? Would a gay member feel comfortable coming out to the group? Would the group feel comfortable with a black or Chicano leader? Do men tend to dominate the discussions or fail to listen to the women in the group? How much latitude exists for all of the group members to express their opinions or feelings?

How many times has the group attempted to participate in people of color, feminist or gay rights actions or tried to learn more about either? If the group's support for other issues is not demonstrated, then it is selfish and probably inaccurate to expect other groups to support *its* cause.

The CIA is only one symptom of a huge, institutionalized system riddled with profound ailments—and it is not necessarily the most important issue to work on. Anti-CIA activists must acknowledge that the work of other activists is just as legitimate as the work that they are doing and understand that coalition building goes both ways. Until white and privileged activists examine their own attitudes and priorities, the student movement will continue to remain divided "along lines of race and ethnicity,"[42] sex and sexual preference. If anything, the situation calls for more efforts to find the common ground on which single-issue groups made up of students of color, white, feminist, gay, bisexual and straight students can meet and work together.

It is essential for students from the dominant power groups in our society—whites, men, the middle class, heterosexuals—to recognize their priviliges and work to empower the oppressed. On a personal level, that means practicing the kind of interpersonal integration that most middle-class whites support theoretically but have little experience with. "A special effort must be made to seek out activists who are people of color," Tracye Matthews notes, "and whites must ask themselves 'What is already being done now by people of color?' They can't assume that they are the only ones addressing the issue." On an organizational level, decision making must be up-front—from setting the agenda to analyzing the strengths and weaknesses of a course of action. "[Whites] also need to put aside their arrogance and respect the opinions of students of color."[43]

Working together is essential "not only to build a more united force on campus, but, more importantly, because the issues and content of the struggle are the same. It's just the form that is different."[44] The CIA Off Campus issue, because of its comprehensive nature, can be a magnet for varying activist organizations and provide a common activity for students of different backgrounds to work on while forging permanent relationships that can only make their voices and their actions on all issues ring truer and stronger.

Strategies

Initial contacts between groups should be made, if they haven't been made already. Representatives can be elected within progressive groups to attend the meetings of other groups. Exchange dates for giving presentations on the kinds of issues you are working on and where you need help the most—or how you think you can work together on at least one action. Strategies for coalition building will vary from school to school depending on each university's structure and campus climate. It may be wiser to retain small groups that have already been recognized by the student government and are receiving funding from it than to merge those groups into one. In a case like this, try establishing an umbrella organization that encompasses different campus groups. Organize a racially-balanced progressive leadership coalition. Then plan an annual or bi-annual conference. In the spring of 1989 at Northwestern University, outreach and educational efforts resulted in what has become an annual progressive students' conference involving seven or eight student groups.

Co-sponsoring speakers, films and symposia is also a good way to connect—both with on-campus groups and community organizations like the Committee in Solidarity with the People of El Salvador (CISPES), churches with a liberation bent, sanctuary networks, and civil liberties advocates like the American Civil Liberties Union (ACLU) or the National Committee Against Repressive Legislation (NCARL).[45] At New York University, a Philip Agee speaking engagement was sponsored by over 20 different groups from the school and the city. Speakers and rallies against the CIA at Penn State were organized by a loose coalition including a Latin American group, a divestment group and a nuclear disarmament group.

Ad hoc committees can be used to join various students and student groups in opposition to the CIA. In 1987, Brown University students—in a pinch—organized an ad hoc committee called "CIA Off Campus." The following fall at Northwestern University, the Committee on Latin America, the International Socialist Organization and Peace Project (a PSN affiliate) co-sponsored the largest anti-CIA demonstration at that school in over seven years. Arrests and an ensuing trial led to the creation of an ad hoc coalition, called "CIA Off Campus" (always a catchy name), that attracted students previously unaffiliated with campus activist groups.

If you are successful in building ties among different campus groups, you may want to consider an umbrella organization or an entirely new and much larger organization. Band together to run for offices in the student government as a progressive party. Election campaigns for individual activists publicize their issues as well. Seats in student governments are a way to raise concerns, bring them to a vote and establish a majority voice on issues like banning the CIA.

A group of activists at the University of Chicago recently sent out a mailing inviting progressive groups at other universities in the Chicago area to form a small network. They also encouraged student groups to get members into their student governments. "The retreat into single issue politics and away from student governments and inter-campus organizations has...fragmented our vision. The nineties call for us to break out of this fragmentation," the mailing advised. Running on a broad progressive agenda, reform-minded students at the University of Chicago recently won 21 out of 50 seats in the Student Assembly. So far, officers in the "Executive Committee" have put forth demands that the university give students and faculty elected seats on the Board of Trustees, provide greater day-care services for staff and students and dispense condoms in campus restrooms.

In March of 1990, at the University of Texas in Austin, a "powerful coalition" that includes the Black Student Alliance, the Gay and Lesbian Student Alliance, MECHA and "numerous others claimed victory in its first major campaign...by electing Toni Luckett as the first African-American president of UT's 48,000-member Student Association." Luckett, a member of the gay rights group and the Texas Rainbow Coalition, and a Central American activist, bases her success on practicing "inclusive" politics and developing the trust of varying contituencies that were "fighting against each other for the same crumbs." After the exhilaration of the election victory, the coalition was back at work, proposing changes in the curriculum with a focus on African-American history and the establishment of an African-American Culture Institute at UT.[46]

Support: Moral and Financial

After an anti-CIA recruiting demonstration in 1987 at Penn State, four students were confronted by university disciplinary action as stringent as suspension and expulsion. Faced with expulsion, Travis Parchman sought the legal advice of the Center for Constitutional Rights (CCR) in New York. With the *pro bono* help of attorney Morton Stavis, each student fought varying charges by questioning the entire university disciplinary code on the grounds of its unconstitutionality. "Here I was, high and dry, alone. Morton helped me deal with the system," Parchman says. Public opinion turned against the administration, which eventually down-graded one activist's suspension to probation and Parchman's expulsion to "disciplinary dismissal." Parchman maintains that "it was Penn State's attempt to do something to me, but not something that looked *totally* devastating to my education." Now he will at least get his diploma.[47]

The support of local, regional or national civil liberties organizations like the CCR is crucial when you face university or municipal justice systems. Activists often bite off a lot more than they can chew on their own, and the advice of experts comes in handy at these more-than-a-mouthful moments. Civil liberties or anti-covert-action groups are often willing to lend a helping hand to students sinking in legal quagmires. The Chicago Committee to Defend the Bill of Rights (CCDBR) sponsored a fundraising benefit for 16 people arrested at an anti-CIA demonstration at Northwestern University to help pay for incurred legal fees of over $2,000. The Committee also booked time on local radio talk shows for the arrestees and invited ex-CIA agent Verne Lyon to come lend his support to the cause.

Parchman's contact with the CCR and Northwestern's contact with the CCDBR actually began somewhat late in the game, after the arrests had happened. Forming *pre-action* coalitions with off-campus, politically experienced groups like these is probably smarter. Their extensive experiences with and knowledge about the CIA, the FBI and the U.S. government in general will help you prepare for the consequences of your activism and can also strengthen your educational campaign. Veteran domestic-surveillance opponent Frank Wilkinson, who fought J. Edgar Hoover and the House Un-American Activities Committee (and spent a year in prison for doing so), is constantly surprised by how little our generation knows about the recent past.

"Some students have even asked me who Hoover was," he marvels. As the executive director emeritus of the National Committee Against Repressive Legislation (NCARL), Wilkinson believes "we need to have more contact with young people."[48]

University of Wisconsin at Madison activist Mark Heimbach notes that within the Madison movement, "community organizations were one glaring thing a lot of students didn't address."[49] And they are usually more than willing to get involved.

Other organizations that will lend their support to your cause can be found right on campus. Even if you haven't gotten involved with your student government, there are usually a few representatives who will lend a sympathetic ear to what you have to say. Request that they raise the CIA issue at a general meeting. You can also request a hearing with the student government and represent yourselves. Eventually, the issue

can be taken to a vote and perhaps a resolution. The University of
Michigan Student Assembly reacted to the violent arrests of anti-CIA
protestors by calling for the resignation of the director of the campus
police. The Assembly also doubled the offer of the graduate student
governing body to reward with $500 any police officer who would give
information on police brutality on the day of the arrests. Finally, it
pledged $1000 to cover one of the victims' lawyer's fees.

As a CIA Off Campus organization made up of students, you may
also be eligible to apply for student government funding. At Brown, the
ad hoc committee "CIA Off Campus" was formally recognized by the
university under the new name "People Against the CIA"—and began
receiving university funds.

Graduate student organizations also tend to sympathize with activists and can often be counted on to sign or endorse petitions and
demands. Grad students at Northwestern organized a CIA recruitment
debate between demonstrators and campus conservatives (the administration refused to participate). The graduate-level Teaching Assistants
Association at the University of Wisconsin at Madison joined an ad hoc
Committee for Academic Responsibility to uproot CIA- and military-
sponsored graduate research. They even threatened the university with
a lawsuit to ban all CIA activity on the campus.

University faculties and staffs are also fertile ground for support.
Professors who are politically oriented, who were perhaps active as
students in the 1960s and '70s, may be itching to get involved again.
Student activists at Rutgers University feel that they have "overwhelming support from professors. Especially in the history, social studies and
psychology departments, nobody likes the CIA," says Rutgers grad
student and Student Action Union member Christine Kelly. She adds
that garnering faculty support is "under-utilized as a tactic" at most
schools.[50]

As members of the university community, professors, assistant
professors, and staff employees are concerned about what goes on in
their working environment. Some professors, especially in political
science and history departments, have studied the CIA and its illicit
activities in detail. They can have a larger perspective on the issue, and
their experience with earlier student movements may provide insight
into how the administration will handle an anti-CIA action, or how the
student body will receive it.

Vernon Elliott of *Campus Watch* reports that faculty at Colby
College voted by a two-to-one margin to ban CIA recruitment there. And
when the Board of Trustees at the University of North Carolina issued
a statement labeling anti-CIA activists "violent terrorists," the faculty

overwhelmingly condemned it.[51] At Northwestern University, over 100 faculty members signed a petition requesting that the university drop charges against anti-CIA arrestees. The petition was published as a half-page ad in the student newspaper. It listed each professor's name and department and publicized an upcoming court date. NU professors also sent letters to the editorial section of the paper and donated money to an arrestee defense fund.

In 1987 at Amherst, 60 faculty and staff members organized the "Committee for Human Rights and a Responsible University," adamantly opposing CIA presence on campus. The group has addressed the Board of Trustees on the issue, initiated discussions in dormitories and brought former CIA officer John Stockwell and former U.S. Attorney General Ramsey Clark to testify in the defense of anti-CIA demonstrators on trial. Faculty organizations like this one prove the potential for faculty support, outspokenness and action. One of its founders, philosophy professor Ann Ferguson, vocalized the group's stand in the *Chronicle of Higher Education*: "There is a distinction between the rights of free speech and rights to recruitment on campus and we feel that the university has systematically confused those issues."[52]

As income earners, teachers and staff members are sometimes willing to donate money to educational or defense funds. Students at the University of Illinois at Chicago sent flyers out to all UIC faculty and staff requesting donations for an anti-CIA speaker and, according to activist Deborah Crawford, raised over $200. Crawford notes that after a demonstration and arrests, UIC professors formed a faculty solidarity group in the students' defense that raised over $500. The group also complained to the university chancellor and sent letters to the university president demanding that charges be dropped.[53]

There are more than ethical reasons for faculty to oppose the Agency. Professors' careers can be threatened by the CIA's presence in their schools. When the CIA sent agent George Chritton to the University of California at Santa Barbara as part of its Officer in Residence program, it was stunned by vociferous opposition from all sectors of the campus community. Students staged demonstrations; the student government voted to rescind Chritton's position; and the faculty at UCSB and other California schools sent objecting letters, initiated petitions of protest and organized meetings where Chritton's position was discussed and voted against.

In particular, the anthropology department "played a critical role" in ousting the schools' Officer in Residence, according to UCSB student activist Dave Karoly.[54] Although Chritton had been assigned to the political science department, the anthropology department claimed that anthropology studies were being overrun by CIA agents, raising suspicion of anthropologists among the people of the Third World. Chritton's presence would just strengthen that suspicion and cause developing nations to refuse U.S. scholars access to their resources. Similarly, Penn State's geography department passed a resolution to ban the CIA from doing business within the department, formerly the Agency's second largest recruiting pool at the university.

To make contacts with your faculty, approach those that seem sympathetic, as judged by the content of their lectures or comments that they have made in class. Some professors may not be willing to participate in demonstrations or civil disobedience for fear of losing their jobs, but will support you in other ways. And, of course, there are those who will pick up a sign and march right along with you. The arrestees at a demonstration against CIA research at the University of Illinois at Champaign-Urbana in February of 1990 included three students and a tenured professor. "Workers, like students, have a major role in the making of a university and its contribution to society."[55]

Staff unions both appreciate student support for their concerns and can further the anti-CIA cause by increasing pressure on the administration and adding credibility and publicity to the issue. When students and staff join together to address the administration, their campaigns can be extremely powerful. The strike at U.C. Berkeley by the United Front coalition, for example, included a staff union demand for an end to sexism, racism and homophobia in the workplace. The strike was observed by 75 percent of the student body.[56] Students occupying a Rutgers administration building for ten days voiced a staff call for the immediate negotiation of fair contracts with university unions.[57] And students at Harvard participated in the successful 1988 campaign for unionization by the Union of Clerical and Technical Workers. University staff have come to the aid of student-initiated campaigns as well. "Despite the administration's efforts to pit students and workers against each other, unions have usually shown support for students...and have often joined students in their demands and actions." In protest of the U.S. invasion of Cambodia in 1970, 350 Harvard staff members agreed to participate in a five-day strike "and to picket their workplaces to convince other workers to join the strike." In 1986, labor activists at Harvard "played a prominent role in protesting the University's engagement in South Africa."[58]

Students seem to be responsive to the opinions of those whom they consider experts in their fields. They also look up to people who are already making their way in the working world. If you can demonstrate faculty and staff support of your student body, you can increase the legitimacy of and interest in the CIA Off Campus issue.

Staff and faculty support and assistance has an advantage in continuity as well. Students may say goodbye to the school after two-, four- or five-year stints. "People are there and then they graduate," Heimbach complains, "and you're dealing with a whole new crop of people." But professors and staff members in active or advisory capacities can continue working on their own or with new students, offering their experienced observations.

Alumni support is another relatively untapped resource. Harvard University has witnessed "the growth of a network of alumni and students concerted in their efforts to fight Harvard, especially its complicity with the rogue regime of South Africa...now students can draw on the resources and organizational skills of a substantial base of alumni from the 1960s and beyond."[59]

Get an alumni mailing or phone list, preferably of graduates who were enrolled in the 1960s and '70s (or even '30s!). It may be worthwhile to enlist their help in either pressuring the university to adopt an anti-CIA resolution or contributing to your educational or defense fund.

High school students have also shown interest in opposing the CIA. The Agency has started recruiting programs aimed at high school seniors (see "Robbing the Cradle" in Chapter Two), and high schools with good history or political science courses (some high school teachers assign Howard Zinn readings) are prime places to find politically conscious allies. A large number of high school students showed up— on their own initiative—for an anti-CIA rally at the University of Minnesota at Minneapolis in the spring of 1987. According to Minnesota activists, "their participation turned out to be crucial to the success of the action."[60] This kind of participation in activism by younger students reflects a heartening trend:

> According to an annual survey by UCLA's Higher Education Research Institute and the American Council of Education, the share of college freshmen who participated in organized demonstrations in their senior year of high school reached a high of 36.7 percent [in the '88-'89 school year], *a percentage even greater than that of the late 1960s.*
>
> The survey...showed that an all time high of 44.1 percent of students feel that it is "very important" to influence "social values." Almost 25 percent of the students said they wanted to participate in community action programs, up from 18.5 percent in 1986.[61]

In Illinois, organized demonstrations included one in which 1,000 high school students walked out of school to protest the firing of a black school district official; one in which another 1,000 high school students walked out to protest outrageous learning conditions and a lack of bilingual teachers (this action resulted in the removal of the school's principal and the arrival of new supplies); and one elementary school protest in which students drafted bilingual issue petitions and marched on City Hall and the Police Department to protest the reassignment of a popular police officer.[62]

The protests show remarkable sophistication and dedication. "In most cases, the students contacted the media in an effort to draw attention to their grievances and enhance their bargaining position." Many of the students involved in the protests "were suspended or faced other disciplinary actions." It is this generation of students that will be marching on university administration buildings in the years to come.

Consider working in conjunction with younger student activists, doing CIA or covert operations workshops in sympathetic high school teacher's classes. Or offer high school seniors the flip side to what high school guidance centers might be promoting as legitimate CIA scholarship programs. A discussion of CIA history with a follow-up on the CIA's academic involvement may be in order. Organize forums. Invite CIA academic representative Michael Turner to the school for a debate or presentation with an anti-CIA speaker.[63] This will provoke some thought on the issue. By the time they hit their college campuses, many high school grads will be ready to take a stand against the CIA in their universities.

Moving beyond campus borders, activists often find local governments sympathetic to anti-CIA actions. The Evanston City Council heard Northwestern arrestees tell their story of police brutality at a public meeting and a few Council members took up the cause, questioning the presence of Evanston city police at the demonstration. One Councilwoman organized the Evanston Democrats and, with the Chicago Committee to Defend the Bill of Rights, set up an art auction fundraiser for the students' defense. At the University of Colorado at Boulder, City Council members joined in civil disobedience actions protesting CIA recruiting. Municipal codes can also be a factor in fighting CIA presence on campus; these will be discussed in Chapter Five.

Although "students are handicapped by the limited duration of their studies, segregation from labor and other social movements can be partly surmounted by 1) maintaining progressive student institutions 2) organizing progressive alumni…and 3) affiliating the student movement with progressive community organizations."[64] Essentially, you are not alone. You do not have to face a heavily backed organization like the Central Intelligence Agency by yourself. In fact, you shouldn't. Gathering support from all reaches of your campus and local community will not only save you from some perilous falls but create strong and valuable affiliations made up of all kinds of people—students, workers, citizens and taxpayers—to really get the CIA off campus and start to address, as a united, majority movement, the extensive social, political and economic predicaments that confront us all.

Sowing Seeds: Education

Self-Education

And ye shall know the truth and the truth shall make you free.
Inscription at CIA headquarters in Langley, VA

A plan of action begins with the people who initiate it and will go as far as their limits. Getting the CIA off your campus will be a difficult task (if you haven't already discovered this) and will bring you face to face with people who have been arguing *for* the CIA's presence for years.

Although knowing just a little about the Agency is enough to turn many against it, those who begin to get active with the issue should learn as much as they can about it. During a CIA recruitment site occupation by students at the University of Minnesota at Minneapolis, activists held a spontaneous "participatory teach-in" for the less informed—which would not have been possible without the prior education of those activists leading the teach-in.[65] An uneducated activist is a weak link in a chain. Someone asks a pointed question that doesn't get a thoughtful and educated response and suddenly the whole movement is discredited. Student body opinion can turn against you. Conservatives can needle at your weak spots. The administration can write you off as a "fringe" group, insinuating that you have nothing better to do than stand around holding signs and passing out leaflets.

So it is important for everyone to do research on the Agency's history, activities, motives and the reasons why they have no place in the university community. There are 101 arguments out there to support the CIA. We must have 102 arguments against it.[66] Being well informed makes persuading others to join you much easier. Your opinions, requests or demands become legitimate and imperative. When people are confronted with the facts, it is difficult for them to argue that the CIA has done the right thing in Chile, Indonesia, Guatemala, South Africa or El Salvador. Knowing these things automatically sets you on the side of the truth.

Educating Others

Organizers...tell me that they are working against a broad political apathy within the student body and certainly within the faculties. But that's what the struggle is all about."

Philip Agee[67]

While those who protest the CIA remain in the minority, educating the uninformed is one of our most compelling tasks. If there is strength in numbers, we are still weak.

Although the information on the Central Intelligence Agency is available to all, we must create easy access to it. Sometimes we even have to hit our fellow citizens over the head with it.

Luckily for campus activists, the overriding theme of a university is education. Granted, some students race through their education with career-track blinders on. But most students enroll in challenging courses and sweat over difficult reading, tests and papers to learn what they can about the world. Take advantage of this natural curiosity to expose the U.S. underworld that is devastating our upper world and our chances for a future on this earth.

Unluckily for all activists, the forces against us are plenty and powerful. Shoddy high school history courses with imperialistic slants lack an economic analysis of our past and, consequently, lack a *meaningful* analysis of our past. The deliberately mindless mass media of 20-second news bites, owned by the very people whose interests the CIA is dedicated to and paid to protect, report State Department news as if it were the Sermon on the Mount.

On top of all this, we are faced with the strange hypocrisy of our First Amendment rights. It is assumed that all speech is free in our society and, therefore, all ideas are heard. At least, people believe, all *important* ideas are heard—broadcast on the Five O'Clock News, explored in depth on the MacNeil-Lehrer Report. Obviously, they're not. But the possibilities of media monopoly and elite media ownership are shocking to most North Americans.

As you go about your educational work, people will ask: "Well, if this is true, how come it's not in the newspapers?" You may have asked yourself this very question early in your own political education and the answer is always disturbing. We are living in a high-gloss, multi-colored version of Orwell's *1984,* complete with an utter vacuum of public information and knowledge. History has been rewritten and a new kind of newspeak or doublespeak has filled the void. Those who care must dig deeply, must see beyond the empty phrases and slogans to become truly informed. You must be prepared to expose this fact to a naive audience.

And Now, Will the Real History Please Stand Up?

The CIA's own record is a trumpet call to action for all who believe in justice, equality and humanity. The problem is how to get the record out on display, how to attract an audience.

Some very basic educational tactics include letters, columns and articles in the local paper, school paper or alternative paper, if you have one. If the university is part of a larger city, what goes on at the school should be of interest to people in the community as well. Local residents as well as students should write letters. Involving community members is also a good way to garner some non-transient support. Some residents may not know that the CIA is present on campus and is therefore a local issue.

Set up a booth or literature table with someone available to answer questions at the student union or wherever there's a crowd. Hang up and hand out posters, flyers or two- or four-page leaflets. Ask sympathetic professors to distribute flyers in their classes or make announcements about events. Post longer educational flyers on the inside of restroom stall doors.

Bring anti-CIA speakers to campus, organize debates on the issue, invite an Agency representative to participate in debates (which they nearly always refuse to do), and then ask the student body who really supports free speech. Sponsor educational forums—perhaps with professors who are willing to speak on the CIA's history. Show movies or video documentaries about the CIA. Students or community members who have visited countries where the CIA is carrying out its dirty work can present slide shows of their trips with follow-up discussions. Initiate a series of dorm discussions or teach-ins that canvass the university.

Don't limit yourself to the nominal topic of "the CIA." The Agency's activities and motives can be brought up in forums on Latin America, domestic and foreign debts, domestic surveillance in the United States, mind-control experiments, national "security" and secrecy, the Executive Office, South Africa, Southeast Asia, Vietnam, the drug epidemic and on and on. Attracting people to your educational events is essential though sometimes difficult. Plug into something you believe a particular audience will respond to. Do a lot of advertising (posters, ads in the paper, flyers, etc.). Include your surrounding area (high schools, coffee shops and bookstores, local papers, radio talk shows, cable television programs). Send press releases and call the local media so they can send a journalist out to cover the event. The more groups on campus and in the community that sponsor any given event, the more draw that event will have.

While it is important to inspire those who are already aware of CIA activities to become active, pulling in the politically unconverted may be the hardest thing to do. Try to find the slant in your event that will bring more of the mainstream population in. For instance, Noam Chomsky, highly regarded as a radical political critic, is also a famous linguist and usually draws entire linguistics departments to speaking engagements.

If your campus is known as conservative or apathetic, gather a crowd with creativity. Most higher education enthusiasts like to consider themselves up-to-date on current events. The video documentary *CoverUp,* released in 1988, was billed as a film on the Iran-contra scandal. Students who went to see it for its coverage of a newsworthy event wound up learning about the history of CIA covert operations and the shadow government that perpetuates them. They were also exposed to the contra-cocaine connection. *CoverUp* was shown all over college campuses in the year of its release and—notably at the University of Iowa and Northwestern University—drew large numbers for anti-CIA demonstrations.

Another way to attract the as yet unconverted and appeal to the converted but inactive is to add some spice to your event, be it art, music, humor or hard-hitting guerrilla theater. Activists with the Progressive Student Organization (PSO) and the Central American Working Group (CAWG) at the University of Minnesota at Minneapolis built their anti-CIA campaign with two goals in mind: "First, to educate and mobilize students against the war that the U.S. is waging on the people of Central America. And second, to politically and physically prevent the CIA from recruiting on campus." According to one activist, "when school began in early October, CIA recruitment was not an issue on the minds of the vast majority of students."[68]

During the three weeks before the CIA was due to recruit, members of the PSO and CAWG hung effigies of Latin American CIA victims from campus trees, erected a mock cemetery outside the student union symbolizing Nicaraguans killed in the contra war, sponsored a debate between an ex-agent and a local reactionary and distributed thousands of leaflets on the CIA's activities in Central America. The intense educational activity culminated in a demonstration of over 100 students at the CIA recruiting site. The demonstration generated both local and national publicity, the PSO experienced a "spurt of growth" as a result and "it will be far more difficult for the CIA to openly recruit on the University of Minnesota campus in the future."[69]

In the spring of 1988, a group of students at the University of Texas at Austin held a CIA Off Campus teach-in on the steps of a university building. Topics of the day were the local Officer in Residence, James McInnis, and the CIA in academia and around the world. The event attracted over 200 people, and passersby lingered to hear a saxophonist and watch guerrilla theater skits. Eventually, the teach-in turned into a demonstration of 150 students that marched through campus and disrupted the CIA's recruiting efforts in another university building.

Guerrilla theater is both attention-getting and educational. Mesmerized by the show, students may inadvertently learn something. From the most dramatic depictions of CIA terrorism to comic pokes at the Agency, employing drama will also give you some credit as an intelligent, creative group of people with flair and a sense of humor. Utilize the talent in your organization by enlisting actors, writers and designers to plan and carry out a guerrilla theater act. Do you want to bring some terror home to the student body, ridicule the Agency or both?

A group of community activists in the Chicago area infiltrated an upper-class, suburban neighborhood and woke residents up with the sound of gunshots at six in the morning. People who ran out of their houses to see what was happening found scattered corpses covered with blood on their front lawns. Accompanying the corpses (activists playing dead) was a banner that read: "You have just experienced a contra attack similar to those experienced in Nicaragua on a daily basis. Stop U.S. support of terrorism. No to contra aid."

A common and very effective guerrilla theater act is the classroom abduction. Activists dressed as Salvadoran death squad members, Guatemalan soldiers, Nicaraguan contras, RENAMO guerrillas (or another CIA-sponsored terrorist organization of your choosing) barge into an ongoing class in full attire: plastic machine guns, bandoliers, fatigues, masks. They announce the name of their organization and read off a list of subversives who they have come to kidnap (the list may include the professor if he or she is cooperative). Charges against the "subversives" can include: organizing a labor union, starting a farm cooperative, belonging to a human rights organization, speaking against the government, writing for an independent newspaper, sympathizing with the Sandinistas, practicing liberation theology, teaching the communist doctrine, fighting for a better life and so on. Those on the hit list may want to plead for their lives or defend their actions by accusing the soldiers of protecting the oligarchy or military and the wealthy businessmen. The soldiers can respond by saying "We are fighting for democracy!" and then dragging the subversives out of the classroom as the victims scream about lack of due process, torture or whatever. You may want to have some kind of narrator or spokesperson stay behind and shout out statistics: "You have just witnessed a 'disappearance.' Over 100 innocent civilians are 'disappeared' in El Salvador every month..." Make sure you have the cooperation and prior knowledge of the class professor before you attempt this one or you may find *yourselves* being abducted by campus security.

Making fun of the CIA is a great way to discredit it. Nobody wants to join up with an organization that is laughed at. Prior to an anti-contra aid rally at Northwestern University, two acting students dressed as a stiff-legged contra puppet and a CIA puppeteer strolled around university grounds, yelling up a storm:

CIA Man: "Who do you hate?"

Contra: "Communists, Reds, Pinkos and Jesse Jackson!"

CIA Man: "Who do you love?"

Contra: "Ronald Reagan, George Bush, John Wayne and Oral Roberts!"

CIA Man: "Who else?"

Contra: "Ronald McDonald, the chief executive of IBM, the board of directors at Nabisco..."

CIA Man: "What are you fighting for?"

Contra: "Money and power."

CIA Man: "No!"

Contra: "I mean, freedom and democracy!"

At the University of Illinois at Chicago, activists paraded through the campus cafeteria dressed as tight-suited, bellicose CIA recruiters, passing out fake recruiting leaflets as they went. ("Did you enjoy bullying your classmates as a child? The CIA is looking for a few good sadists...")

Acting aside, there is nothing more effective than getting the truth from someone who has been there. Students can be inspired by the story of someone who has been directly affected by the CIA's activities. Invite a Salvadoran, Chilean or Guatemalan national to speak at your school in a public forum. Be aware that sometimes these people are placing themselves at risk (they may be undocumented refugees) by speaking in the United States about U.S. terrorism. Make sure to ask if they have any concerns about the audience or about being identified in a particular way and accommodate accordingly.

Bring an ex-CIA agent to town. People like Philip Agee, Verne Lyon, David MacMichael, Ralph McGehee and John Stockwell, who have had personal experiences with the Agency, have much to say about it. Vietnam veterans who are now opposed to U.S. intervention can also speak with the authority of personal experience.

With enough educational work, you should develop a good base from which to take action. Education, however, does not end with a demonstration. The purpose of most actions is to draw more attention to the issue of the CIA, if not actually hinder the CIA's activities. Two students in a sit-in at the recruiting office at Rutgers used a school phone to call a local radio station whose disc jockey, Steve Capen, broadcast the event live to the people of New York—as a Rutgers dean read the Riot Act. (Capen, who had frequently supported the activists, was later fired by the station, KROCK.)

Your efforts to educate others should increase in proportion to the attention you may be receiving from the media and the student body. After the Minneapolis demonstration at which glass doors were broken by activists in response to police clubbing and macing, the students involved defended the action. "We used it as a pole to further discussion on the CIA, to raise the interest level of the student body. Though there was controversy about the tactics used at the demonstration, we forced the question back on the CIA issue," Minneapolis senior Mike Turner explains.

The CIA issue is where the question should always remain. It is easy to get caught up in smaller arguments about logistics, tactics or the infamous freedom of speech debate. And the mainstream media (which includes most college papers) will tend to deal with superficialities rather than the glaring and immediate problem: *the CIA is killing people and undermining, not protecting, democracy.* Use every opportunity that you can to get back to this fact. It is this fact that you are acting on and unless your audience is aware of this, it will never understand you or your actions.

CHAPTER FOUR

Q & A on the CIA:
Nine Infamous Questions
Get Answered

We need not deceive ourselves that we can afford today the luxury
of altruism and world benefaction...We should cease to talk about
vague and...unreal objectives such as human rights, the raising of
living standards and democratization.

Former State Department official George Kennan[1]

There are a number of questions—some more profound than
others—that students will ask regarding the CIA in general and, specifically, about banning CIA campus presence. These questions become
part of the general tempest that swirls around anti-CIA actions and are
essential for the activist or spokesperson to be able to answer.

Don't get caught with your political pants down! Prepare yourself
to encounter these questions about the CIA's activities:

Isn't the CIA Saving the World?

*Q: Don't we need the CIA to counter Soviet/Cuban/Arab/drug lord/ter-
rorist spying and attack? Don't some less powerful countries need us to help
them fight imported communism and lawless aggression?*

A: Now that the "Soviet threat" has diminished considerably with the
advent of Glasnost and the retreat of Soviet forces from Eastern Europe,
the official rhetoric will focus more on a "terrorist," drug or Cuban
threat—especially regarding Latin America. As career defense strate-

gist and diplomat Paul H. Nitze has noted, "There will be all kinds of contestants for that honor of being 'the enemy' or 'the problem.'"[2] Historically, however, the Soviet threat has been used as a justification for U.S. military intervention throughout the world.

The question implies that the "threat" is or was real and also that the CIA and the U.S. government are interested in fighting this threat. These assumptions, though understandable, must be re-examined according to the facts of actual CIA operations.

In the case of the 1973 Chilean coup, even the CIA admitted that Salvador Allende was pursuing a policy of neutrality. Internal CIA documents concluded that Allende "would not pose any likely threat to the peace of the region." However the "negative drawbacks" of his presidency included "the advance of the Marxist *idea* and a *psychological setback* for the United States."[3]

It was Allende's decision to nationalize major industry that prodded the CIA to action, along with the threat to U.S. hegemony in the region. Senator Frank Church's 1975 committee report on intelligence activities explicates the motives behind the CIA's covert operations in Chile. According to the Church report, the CIA was activated by "the determination to sustain the principle of compensation for U.S. firms nationalized by the Allende government."[4] Journalist Penny Lernoux notes that, "with few exceptions, the military coups of the past fifteen years in Latin America have been related in some way to U.S. business, the payoff after the coup—as in Brazil, Bolivia, and Chile—being special concessions to U.S. companies."[5]

In the face of the Cold War meltdown, current CIA director William Webster has attempted to reframe CIA activities by describing what the CIA has actually been doing all along. One of the primary responsiblities of the intelligence community, he ventures, is to "identify opportunities" for private industry.[6] Although he and George Bush present the idea as a new one, and the media obediently follows suit, Webster's comments are an effort to come out of the closet with the CIA's historical agenda.

In some cases, the CIA has falsified a Soviet threat to justify its profit-motivated actions. Former CIA analyst David MacMichael resigned from the Agency when he was asked to falsify a Sandinista arms flow to Salvadoran rebels (FMLN). Ironically, near the end of the anti-Sandinista war, the *contras* were accused of selling arms to the FMLN.[7]

As for "weak" nations that need our help against the Russians, Cubans or Marxist guerrillas, the CIA's activities tend to create the kind of poverty and instability that invite hostility toward the United States and toward imported capitalism. More important, CIA actions create a need for self defense, thus ensuring alignment with the "other" super-power or with extreme political forces. This alignment is then used to justify continued U.S. interference. It is a continuous—and, for its human victims, a brutal and terrifying—cycle.

CIA support of the Shah in Iran, for instance, led to conditions ripe for the Ayatollah Khomeini to take power. The CIA both installed the Shah and organized his secret police force, SAVAK, to terrorize his opponents.[8] Iranians began to hate the United States—justifiably so. The Ayatollah took advantage of that hatred to become their leader.

The CIA-led contra war aginst Nicaragua reflects the same process: "the point is that by attacking the country you can force the Sandinistas into a more radical position from which you have more ammunition to attack them."[9]

Ultimately, we must examine the essential motives of the CIA. Whose interests does the Agency really protect? More often than not, the CIA is doing the dirty work of major corporations and big capital at the *expense* of democracy and freedom, not to mention human lives. John Stockwell adds that "it is the function...of the CIA, with its...destabilization programs going on around the world today, to keep the world unstable, and to propagandize the American people to hate, so we will let the establishment spend any amount of money on arms."[10]

The CIA is not defending little countries from bigger ones, or good guys from bad guys. Many smaller countries have shown that they can hold their own against both superpowers (Vietnam, Cuba and Afghanistan, for instance). The point is that it is the *people's* option to do what they want in their own country, and it should never be the option of a privileged U.S. minority composed of the business and political elite.

Q: But the CIA is a legal organization headed by the National Security Council and the President of the United States. Isn't it just doing its job?

A: Good point. Being a legally constituted part of the U.S. government does not, however, justify the CIA's illegal activities. We oppose the CIA precisely because it is the active arm of U.S. foreign policy.

This policy is cloaked under the rhetoric of "fighting for democracy" and protecting our "national security" but is really only protecting the interests of a very few and creating chaos and suffering throughout the world. The planet's economies are heavily interdependent, and the U.S. multinational corporations' gobbling of natural resources and cheap labor (protected by the CIA) may put us all in the hole. Covert operations, McGehee asserts, "are destructive for our own interests.

Inevitably, the result of those actions impact negatively on our economy and on our democratic principles."[11]

The Latin American debt is a good example of the ramifications of U.S. neo-colonial policies. Rich in natural resources, Latin American nations are some of the poorest in the world due to improper distribution of raw materials and an emphasis on export-based economies. The International Monetary Fund (IMF)—dominated by the United States—has only intensified the problem by forcing debtor nations to cut back on social programs and increase exports. However, "these nations represent a significant market for American goods, normally accounting for up to a third of United States exports,"[12] and the loss of their buying power increases our trade deficit.

The Third World's problems are not natural; rather, they are political. And the United States has helped sustain the inequity for over a century—in El Salvador, for instance, by "propping up a corrupt and violent authoritarian regime."[13] In Haiti, the poorest country in the Western hemisphere, former dictator Jean Claude Duvalier "could count on Washington's firm support" despite an egregious record of human rights abuses, as long as U.S. investors could "take advantage of the country's cheap labor."[14] As one Haitian peasant commented to a reporter for the the *New York Review of Books* in 1987, "...the American government doesn't care about the poor people—only the high classes."[15]

Although there is much the people of the United States have accomplished in the areas of domestic freedom and equality, economic and political motives have been a driving force in the history of this nation. Though the United States has always called itself democratic and freedom-loving, how did it get from "sea to shining sea?" Partially by exploiting Africans as slaves and devastating the indigenous populations. That was even before Karl Marx was a gleam in his mother's eye; the word of the day was "savages" rather than "communists." As Jeanne Woods, legislative counsel to the ACLU, notes, "Today's 'terrorists' are yesterday's 'communists.' "[16]

The harsh reality of the nation's foreign policy objectives has not been lost on its policy makers. Rather than delude themselves with the precept of humanitarianism, some officials have accepted the situation as purely Machiavellian. George Kennan put it quite succinctly in a 1948 top secret State Department document, as the U.S. was realizing its dominant position in the world economy:

> We have about 50 percent of the world's wealth, but only 6.3 percent of its population...in this situation, we cannot fail to be the object of envy and resentment. Our real task in the

coming period is to devise a pattern of relationships which will permit us to maintain this position of disparity...to do so, we will have to dispense with all sentimentality and daydreaming...We need not deceive ourselves that we can afford today the luxury of altruism and world benefaction...We should cease to talk about vague and—for the Far East—unreal objectives such as human rights, the raising of living standards and democratization. The day is not far off when we are going to have to deal in straight power concepts. The less we are then hampered by idealistic slogans, the better.[17]

Kennan is now a highly respected scholar at Princeton's Institute for Advanced Studies. It seems the only flaw in his theory has been the need to dispense with "idealistic slogans." Our policy makers have found that the American people are truly idealistic. Thus, the powers-that-be perceive the need for an arm of the government whose activities are hidden from our view: the Central Intelligence Agency.

The history of the world is the history of people with money and power oppressing the weaker majority which struggles for its rights. And it is always most difficult for those with the most money and power to recognize this fact. "Ideology and [corporate] profits become interwoven," McGehee says, "until even policymakers aren't sure what is the truth and what is not."[18]

Though the CIA has occasionally strayed from the guidance of the President and more frequently from Congress (it has lied to Congress more than once), it is usually just "doing its job."

That is the problem.

Opposing the CIA is one way to protest the inhumane and destructive policies of the National Security Council, the President of the United States and the businesses to which they are beholden.

Q: If Congress is aware of the CIA's activities, why not lobby your representative? Change comes through working within the system, not forcing your opinion at lower levels.

A: Within every group of people working against the CIA and covert operations, there are widely differing opinions on how best to change this particular aspect of the government. Many anti-CIA folks are lobbying Congress to pass laws restricting or abolishing covert operations.

Others feel that Congress is too entrenched in the "business" of the nation (i.e., many legislators are major stockholders in large corporations or are bought off by lobbies) to really do anything about it.

One thing is certainly true: if covert operations remain hidden from the American public, there will be little democratic decision making going on regarding some of our most important foreign policy questions.

The activities of the CIA have been condemned in the World Court and the United Nations. These activities have violated numerous international treaties, signed by the United States, that are designed to keep peace on the planet. According to John Stockwell, CIA actions around the world have resulted in the deaths of at least six million people—an astounding toll.[19]

> The people that are dying in these things are people of the Third World…people who have the misfortune of being born in the Mtumba mountains of the Congo, in the jungles of southeast Asia,…in the hills of northern Nicaragua. Far more Catholics than communists, far more Buddhists than communists; most of them couldn't give you an intelligent definition of communism or capitalism.[20]

Whether or not our government is willing to act, we have a responsibility to stop the atrocities being committed in our name and with our tax dollars. When the legislative arena is stymied, our responsibility naturally extends to more dramatic grassroots tactics.

The Chicago Religious Task Force on Central America (CRTFCA), an organization founded in 1980 in response to the murder of four North American church women by death squads in El Salvador, is committed to civil disobedience in the face of unjust and murderous U.S. policy in Latin America. To quote a CRTFCA publication, "Law is a human construct…subject to the race, class and sex biases prevalent in the culture…When law does not serve justice, law should be disobeyed."[21]

The struggles for civil rights, women's voting rights and an end to the war in Vietnam began with the grassroots, the people, not Congress. The people demonstrated their opposition in the streets and pressured the government until it finally reacted.

Thousands are dying in El Salvador, Guatemala, Indonesia and South Africa. As author Hortensia Bussi De Allende, wife of the late Salvador Allende, said at a conference on the CIA and world peace at Yale University: "the so-called silent majority must convert itself into an active, thundering majority for democracy."[22] Our responsibilities are to act now in our fullest local capacities to stop the Central Intelligence Agency.

Q: But don't we need some kind of intelligence gathering?

A: We do need intelligence gathering, but the CIA's primary function is not to gather intelligence.

Ralph McGehee puts the number of U.S. intelligence agencies at 28, with the great bulk of intelligence gathering and analysis being done by the National Security Agency and the various military intelligence units.[23]

According to Victor Marchetti, former executive assistant to the deputy director of the CIA, "the Agency uses about two-thirds of its funds for covert operations and their support...Only about 20 percent of the CIA's career employees (spending less than 10 percent of the budget) work on intelligence analysis and information processing."[24] Marchetti was referring roughly to the period between 1965 and 1975. Given that the CIA budget increased 25 to 35 percent under William Casey,[25] it is unlikely that the 20/80 ratio of intelligence analysis to covert operations has changed. From what we know of the CIA under Reagan and Casey, covert operations probably claimed an even *higher* percentage of the Agency budget in the 1980s.

The CIA's real job is less to gather intelligence, than to manufacture it. According to the testimony of ex-agent Ralph McGehee, the CIA consistently falsifies information regarding "communist threats," and "the Agency's misinformation is handed to the American people"[26] that they might better digest their government's actions.

Case in point: in order to escalate the Vietnamese conflict in 1965, the CIA "took tons of Communist-made weapons out of [CIA] warehouses, loaded them on a Vietnamese coastal vessel, faked a firefight, and then called in Western reporters and International Control Commission observers to 'prove' North Vietnamese aid to the Viet Cong."[27] The falsified evidence was published in the CIA White Paper on Vietnam in a seven-page spread including photographs of the second-hand communist ammunition. One week after the White Paper was published, President Johnson initiated the systematic bombing of North Vietnam.

In the CIA's Angolan operation, Stockwell reflects, "one-third of my staff were propagandists who were working in every way they could think of to get stories into the United States press, the world press, to create this picture of Cubans raping Angolans; Cubans and Soviets introducing arms into the conflict; Cubans and Russians trying to take over the world."[28] That was over ten years and 10,000 deaths ago.

We are the ones being deceived, not the "enemy." Covert operations are covert because most people have an innate sense of decency and a strong belief in national self-determination and would object to them. Surely the Sandinistas knew about the contras and their North American backers as soon as they started attacking Nicaraguan villages with U.S. weaponry. It was the North American people who found out last.

The real question is, as long as the CIA's motives are economic and not democratic, what good is the intelligence gathered—or manufactured? Currently, it is being used to suppress popular movements around the world.

Q: Does the CIA do anything good? You're just talking about the bad things.

A: Central Intelligence Agency activities that sound like "bad" things to us are considered successful by the Agency. Though CIA officials complain that "the hundreds of successes [the American public has] not heard of are the operations done right,"[29] these operations are actually well known to those who have looked into them.

The 1953 overthrow of Iranian Prime Minister Mossadegh—who, according to the CIA, "threatened American and British interests"[30]— and his replacement with the dictatorial Shah are among what the Agency would call its finest achievements. According to John Quirk, an avid CIA supporter and author of a number of pro-CIA books, the CIA paid protesters and "organized the riots"[31] that led to Mossadegh's flight from the country. These are supposed to be laudatory actions. Out of that great Agency success, we got the rise to power of the Ayatollah Khomeini, one of our greatest international friends.

Another CIA "success": the overthrow of elected, reformist president Jacobo Arbenz in Guatemala in 1954 and the installation of a military dictatorship headed by Castillo Armas. Over 100,000 civilians have been killed, over 38,000 abducted or "disappeared" by the army in that country since the coup.[32] Quirk relates the action as a success by quoting President Eisenhower's remarks to then-CIA director Allen Dulles: "Thank you, Allen. You have averted a Soviet beachhead in Central America." Odd thing to say, given that Arbenz greatly admired the policies of Franklin Roosevelt and was attempting to carry them out in Guatemala when the CIA forced him out of the country.[33]

The CIA counts as a success every action in which it "wins" or achieves its initial goal. The Agency is embarrassed only by its "losses" (Vietnam, Angola, the Bay of Pigs), not by atrocities committed in the process or dictators installed. When your motto is to fight fire with fire (though there may be no fire to begin with), there is little to be concerned about in the area of human rights. It's a question of objectives.

From Foreign Policy to Freedom of Speech

As you can see, discussions about the CIA become discussions about foreign policy in general, the United States, the media, centralized power and political ideology. It is important to think these issues through on a personal level so that you are not caught contradicting yourself before a group of people you may be hoping to persuade (e.g., you may be arguing that the CIA is disobeying Congress and get locked into a "Congress knows best" opinion which you may not really believe). It is also wise to admit that you don't know everything about the world either. Refusing to be vulnerable can become a sort of dogmatism that turns people off.

In addition to arguments about the CIA in general, you will encounter some very difficult arguments supporting the CIA's presence on campus. Though many people will agree with you that the CIA is a horrible organization, most North Americans take the word "freedom" very seriously and jump when anyone mentions restricting it.

Here are the most common questions students will have about banning the CIA from the university:

Q: Isn't banning the CIA the same as restricting their freedom of speech? If we keep them from coming to campus to recruit, we are losing their point of view.

A: Granting university facilities to employers is a privilege, a part of a mutually beneficial arrangement, not the "right" of anyone. Recruiting at a university is not protected under the Bill of Rights. The Bill of Rights was written *to protect the people from the government, not the government from the people.* It was not designed to shelter federal agencies from public scrutiny and criticism. Legally, the CIA has no specific rights under the Constitution.

The CIA is welcome to come here and give a speech about activities or participate in an open debate with opponents. The "speech" that goes on in an interview, however, is not for the education of the general public, nor is it for the education of the potential recruit: "they don't tell [interviewees] that the CIA is geared for subverting treaties and circumventing international law, that it is a criminal organization, that it has participated in drug dealing. Of course they can't tell students this," Verne Lyon points out.[34] The CIA hides its activities, puts up a false front, manufactures information; indeed, its stock and trade is to lie. It does not participate in free and open speech.

We welcome the opportunity to talk to the CIA. However, given the serious questions raised about its history, purpose and current activities, we must make the decision within our community, the campus community, that the CIA has no place here. Murderers have every right to write books and publish them; however, they should certainly not be aided and abetted in recruiting others to help commit more murders.

The CIA has stripped millions of their right not only to speech but to life as well. These activities are fact and are documented even by our own government. For whatever reasons, our government has chosen *not* to rule the CIA an illegal institution; we, therefore, have a moral obligation to curtail its activities within our own community, based on our own sense of ethics and morality.

Q: What about students and professors who want to work for the CIA? Aren't we infringing on their rights?

A: We have the right to choose our religion or no religion. We have the right to speak freely. We have the right to "pursue happiness." Nowhere in the Constitution is there a clause protecting the right to kill, torture, abduct, steal, cheat or lie.

Those who wish to work for the Agency are usually misinterpreting what the Agency is and does (understandably). Or they are persuaded by money to do it (not so understandably). Most of the agents who started with the Agency and became shocked and angered enough to leave and write books condemning what they saw started out as very patriotic, idealistic, anti-communist students. They believed in the CIA. Now they warn others away.

We encourage all who would consider applying for a job with the Central Intelligence Agency to read all they can, talk to as many people as they can, visit as many countries as they can to learn about its actions before they actually join up with the Company.

You may think that what we are saying is not true. *But what if it is?* Isn't that thought alone enough for you to go out and do some of your own research? "The only way you can figure it out for yourself is to educate yourself."[35] Prove or disprove it on your own. But find the truth.

Q: But if we ban the CIA from recruiting, who is to say who else will be banned? We will be setting a dangerous precedent.

A: People tend to forget that almost all universities have some sort of guidelines or conditions an employer must meet before it can come and recruit. For example, organizations and companies must be equal opportunity employers and at some schools cannot practice sexual-preference discrimination.

So the recruiting office is not willing to open its doors to just any organization. What if the Mafia wanted to come and recruit? Or how about the Nazi party or the Ku Klux Klan? An escort service? Any organization should have the right to pass out pamphlets on school grounds, but schools generally follow some sort of "moral" or legal code in choosing who may use their recruiting facilities.

The CIA, unfortunately, has not been subjected to close scrutiny by our university administrations. Surely, creating the conditions for the murder of over 100,000 people in Guatemala, or an estimated 10,000 to 30,000 in Chile (more than 80,000 were imprisoned and tortured; 200,000 were exiled by the government[36]) is a criminal act—in direct violation of the United Nations Charter stating: "All Members shall refrain in their international relations from the threat or use of force against the territorial integrity or political independence of any state."

Torture training, support for drug running, subverting the Constitution and international law, overthrowing sovereign governments...these are all crimes, more severe than hiring discrimination.

We are, as citizens, subject to the laws governing crime in this country and in the world. If we murder someone we are sent to prison. Our freedom is revoked as soon as we take away someone else's freedom to live. The CIA has stripped so many people of their freedoms and escaped with impunity because most of those who would object never hear of its atrocities.

Well, we have heard and now we must act. It's bad enough that the organization that ought to be sent to trial is being sent all over the world with our tax dollars. Let's not make it worse by helping them recruit agents or bureaucrats for their dirty work.

Finally, since we have already established rules about equal opportunity employment and sexual-preference discrimination, why not add what seems to be missing and what may be the most sorely needed? Let's propose that no organization or agency committing infractions against the universal Code of Human Rights, established by the United Nations, or against the Charter of the United Nations or the Organization of American States, or in violation of the Geneva Convention or the Nuremberg Principles be allowed to recruit at, use the facilities of or contract personnel from our university. The U.S. government is a signatory to all of these agreements. The U.S. Constitution assigns them supremacy over state and local law. We are choosing to do a little law enforcement.

Q: Well, if you are the only ones who are saying the CIA is bad, you're in the minority. Isn't it undemocratic to let a few people dictate what the whole school does?

A: If everyone knew what the CIA was doing, it is unlikely that the CIA would be allowed to recruit here in the first place. Not everyone knows. We are trying to spread the word.

As mentioned previously, the CIA is breaking international laws. This may not be recognized by the student body, but it is recognized by the World Court. Is it undemocratic to ask that we obey international law? If need be, we can take this to some kind of democratic forum: research it, debate it and vote on it. But right now, people don't know enough about it. Let's get it on the agenda.

As for blocking recruiting sites and attempting to keep students from recruiting with the CIA, there are those that feel the CIA must be stopped at all costs—even to the extent of disobeying the rules of the university. The reasoning is the same as for any civil disobedience action. If the laws are unjust, people must disobey the laws and risk the consequences. Civil disobedience is a matter of individual principle.

Many minority groups have challenged unjust laws and won on the grounds of morality rather than on the basis of possessing a majority. African-Americans, for instance, had to fight—as a minority—for their rights, though in some places, a "majority" would very democratically oppose them. Perhaps democracy would really be served if all the people of the Third World were able to vote for or against the existence of the CIA. Is the "security" and "stability" it offers more valuable than the havoc it wreaks?

Ask yourself this: would it have been wrong to attempt to stop the Nazis from recruiting soldiers at German universities because most people at the university supported the Nazis? Would it have been undemocratic? Let's not deceive ourselves. The Nazis and the Germans who supported them were not somehow genetically flawed or more inclined toward hatred than other human beings. They were manipulated and lied to by their leaders. *We are not above this.* And yet we act as if we are. People are dying. And many activists don't really care if anyone believes them or not. They have a job to do.

We are a minority representing those who are victimized by the CIA and we are claiming the right to be free from CIA interference by stopping the CIA here, at the university. In order to create a more humane and peaceful world, we must have a place to start. Local institutions like city councils, churches, temples, unions and universities can be instrumental in initiating the kind of change that starts slowly but ultimately transforms society.

What do we want this university to stand for?

CHAPTER FIVE

Word and Action:
Building the Most Effective
CIA Off Campus Campaign

Before You Begin: Media Relations

Unfortunately, it is often true that "in America, an event hasn't actually 'happened' unless it has been covered in the press."[1] News coverage acts as publicity for demands or actions and can educate readers and viewers on the issues involved. It also increases the pressure on the administration or Trustees to respond to activist initiatives. The slant of the coverage can turn audiences against or motivate them to support a cause. For better or worse, media coverage is an important element in activist organizing.

As you search for and act against CIA activity at your school, keep in contact with the media and try to develop an ongoing, positive relationship with reporters. Issue press releases to the school and local newspapers. Phone television news stations and inform them of developing events. Use the media to augment your educational effort: employ every minute you get at the microphone, before cameras or with journalists to explain to the community and possibly to the nation what you are doing and why you are doing it. Activists at Ohio University in Athens contacted sympathetic journalists who put their story on the front page of their local paper. Other actions at Boulder, Minneapolis, Northwestern and Santa Barbara made national and international news with spots on *Good Morning America,* network newscasts and stories in European and Latin American dailies. Elect people in your organization to keep in contact with the press by writing press releases and phoning television shows. Try for interviews on local television and radio talk shows. Generally, on issues like this the media will not come to you; you must go to the media.

Even when reporters do cover the event, however, they usually do it poorly and resist speaking directly to the CIA issue. "Indeed, this country's so-called Fourth Estate has, for the most part, debased itself into becoming the [government's] compliant lapdog."[2] Published or televised reports on the student movement or student protests are often superficial and patronizing. "On the whole, sixties comparisons, personality emphasis and poor research mark most reporting on campus activism."[3]

Even campus papers will follow the mainstream model and, in their efforts to be "objective," will side with the status quo, portraying activists as extremists who operate on opinion rather than fact. To mainstream campus papers, CIA crimes are always "alleged" even though extensive and incontrovertable documentation proves them to be true. Campus conservatives may give you more credit than the school newspaper: at least they sometimes concede CIA activities while arguing motive.

You can assume that many articles and news stories will be biased against you. However, it is certainly within your rights to confront the bias of these reports. Northwestern activists found so many errors of fact in their school newspaper that they requested a private meeting with the editor and presented him with a list of inaccuracies from stories on their demonstration. They also asked him to print the many letters to the editor submitted in support of their case, which he finally agreed to do.

Dealing with the media can be a hassle, but is well worth the effort. Citizens must know that people are going to great lengths to oppose the CIA so that, even if they are not presented with the facts, they will at least ask themselves, "Why?"[4]

Discovering CIA Activities on Campus Above and Below the Floorboards

If your university is like many universities in the United States, the Central Intelligence Agency is carrying on some kind of business at it.

Recruiting

If the CIA is recruiting openly through your placement services office, you can check with the office and find out quite easily. When confronted with protest, the Agency has been known to switch its recruiting dates at the last minute. Try to be in constant contact with someone who has a scheduled interview with the CIA. They may be told to come to the placement office on a day other than the one officially scheduled.

The CIA may also be doing covert recruiting. In this case, the Agency sends out mailings or "invitations" to students in various departments. The mailing may be sent randomly to students majoring in fields the CIA is particularly interested in at the time or it may go to students the CIA has already hand-picked.

To find out whether the CIA covertly comes to your campus to recruit, have someone with no background in activism (author and activist Bob Witanek suggests "a low-profile senior") approach the placement office or their major department's career guidance office and display some enthusiasm for a career with the Agency. He or she should ask whether or not the CIA comes or how to get in touch with the Agency if it does not come. That person may be sent an interview invitation or be approached by someone in the department with an invitation. On the other hand, they may only get the local CIA recruiter's office number. These numbers are practically public knowledge and, when called, are usually answered by a machine. Have the "mole" leave his or her name and number on the machine, and if and when a recruiter calls, find out whether or not the CIA will be coming to the university.

Moles can also find out if there are any co-op programs with the CIA at the university, graduate studies programs or foreign student recruiting programs. For instance, an undergraduate mole in a CIA interview can ask to do some kind of CIA traineeship while still in school and note the recruiter's response. If you can find a graduate student willing to participate (and who wouldn't already have a file with the CIA), have her or him ask the CIA about the possibility of doing research for the Agency while still in school.

Finding out about foreign student recruiting may be a bit trickier. This kind of recruiting is done secretly. Traditionally, foreign students are approached very carefully by the CIA after being screened by a professor or another student already working for the Agency. The student is usually introduced to the CIA recruiter through a go-between with whom the student is already familiar.

Activist foreign students can discreetly ask students from their own countries if they have ever been approached by the CIA. Many foreign nationals who are offered jobs with the Agency turn them down and never tell anyone about the offer for fear of recriminations. They might unload the information if they can retain their anonymity. Then again, they might be angry about the offer and want to tell their story to the public.

In general, making the existence of these kinds of recruiting programs known to the campus community may turn up a few people who were once afraid to talk because they were alone with their information. "Put out a call to professors and graduate students to blow the whistle," Witanek says.[5] Knowing that *you* know about what's going on could be the cue they've been waiting for. Publicly encourage everyone on campus to reveal information about CIA ties to the university. You may want to place an advertisement in the school paper with an address to which people can send anonymous tips.

Research and CIA-Paid Professors

CIA-sponsored research and professors on the Agency's payroll will be even more difficult to discover. Travis Parchman claims "the only way to get some of this information is to have people on the inside who can get it for you, like friends in different departments."[6]

Ex-agent Verne Lyon suggests approaching the university administration with the blunt question: does the CIA sponsor any research here? This could be submitted in the form of a written request for information or within the context of a personal meeting. Some university administrations will be more willing to divulge than others—that is, if they even know about CIA research. Once you begin requesting information from the university, publicize your requests in the school and local papers so that pressure will be on the administration to give out the information.

Administrators may not know about the existence or extent of CIA research going on in their facilities because of the many and varied front companies the Agency uses to disguise its presence.

Ramparts magazine turned up a number of CIA front companies and foundations by checking into their sources of revenue. The funding trail always led to a twilight zone of post office boxes, non-existent agencies and eventually straight into the public pocket. Ask your administration or Board of Trustees for a list of the federal, state and private organizations and businesses that are sponsoring university research. Then check into their financial channels. Concentrate on those areas where the CIA would most likely be concentrating: engineering, political science, foreign studies, foreign language studies and so on.

Or you can go straight to the source and ask the CIA. Lyon recommends filing a Freedom of Information Act (FOIA) request asking for all information about CIA-funded research and professors at your school. Vernon Elliott, co-editor of *Campus Watch,* suggests filing the request with the cooperation of a professor. "If the request is 'in furtherance of scholarly or scientific research,'" he says, "students will have a much easier time avoiding FOIA fees (search charges)...[also] if students file a request through a professor, the Agency is less likely to challenge the validity of the request."[7] Information on how to file an FOIA request is located in Appendix B.

Though an FOIA request is always worth a try, the information released under the Act—at times substantial—was severely curtailed by the Reagan administration under the catch-all reasoning of "national security." George Bush has made no moves to repeal any of Ronald Reagan's Executive Orders, and Lyon notes that on this issue, Bush's presidency "is basically a continuation of Reagan administration policies." Although filing an FOIA request "doesn't mean the CIA is going to cough up any information, you can badger them a little," Lyon says. And you may come up with something.

Officer in Residence

If there is an Officer in Residence at your school, you should know about it. If not, ask around or check the class schedule for courses on intelligence or national security. The professors of these courses may be Officers in Residence or may formerly have been with the Agency or another government intelligence organization.[8]

When the CIA is exposed as operating an Officer in Residence program at a university, it comes out with a lot of hoopla about the overt and open relationship the officer has with the school. But when most of the programs are started, the officer is not announced and the program is only discovered by inquisitive students or faculty members. At George Washington University, the appointment of CIA officer Laurie Kurtzweg was brought to light in a xeroxed flyer distributed by a student. Students and faculty at the Rochester Institute of Technology learned about the CIA program there only after a reporter for *Campus Watch* called to question the administration about it.[9]

The initiation of the Officer in Residence program at the University of California at Santa Barbara (UCSB) was also less than overt. CIA representatives brought up the idea of establishing an Officer in Residence program with the UCSB chancellor at a dinner party in the summer of 1987. The chancellor took the issue up with then head of the political science department, Dean Mann. Mann approved the program, consulting only a few department faculty members, and the next class schedule listed a national security course taught by a new lecturer named George Chritton. Chritton, of course, was CIA, but no one except the chancellor, Mann and three or four political science professors were aware of his affiliation. Fortunately for UCSB student activists, Mann was replaced as department chair by Cedric Robinson in the same year. Upon entering his new position, Robinson found a letter from the Agency to Mann about the CIA program and released it to the local press. Whether or not Chritton's CIA background was going to be revealed to the campus community at some future date, UCSB activist Dave Karloy notes that the administration "was not exactly open about it" at the initiation of the program.[10]

Programs and Institutes

If there is some kind of government or foreign studies institute at your university that is particularly well-funded, you can almost count on the guiding hand of the State Department, the Pentagon or the CIA. In addition to those CIA-sponsored university research programs and departments mentioned in Chapter Two, the following programs and departments are known to have accepted some kind of funding, contracting or counseling from the CIA:

- A project at the University of Illinois at Chicago to "develop statistical models of governability on a global basis."[11]
- Research into the Filipino Communist Party's New People's Army with professor Justin Green at Villanova University in Pennsylvania.[12]
- Quite a few programs at the Massachusetts Institute of Technology and at Johns Hopkins University, the two schools that pulled in almost half of the Pentagon money available for university research in 1980 and 1981.[13]
- The Ethics and Public Policy Center at Georgetown University.[14]
- Tufts University's Fletcher School of Law and Diplomacy, specifically, the Murrow Center for Public Diplomacy.[15]
- The University of Pennsylvania's Foreign Policy Research Institute. According to activist Gerry O'Sullivan, the Institute is a "revolving door" for the CIA.[16]
- Any program funded or sponsored by the National Strategy Information Center or Roy Godson's Consortium for the Study of Intelligence.[17] Godson chairs the Labor Studies Program at Georgetown University—reputed to be an active recruitment operation for the intelligence profession among its foreign and U.S. students.

- Possibly, programs receiving funds from the Scaife Foundation or the Scaife Family Charitable Trusts and Allegheny Foundations, or the Smith-Richardson Foundation—all of which have contributed to pro-CIA research and public opinion making.[18]
- Programs at M.I.T. and elsewhere funded by the Defense Supply Service. Two M.I.T. professors running a program funded by this Service have been identified as consultants to the CIA.[19]

There are definitely dozens and possibly hundreds of universities doing business with the Central Intelligence Agency, most of which are not listed here. Research may turn up some connections at your school.

"Consensual Strategy": Legitimizing Before Hell Raising

Once you have found CIA connections to target for protest at your school, you should come up with a definite goal and a solid strategy to achieve that goal. One of the common mistakes anti-CIA activists make is setting short-term, immediate goals without considering their effects 1) over a longer time period and 2) on student body and community opinion. Many activist groups, fueled by their knowledge of horrible CIA atrocities, take it upon themselves to stop the CIA immediately and in any way they can. But without developing the support of the campus community, immediate successes—for example, stopping a recruiting session—do little to hinder the Agency's activities. When those activists graduate, the CIA will come back. In the meantime, nothing has been done to gain a majority opinion on CIA recruiting and further the progressive movement as a whole. Few, if any, new people have been educated or radicalized by the action.

> Separatism…or actions that remain meaningless or offensive to much of the population [and]…lack of an articulate vision of the future…are among the many reflections of the enormous power of the Western system of fragmentation and ideological control.[20]

Although activists might feel frustrated that so few of their peers know about the suffering of others at the hands of the CIA, "student exclusivism or putschism will hardly do as a political strategy."[21]

The most successful campaigns against the CIA involve strategized stages that can span years. Activists who have waged these campaigns call them "consensual strategies," or "legitimization processes." Our generation of activists benefits today from the same kinds of campaigns waged in the '50s and '60s. The anti-discrimination restrictions that govern our placement centers, and those that we use to point out existing ethical codes in the university as we struggle to ban the CIA, are in place because of previous consensual campaigns. These kinds of campaigns do not rule out militant action. Rather, they lay the groundwork for militant action to be fully effective and successful. Basically, consensual strategy involves exhausting all the "legitimate" channels for proposing changes in university policy before carrying out militant actions. This legitimization inevitably involves consistent educational appeals to the campus community for agreement on the issue—pulling in members of voting bodies that must research the CIA's history to make a decision. Eventually the decision will go to the Board of Trustees, which will probably reject banning the Agency. Then, whether or not a previous majority agreement has been reached, by the time a militant action is carried out the community will understand the necessity for the action rather than view it as extremist and out of line. "In contrast, without a background of popular understanding, [action] may be only a form of self-indulgent and possibly quite harmful adventurism."[22]

Another benefit of a consensual campaign is that it can happen at any time. Caryl Sortwell, an activist at the University of Illinois at Chicago and a member of the Progressive Student Network, describes the campaign against the Agency at UIC as "pro-active."

"It's not reactive to the CIA, meaning the CIA does not determine our agenda. We are attacking the attitude of the university and its recruiting policy rather than waiting for the CIA to show up in order to act," she says. With the initiation of the pro-active approach at UIC, the administration agreed to sponsor and fund a CIA campus forum that included John Stockwell and FMLN/FDR spokesperson Arnoldo Ramos, among others.

Sortwell's organization plans to bring the issue to a vote eventually. "When the matter is taken to a vote, all of a sudden, everyone involved has to have an opinion," she says.[23] And to have an opinion, the voting body must do research and educate itself. At the University of Maine and the University of Colorado at Boulder, consensual strategy won activists majority votes in faculty and student governing bodies to ban the CIA. Militant actions following legitimization chased the CIA out of Boulder. By rejecting vanguardism and carefully refusing to be coopted, activists can radicalize community opinion *and* stop the CIA from recruiting and researching at their schools.

Legitimization:
Set Your Goals and Make Them Known

Going to your administration and Trustees with your concerns before you begin more serious actions is a good idea for two reasons. One: sometimes, however rarely, university administrators are willing to concede to students when they feel that the students' requests are legitimate. At many smaller schools and at religious-based institutions, administrators are dedicated to a code of ethics or to the idea that the student body should have a voice in the basic functions of the university. Even at larger schools, guidelines for employment that may have been instituted in the 1960s or '70s can be invoked today to relieve the university of organizations like the CIA.

Two: when you have made your demands to the administration, you have set your goals. Your actions can then be focused on achieving those goals and the campus community will understand why the actions are taking place. It is a common argument of administration officials to say that activists who are arrested or charged with university disciplinary violations never came to them beforehand to discuss the issue. "Well, we could have talked about this," the argument goes, "but these misfits just took it upon themselves to stop the CIA from coming." The inference is that they are reasonable people and you are dictatorial tyrants.

From the first time you make your goals known to university officials, start keeping extensive notes. Document all of your communications with the administration or Trustees. Elliott recommends keeping a "detailed chronology of all letters, calls and meetings" with school representatives.[24] Note the date, content and outcome, if any, of each communication and keep the records (duplicates if necessary) in a safe place. You can present this list to the media later for reference or if administrators claim that you did not go through instituted channels for raising issues with the school.

Before you go to the administration or boards of your university, however, formulate your demands thoughtfully in the context of pre-established rules and guidelines; or make demands for new guidelines. Then garner the sympathy of all the campus and community organizations that you possibly can so that you present the administration with solid support for banning the CIA.

Use Existing Guidelines

Try to base your demands on your school's existing guidelines for
recruiting and research. For example, at Northwestern University Law
School, the recruiting guidelines exclude all employers who discriminate against potential employees on the basis of their sexual orientation.
When the CIA requested permission to recruit at the N.U. Law School
placement office, it was flatly denied. According to Cindy Rold of placement services, the decision was made on the basis of a CIA recruiting
policy publication sent to the office at her request and titled the "Policy
on Certain Sexual Conduct." The publication stated that sexual orientation was "one factor" in the CIA's employment decision making, and that
was enough to bar representatives from coming.

The same tactic was used by activists at Princeton University to
get the CIA off campus, as mentioned earlier. Princeton student activist
Suju Vijayan found that his anti-CIA group "brought in a lot more support
and certainly a lot more interest and press coverage" by focusing on the
CIA's sexual-orientation discrimination.[25] The media and the governing
bodies of your school might find the discrimination issue easier to tackle
than a full-scale indictment of our government's international objectives.

Kate Hill, an activist at Columbia University, warns that the plan
to exclude the CIA solely on the basis of sexual-orientation discrimination, though often successful, can be "dangerous to use. The implication
is that if they eliminate these problems [the discrimination] they can
come on campus."[26] You also lose the opportunity for valuable education
on U.S. foreign policy if you concentrate on the discrimination issue
alone.

A "two-pronged effort" encompasses both covert action and discrimination. "Then even if the CIA some day changes its recruitment
policy and didn't discriminate, we would still continue fighting on the
covert action issue," Vijayan points out.[27]

Greg Christiansen is one of the students in Princeton's Coalition
Against Homophobia that fought CIA recruiting. "It's important...that
it [anti-CIA organizing on sexual-orientation discrimination grounds] is
done through a gay-lesbian alliance or through a coalition against
homophobia," he says, "because that is where the expertise is regarding
sexual orientation discrimination."[28] In other words, those who are most
affected by the issue should make the primary decisions about how to
handle it and should be within the leadership of a discrimination campaign. If your university does not have a guideline regarding sexual-orientation discrimination, an anti-CIA group could work with a gay-lesbian
group to propose one and pressure the administration to adopt it.

Most universities restrict recruiting opportunities to non-equal-opportunity employers. Some also state that companies or organizations that are not "legal," "lawful" or "legitimate" cannot come to the campus to recruit. Operating on the premise that creating restrictions to weed out unfair, unjust or criminal institutions is a step in the right direction (noting also that equal opportunity was won through struggle), you can point out that crimes against humanity and violations of international and domestic law should exclude the CIA under existing guidelines.

In 1985, a "Citizens Coalition Against the CIA" at the University of Wisconsin at Madison questioned university practices that allowed the CIA to recruit on campus. The group presented to faculty committees proposals that criticized the school for violating both university and city codes. According to the Coalition, CIA recruiting at Madison violated a "Faculty Document" stating that all recruiters at the school must provide "legitimate employment." The CIA, they argued, hardly offered "legitimate employment" for graduating students.[29]

In addition to breaching the Faculty Document, CIA recruiting at Madison violated Wisconsin State Statute #939.05 regarding "Parties to Crime." The Citizens Coalition documented CIA participation in criminal activity—making CIA recruiting "soliciting for the commission of a crime," an illegal activity according to the state's attorney general. By abetting the Agency in its search for employees, the university was a party to crime.[30] Finally, the Coalition "respectfully insisted" that the faculty senate "implement a moratorium on CIA recruitment" at the university, "execute a full-scale investigation as to the criminal nature of the CIA and cease and desist assistance in the solicitation of students to commit illegal acts."[31]

The successful defense of anti-CIA activists from the University of Massachusetts at Amherst rested partially on the university's recruitment policy which prohibits employers who are not "law abiding" and do not conduct "legitimate business" from using placement facilities. Defendant Mark Caldiera reflects that it was "pretty easy" to prove to the jurors that the CIA lacked both qualifications.[32]

Research City, State and International Law

In addition to university guidelines, many cities and states have employment regulations. Your targeted school may be in violation of one or more municipal or state laws by allowing the CIA to recruit at its facilities. At the University of Pennsylvania, lesbian and gay activists used Philadelphia's city law, the "Fair Practices Act," to file suit against the university for assisting the CIA in recruiting. They achieved a victory by getting the CIA off campus, though activist Gerry O'Sullivan claims that "all [the administration] did was move the CIA recruiter out of the campus placement office" and underground.[33]

International law is also relevant to city or state law. Since treaties signed by the United States have supremacy over local laws, they are binding on local citizens and on the university. Prove that the university is in violation of the law by aiding and abetting an international criminal organization. If your city council is more reform-minded than your university administration (e.g., if the city is a nuclear-free zone or sanctuary city), it might be worthwhile to approach local politicians and community members and propose a "CIA-free zone" that would include university grounds. Local churches and temples, including your campus ministry, might also be able to help. After all, the CIA on campus is a local issue that should concern everyone in the area.

Academic Codes

CIA-sponsored research and training programs or the presence of an Officer in Residence are in direct contradiction to the academic freedom and integrity codes at most universities. A graduate organization at Madison challenged CIA research funding on the grounds that it violated the stated purpose of the university to "provide a learning environment in which faculty, staff and students can discover...and transmit...knowledge, wisdom, and values...to improve the quality of life [of the society]...to have respect for and commitment to the ideals of a pluralistic, multiracial, open and democratic society." The CIA, the organization noted, undermines intellectual integrity and steers the university from its "purported goals of 'improving the quality of life of society.'"[34] This campaign against CIA-sponsored research was built on a resolution passed in the mid-1980s by the university's Board of Trustees that banned all covert research on campus. According to Mark Heimbach, the university endorsed the resolution "not so much because they felt a sense of moral outrage" about the CIA, but because the Trustees felt that the CIA would damage the "academic excellence of the university. They were concerned that the results of university research would go unpublished and unpublicized," Heimbach says.[35]

Your efforts, however, to promote the fundamental, more compelling reasons to ban the Agency must continue. The Student Cooperative Union at the University of California advanced some of the most pressing arguments against CIA complicity in campus research. Its report on the "Censored History of Relations Between the University of California and the Central Intelligence Agency" concluded:

[The] university cannot collaborate with the CIA without sharing culpability for its actions. Research done for the CIA *has direct impact on the lives of people around the world...*As long as the university functions as a service agency for the CIA, or as a cover for its "academic" and propaganda purposes, any claim to the university's role as an open and democratic institution is farce.[36]

Arguments for academic integrity and independence that apply to CIA-funded research also apply to the CIA's Officer in Residence program. *Campus Watch* summarizes the major condemnations of the Officer in Residence program according to the academic standards of an independent university:

- Officers in Residence, as active employees of the CIA, may be inclined to speak under the direction and influence of the Agency, rather than speaking freely under the principle of academic freedom.
- Officers in Residence, acting in accordance with their secrecy oaths, may be inclined to omit, misrepresent, or distort certain information during their class presentations.
- The Officer in Residence program may be used to provide the CIA with enhanced capability to covertly recruit foreign students . . .
- The Officer in Residence program may provide the Agency with a convenient means for supporting domestic surveillance operations targeted at student groups...[37]

The political science department at the University of California at Santa Barbara, under its chairman, Cedric Robinson, voted overwhelmingly to downgrade Officer in Residence Chritton's status from "lecturer" to the department's lowest formal position, "academic miscellany"—based on some of the arguments listed above. Although there was some faculty sentiment to ask Chritton to leave the university altogether, Chritton had already signed a contract with the university that some felt should not be broken.

Former CIA academic affairs coordinator and current Officer in Residence at Boston University, Arthur Hulnick, defends the program, stating that many professions require secrecy oaths—law and psychology, for example—which forbid professors in those fields from discussing ongoing cases. Furthermore, Hulnick claims "it's up to students to make their own judgments about the objectivity of their professors." According to Hulnick, the overwhelming opposition to the program at

UCSB was the result of "a disinformation campaign waged by [John] Stockwell and Philip Agee."[38]

Cedric Robinson calls Hulnick's accusation "absurd." Regarding Hulnick's arguments about the relative normalcy of secrecy oaths among professionals, Robinson says, "I spent a long time talking with Chritton. He could not substantiate events that the *New York Times* reported as fact 20 years ago. The blanks [in CIA officers' lecture materials] are extensive. They're not just blanks about current activity, but about generally accepted historical fact. If they are not able to talk about recognized events, then they are not going to be able to teach with candidness. Their courses will be extremely prejudicial because they can only offer the CIA's self-serving accounts of history."[39]

Ironically, when activists rightly oppose CIA research funding on the basis of the CIA's very blatant, extremist political agenda, critics accuse the *activists* of injecting politics into guidelines on academic research. Counter by pointing out that you are seeking to create an independent and moral university atmosphere by ridding it of a highly political and immoral organization. CIA research funding and CIA-directed programs at U.S. universities have contributed directly to covert actions in Vietnam, Indonesia and Latin America that killed thousands. If the university will allow contracts with the CIA, will it also allow contracts with organizations in opposition to the CIA like the ANC or the FMLN? If you find that your school has no codes or regulations regarding recruiting, research funding or professorial status, or if the existing rules are insufficient, create new ones. Every university needs a rule barring any relationship with an organization that commits crimes against humanity—whether those crimes are torture, murder, genocide or manufacturing the tools of torture, murder or genocide.

A very small group of students at Chico State University in California managed to gain the support of the school paper when they proposed a change in recruiting policy "requiring all recruiting organizations to sign a statement saying that they agree to abide by all university regulations, local ordinances, state and federal laws, the U.S. Constitution and international law."[40] If a significant portion of the university community questions the compliance of a specific organization, the issue would be researched by a student-faculty committee with authority to revoke recruiting priviliges from non-compliant organizations. Reviews of specific organizations would be public, contributing to the educational process of the entire student body.

If you make your demands specific and appeal to laws and ethical or moral values *that are already agreed upon by our society* then you have built an appealing case for yourself that is difficult to refute.

Student Government and Faculty Bodies

Once you have built a strong case for yourself, grounded in the existing recruiting guidelines, city or state law (and thus, international law) and the ethical codes of the university, take the issue to the student and faculty governments. At the University of Minnesota at Minneapolis, the Progressive Student Organization sponsored a resolution which called for the banning of CIA recruitment. The PSO's resolution passed—somewhat watered down—as a call for an "open debate" on the issue.[41] If progressive students are already on the student government, the body will be more likely to consider and perhaps pass your resolutions. In April 1990 the vice-president of the Associated Student Body at Humboldt State University not only joined in a protest against CIA recruiters but resolved to "develop legislation on the student level banning the CIA from HSU."[42] At the University of California at Santa Barbara, five activists held positions in the student government. Their influence helped persuade the student government's vote to recommend revoking Officer in Residence George Chritton's appointment to the university staff. At Boulder, a majority of the student governing body voted to ban CIA recruiting altogether.

Faculty governing bodies tend to be even more responsive than student governments to issues like banning the CIA because faculty members are usually more familiar with Agency activities. At the University of Maine, for example, a vote in the faculty senate to end university complicity with the Agency was defeated by two votes: the two student representatives on the senate. At Maine, an "Ad Hoc Committee on the CIA and University Recruiting Policy" charged by the senate to research the issue had previously voted six to two in favor of recommending "that the CIA, as a result of its disregard of federal and international law, and its violations of human rights, be barred from using University of Maine resources in its efforts to recruit new personnel."[43] The report by the Committee (made up of administration officials, faculty and students) was the result of an educational campaign the Committee organized on behalf of the faculty senate. Panels, debates, ex-agent speakers, Agency presentations and community forums were all sponsored as part of the Committee's research. Maine activists claim that the sponsored, participatory nature of the educational campaign supported their consensual strategy to turn campus opinion against the Agency. The success of the campaign is reflected in the language of the report itself:

> Our inquiry revealed violations of international law, as judged by the International Court of Justice, as recently as

the last administration, probable violations of federal laws, and operating rules allowing violations of fundamental rights to privacy, a long history of inhumane and anti-democratic practices which have been well documented and are inconsistent with the values of a public university in a democratic society... [Some] have voiced the opinion that such activities were regrettable but temporary aberrations of CIA practice, a position, however, which is difficult to sustain after examining the history of the agency... [The argument that only a small percentage of the agency's activities are illegal or unethical] is difficult to verify...but even if true it is not relevant to our evaluation of the agency, any more than a high percentage of bookkeeping jobs in the Mafia would qualify that organization for access to recruiting privileges...Based on consultations with Louis Menand and informal discussions with constitutional lawyers, our committee concludes that a ban on CIA recruiting would not violate the agency's First Amendment rights. Recruitment, unlike speech, is not a right but a privilige...recruitment priviliges can be withheld...for any reason the university considers relevant and embodies in its access guidelines...At the same time, opportunity to interview with potential employers through the Career Center is not a right, even under current policy...Student opportunity is inevitably constrained by considerations of legality, equity and university policy. The question is what that policy should be.[44]

Activists should assume that student governments and faculty bodies can come to the same conclusions that they have regarding the CIA's campus presence. By bringing the issue up to these organizations, activists distribute the responsibilty of upholding morality and legality for the university. In the process of making decisions on the issues, "legitimate" university organizations can become educated and radicalized. Soon enough, activists' concerns become everybody's concerns. And then you have only two more groups to deal with...

The Administration and Board

Administrations and Regent, Governor or Trustee boards will be the least receptive to anti-CIA proposals. In November of 1987 at Colby College, faculty members voted 49 to 22 in favor of adopting a resolution to ban CIA recruiting on the campus. The Board of Trustees responded with the decision not to ban the CIA from recruiting, but to formulate a general rule that all potential employers must be willing, if requested, to discuss their policies in an open forum before recruiting at the university. "It will then be for the individual student to determine whether he or she is satisfied with the adequacy of what is presented."[45] It seems that at Colby, and in schools across the country, college students have been granted judicial powers that supercede those of the International Court of Justice.

Unfortunately, most activists' experiences with college boards and administrations reveal a poor track record in responding to student concerns. Madison's Citizens Coalition Against the CIA, despite hard work and a willingness to reason with the university administration, despite lengthy documentation of CIA crimes and an effort to utilize existing recruiting regulations and city laws, met with the businesslike, cold shoulder of the university. The Coalition was refused a moratorium on CIA recruitment and the Agency was welcomed to the campus in 1986.

Activists at the University of Illinois addressed a university Trustee meeting in April of 1990 only to hear the board's president conclude that he "heard nothing...that made me believe we had to change our policies."[46]

At Rutgers, activists were refused even a meeting with university president Edward Bloustein. Instead, they received a position paper from the assistant provost for student affairs stating that "for Rutgers University to ban a legitimate organization engaged in lawful activities on campus on the basis of a philosophical judgement about its goals and methods would be an arrogant and presumptuous form of political censorship."[47] Rutgers students were actively *questioning* the legitimacy and legality of the CIA, and the issue at hand was as "philosophical" as torture training, direct assistance to criminal bodies and blatant violations of domestic and international law. But the university administration was consciously avoiding the real issue.

Why? True, the Central Intelligence Agency brings dollars to university programs. But is the financing enough to justify what those programs may eventually be used for? The campus-CIA nexus runs deeper than a few hefty grants. CIA connections to university administrations and faculties tie into the personal and political as well, into an intricate web of old relationships and former allegiances. Especially at large and well-funded institutions, many administrators, Trustees, Regents and Governors have individual histories with the State Department, the CIA, the FBI and other government agencies. Was it a coincidence that Rutgers president Edward Bloustein, nominated for the CIA directorship under Jimmy Carter in 1977, refused to meet with student activists regarding the CIA's status as a "legitimate" employer? According to Christine Kelly, Bloustein "wrote the book on how to counter student demonstrators."[48] Should activists at the University of Illinois at Chicago have been surprised when the vice-chancellor for administrative affairs ordered their arrest at a peaceful demonstration, given that the vice-chancellor participated in the CIA's invasion of Cuba in 1961? While a U.S. college education continues to be mainly a luxury of the middle and upper classes, the owners and administrators of our universities will continue to be functionaries of a state that, for the most part, represents the interests of the wealthy. The overlapping of government and university officials is so common that it is rare to find a school where none of the administrators have ties to the government. Most universities are built on these kinds of affiliations.

Case in point: Tufts University's Board of Visitors and its Advisory Councils consist of the following notables: Senator Daniel Patrick Moynihan, Henry Cabot Lodge, Stansfield Turner, former CIA deputy director Bobby Inman and National Security Council member Alexis Johnson.[49] Princeton president Harold Shapiro has been known to consult for the CIA. Northwestern University president and former University of Colorado president Arnold Webber, once with the State Department, is still a friend of George Shultz. Northwestern's chief of campus police lists the FBI as a former employer. "Chico State President Robin Wilson worked as a CIA foreign intelligence estimates officer and operations officer from 1959 to 1967."[50]

In addition to occupational or personal bonds, there are direct financial connections between university funders and CIA operations. Northwestern University's Board of Trustees includes current and former presidents, chairpersons and board directors of the First National Bank of Chicago, G.D. Searle Incorporated, Cessna Aircraft, Inland Steel, Firestone Tire and Rubber, Lone Star Steel, Morgan Guaranty Trust, Zenith Radio Corporation, Harris Trust and Savings Bank, Texaco, Arthur Anderson and Company, Pan Am, Kraft and International Telephone and Telegraph (ITT), among others.[51]

Many of these companies continue to invest, notably in South Africa, and in a number of countries where the CIA is currently engaged in covert operations. ITT issued funds directly to the Central Intelligence Agency to bolster anti-Allende factions in Chile before the violent coup in 1973. It is reasonable to say that in the Chilean coup, the CIA was the covert action arm of ITT and the Anaconda and Kennecott Corporations. The Cessna Aircraft Company's A-37s are used by the El

Salvadoran military to bomb and strafe densely populated mountainous areas. Even "a U.S. Defense Department panel of military experts recommended against the A-37 in El Salvador because of mounting criticism of the civilian casualties it inflicts."[52]

Therefore, in many cases, activists are appealing to those very people whose financial interests the CIA is ordered to protect. We can assume that in our negotiations with our boards and administrations we will not get very far at all. This assumption, however, should not exclude our attempts. The reluctance of the power wielders to respond to student concerns effectively illustrates the undemocratic structure of most universities and will help to pull others into empowerment struggles.

Regent, Governor and Trustee boards are likely to put a screeching halt to the legitimization process of consensual strategy. Build all the possible support you can from all sectors of the campus and local community before you take the issue to those with real decision-making power. Then, by the time you get there, you arrive with the strongest possible coalition behind you. If and when the board rejects your proposals, your next actions will be understood and supported by more of the community. The important thing to remember is that your tactical options are not limited to asking nicely. As Minneapolis activist Mike Turner comments regarding the CIA on campus: "You can raise the issue with the university, but demonstrations will get them off."

No More Mister Nice Guy: Agitation and Action

> You can't always get what you want. But if you try sometimes, you just might find, you get what you need.
>   Mick Jagger and Keith Richards, 1969.

So you put on your best dress and the administration still won't listen to you? You worked hard for umpteen thousand signatures on a petition that is now worth about as much as a cancelled check? Your Trustees can't get out from behind their polished walnut CEO desks?

Cheer up.

Where there are numbers and where there is a will, there is the potential to accomplish anything. You have appealed to the student body, the faculty, staff, administration and Trustees. You have exhausted all possible "proper" channels. Your campaign has been totally legit. Your consensual educational efforts have pulled in a good number of students and you are ready to act on what you have been talking about all this time.

We come now to a highly controversial point in the struggle against the CIA on campus. How far do you go to get the CIA off campus? At what point do you lose your appeal? At what point do you lose your principles? And how much does it take to get the job done?

The answers to these questions vary from individual to individual and center on what is usually called the level of "militancy" of an action carried out. In the dictionary, "militant" is defined in two ways: "1. prepared to take aggressive action in support of a cause. 2. involved in warfare or fighting."53 Most activists prefer the former definition. However, it is the latter definition that gives the word a bad name. The militaristic connotations of "militant" are combined with the question: how aggressive is "aggressive" action? In the United States, where the direct effects of CIA actions are seldom felt, will highly aggressive tactics turn more people off than on? And will the State (the administration, the court system) be able to use those tactics to turn the public against activists? Ultimately, if we are working for a peaceful and just society, should we be peaceful in our struggle? Or should we attack an unjust system with the same kind of force the system itself uses?

In the campus struggle against the Central Intelligence Agency, these questions arise again and again. When a group is deciding whether to educate quietly with a protest and signs, to commit civil disobedience or "passive" resistance to the State or to actively stop the CIA from recruiting by blocking doors, disrupting interviews, damaging property, resisting arrest and avoiding or fighting police attacks ("aggressive" resistance), a general agreement on the relative militancy of the action planned is desirable and often hard-won. There are a number of factors to take into account when you are going into an action, and the experiences of other schools should play into your strategy.

Consensual Strategy and Militant Action: The Story of Boulder

In 1984, the Central Intelligence Agency made its first public appearance at the University of Colorado at Boulder since the 1970s. Students and community members active in the local CISPES chapter raised their eyebrows. The CIA had taken a bold step in coming to a school and a community known for its progressive climate. The action would be met with even "boulder" steps.

From the fall of 1985 to the fall of 1986, a series of events unfolded at UCB that transformed the community and the activists in it. It began with the first anti-CIA demonstration in November 1985, a civil disobedience (CD) marathon that lasted for three days while the CIA recruited in a university building. Boulder resident and activist Jimmy Walker describes the experience as "magical...Something was right about the whole event."[54]

Boulder students and CISPES members formed "Community In Action" (CIA, to make things confusing) and voiced their concerns to the career counseling office, the administration and the local district attorney. They told the D.A. that he had an obligation to arrest the CIA for solicitation to commit crimes—illegal according to a Colorado statute. The "CIA" group then invited the CIA to send a representative to speak on campus, thereby refuting charges of breaching the Agency's freedoms. "During the representative's presentation, we were very respectful and very polite," Walker recalls. "But we were forceful and clear about our own opinion as to what the CIA was doing."

Before the day the CIA was scheduled to recruit, activists spoke with the local police department and stated their intention to make a citizen's arrest of the CIA agents in the building. If the police were planning to protect the agents, they could demarcate an "arrest" zone into which activists who were willing to risk arrest could pass and go willingly with police to waiting vans. Approximately 15 activists, students and residents of Boulder were prepared for arrest on the first day of the demonstration. A microphone was set up and as each CD candidate made his or her way to the arrest zone, they stopped at the microphone and explained the reasons for their actions.

A large crowd gathered to hear the stories. Some applauded. Some heckled. Some made the spontaneous decision to participate. By the end of the first day, 140 people had been arrested. Activists overheard other students discussing the event that evening, asking each other if they were going to go "do it."

The next day, more people showed. More were arrested. On the final day, even hecklers had experienced a change of heart and were sitting in police vans. Student Council members were arrested. City Council members were arrested. It seemed that the whole town was going to get arrested. At times the line to the microphone swelled to 100 and the number of onlookers to 2,000. By the end of the third day, when the CIA agents were packing up their questionnaires and literature and stuffing them back into their briefcases, 478 people had been arrested by Boulder police, some twice. "It was quite an incredible dynamic, an incredibly successful action. People were really amazed," Walker says.

The UC Boulder administration, however, was not. It refused to bar the CIA from coming back, claiming that to do so would be to obstruct the rights of students who wished to recruit with the Agency. The CIA was duly invited back and accepted the invitation. Agency recruiters announced their intention to return the following semester.

When the following semester came, Boulder activists struggled for unity within the group. At the Community In Action planning meeting, democratic centralists argued with anarchists. Some wanted to take more direct action against the CIA than legal self-sacrifice. They complained that the previous demonstration was "drive-through civil disobedience," a "K-Mart" action that hindered neither the CIA nor students recruiting with the CIA.

"It was a crazy meeting," Walker recalls, "We were roadblocked." Most of the activists favored non-violent techniques for practical as well as philosophical reasons. The group finally reached an agreement to attempt to get inside the recruiting building and perform a citizen's arrest.

On recruiting day, the lack of a solid consensus was apparent. Elected leaders of Community in Action tried to exercise some control while anarchists refused to follow orders. Some demonstrators attempted to block doors while others tried to find ways into the building. Rock climbers scaled the walls of the building and climbed in through windows. A citizen's arrest was unsuccessfully attempted and the previously cooperative relationship the activists had established with police disintegrated. Leaders told the police to demarcate another arrest zone and then said that they were not responsible for what would happen and were not claiming to know what would happen. The situation was no longer "drive-through"; it was bumper cars. The police arrested 200 people in four hours. Predictably, no one was charged.

And the CIA announced its intentions to return to campus the following fall.

This time, Community In Action members shared their feelings of frustration. They announced to the press that they planned to "get tougher." A vote to allow the use of property destruction during the demonstration was passed. Administration officials opened their front doors in the mornings to pools of bovine blood on their steps. They raised their shades to find pictures of contra atrocities plastered to their windows. The local media painted a dark picture of what might happen on recruiting day. "We scared a lot of people away," Walker says. Evidently, they scared the university enough to move the recruiting site from a relatively average-looking college building to what activists called "Fort Somoza," a large, windowless, cement basketball stadium on the other side of campus.

On the big day, police erected chain-link fences around the structure and blockaded the entrances. Recruitees were bussed in from the career counseling office and met by about 500 demonstrators. Some pulled the valve stems out of the university van wheels so they could not return to pick up more students. Amidst the wheezing of deflating tires, activists attempted to block the open entrances to the stadium. The police responded by macing and beating the demonstrators with their batons. Angered, the activists started to tear down the chain fences and the police released their guard dogs. General chaos ensued.

Walker describes the scene as "completely out of control." People arrested by the police and taken into custody inside the stadium disappeared—climbing into the roof rafters. "The police were freaking out," Walker says, and casual observers were compelled by the brutality to jump into the fracas. "None of us are militant yahoos," Walker explains. "We're not street fighters." The situation, however, had escalated beyond anyone's control.

In the aftermath, "we faced a lot of grief from the community." Critics, Walker points out, tend to be far more vocal than supporters. But Community In Action defended the actions of those present. Walker explains:

> Our basic point was that when the government is doing something horrible in another part of the world, we must make those actions socially expensive, domestically expensive here. Society must become unmanageable. Yes, the tactics seemed extreme. But when Martin Luther King first began his kind of resistance, everyone was saying he was so extreme. Then came the Black Panthers. At that point the government says "Why can't you go back to what you were doing before and not be so extreme?" Like the university was saying to us, "Can't you go back to what you were doing before so we can go on with our business? Can't you be more manageable?" Well, we don't want to be so easily controlled.
>
> On the other hand, we didn't want to become some kind of ridiculous vanguard—righteous and small. We weaned people along with us. The action widened the gap of acceptable tactics.

The action certainly generated a lot of press coverage and the debate around the issue following the demonstration became more substantive. Suddenly, there was more at stake than a few hours at the

Boulder police station. When the state prosecution learned that activists faced with criminal offenses would be allowed the necessity defense (explained more in Chapter Six), it immediately dropped all charges.

The CIA has not come back to Boulder since.

The Boulder action may have stretched the limits of acceptable tactics, as Walker believes. On the other hand, Boulder students were essentially responding to police mace and batons. Former Boulder student and current United States Student Association (USSA) organizer Kevin Harris points out that activists "did feel it was necessary to escalate our tactics, and we did plan for that, but *no one* planned for what actually happened. It's important to see the student actions in the context of what the police were doing. Students were mostly acting out of response."[55]

According to Harris, the final action was successful mostly because the Community In Action group had already been through a legitimization process during the previous year that included education, exhausting all "proper" channels and risking arrest at the CD action. Legitimization, he says, "was crucial to our success. We laid the groundwork for what might happen later...It was a real, community based effort" that focused not just on the CIA but on education and community empowerment. By the time the final action occurred at the basketball stadium, a majority of students at Boulder had already voted "no" to CIA recruiting in a campus referendum.

Another hectic demonstration (again, provoked by police mace and clubs) at the University of Minnesota at Minneapolis resulted in damaged property, but attracted publicity from around the world. The action was reported on all the domestic network news programs, cable news, major domestic newspapers and foreign newspapers—specifically, in Chilean papers and in Nicaragua's *Barricada*.

Minneapolis Progressive Student Organization member Jill Zemke claims "just the picture and caption in *Barricada* made it worthwhile to us."[56] She says "the action did cause a lot of debate. But I wouldn't necessarily call the action 'violent.' Destruction of property is not the same as causing harm to people." The police seem to be taking care of that. Though the relative heat of the Minneapolis action served to push the issue forward, the CIA returned twice more before the actual disruption of interviews finally forced them off. At some schools, the disruption of student interviews with employers would be met with the outrage of the campus paper at the lack of respect for students' rights shown by the offending organization. But the continuous efforts of Minneapolis activists had turned the school paper against CIA on-campus recruiting.

Militancy (perhaps a better term in these cases is "assertive self-defense") has been successful in getting the CIA off campus at schools like Minneapolis and at the University of Colorado—where extensive education was done, where the president of the student body was participating in demonstrations, where about a third of the Student Council sympathized with protesters or protested themselves, where Boulder's mayor gave speeches at anti-CIA rallies. Would the same kind of action have been as effective at a place like Princeton?

As you plan your actions, take into account the political atmosphere of your school. Weigh your support against your relative isolation. Perhaps a civil disobedience action like the first one at Boulder is more suited to the current stage of your campaign. That kind of civil disobedience action could be your first step, and your actions can become more militant as you gain support through education. Just remember that educating and involving the community should be one of your primary goals. Then the community will support and become a part of your actions, increasing their chances for success.

Be aware, though, that your actions are not without ramifications—both on student body and community opinion and on your personal welfare. Before you go into any action that may involve breaching laws of the state or of the school, know what the possible consequences may be. With this warning, we move on to Chapter Six.

CHAPTER SIX

It's a Jungle Out There:
The Consequences of Activism
and How to Deal With Them

Individuals who violate University policy are subject to disciplinary action in accordance with campus disciplinary procedures. Individuals in violation of the law are subject to arrest and prosecution. Organizations which violate University policy are subject to sanctions provided for by the Student Code.

Memo to student groups at the University of Illinois, Chicago from the Vice Chancellor for Administration, 1989.

Failing to plan for the worst usually leads to the worst. As activists in the 1990s, we are akin to David facing the mighty Goliath. Of course, David's stone hit its mark. But what if it hadn't? What would David have done? Run? Begged forgiveness? Picked up another stone? Fainted? We are the modern David, and yet we are fallible. We are vulnerable to slander, attack and persecution. The rival that we are facing is, like Goliath, monolithic if not far-sighted.

We are playing with fire and should be fully aware of this fact as we do so. If we are lucky, we will suffer only a few blisters: lack of time for school or work, some peer harassment, stress. If we are unlucky, we can get badly burned: physical abuse, suspension, expulsion, arrest, prosecution, even prison. The CIA has done some nasty things to protect financial interests. What will the CIA do to protect its access to academia—a crucial element of its existence?

This chapter will explore some of the ramifications of student dissent, from blisters to third-degree burns. But this *caveat* is by no means complete. As the situation at every U.S. university waxes and wanes in intensity, so do the possible consequences of activism. No one can claim to know all the possibilities. Find out as much as you can about the consequences you may face at your school or in your city before you wing that first stone at Goliath.

Counter-Demonstrators: Why Don't You Go Get Your Own Issue?

Perhaps as an effect of the Reagan-Bush Era, counter-demonstrators seem to make an appearance at almost every anti-CIA demonstration that goes on these days. Usually, the pro-CIA folks are a contingent from the College Republicans, Students for America, Young Americans for Freedom (YAF) or another right-wing campus group. Sometimes, superficial-thinking "freedom-before-justice" advocates—economic libertarians or objectivists, for instance—join the hecklers with signs saying "Freedom for the CIA" or, as one civil libertarian's sign at a Northwestern University demonstration stated: "CIA Off the Planet, But Not Off Campus," whatever that means.

The counter-demonstrators may, if their numbers are great enough, form their own picket line and stay relatively out of sight and mind. More often, they attempt to disrupt your demonstration by distracting and provoking your group with insults and taunts or, worse, by physically accosting you, drowning out your speeches with their own or preventing you from attempting your planned action.

At Northwestern University, anti-CIA demonstrators arrived at a rally in front of the campus placement office and were met by a very loud broadcast of Bush's 1988 campaign song: "I'm Proud to Be an American." The College Republicans and friends had also hung a huge banner from a dormitory window calling for "Free Speech for the CIA." The music continued throughout the day, alternating between "Proud to Be an American" and "Born in the U.S.A."

Initially, anti-CIA protesters put up with the noise and tedium, marching in a circle around the cul-de-sac before the placement office. When the counter-protesters broke through the circle and formed their own inside of the larger one, some of the protesters got angry and started to push and shove the counter-demonstrators. A scuffle ensued, broken up by the campus police. The antagonism continued and culminated in the tearing up and burning of a Republican's U.S. flag—an action that incited controversy in the demonstration's aftermath.

At other schools, counter-demonstrators have regressed from heckling to throwing eggs and yogurt at protesters.[1] In one of their more disturbing exhibitions, counter-protesters at a Minneapolis demonstration encouraged police to "use [their] guns" against anti-CIA students and chanted for "another Kent State!"[2]

To some extent, activists are protected from counter-demonstrators by the laws that govern freedom of speech and assembly. If CIA proponents disrupt your demonstration or interrupt speeches, the campus police may be called upon to stop them. However, the campus police are usually there to protect the CIA recruiters from you. The administration may have no quarrel with the counter-demonstrators; they are sustaining the status quo. You can expect the school and the police to be far more lenient with pro-CIA student agitators than with anti-CIA student agitators. Toward the end of the Northwestern demonstration, protesters were arrested for expired sound and gathering permits. The counter-protesters never had the same permits to begin with and were never asked whether or not they did, though the music blaring from their speakers unquestionably exceeded the city's legal decibel level.

You are participating in a political action. The police, the administration and affiliates will act along political lines. Essentially, the *issue* is of the utmost importance, and one of the worst things counter-demonstrators can do to a rally is successfully distract it from the issue of what the CIA is and does. Hecklers may try to engage you in a debate about freedom of speech. Or they may try to make you angry enough to attack them, rather than the Agency. If there is still confusion about the CIA's "freedom of speech" on your campus, you may want to address some of the questions the counter-demonstrators bring up. Just make sure you have control of the megaphone or microphone.

Another tactic is to ignore the counter-protesters completely. Or mention their arguments and defeat them, but never speak directly to them. Address your voice to the general crowd instead. If you do let them get to you, you can easily lose control of the situation.

A few activists at almost every demonstration seem to be itching for some kind of aggressive confrontation with *anybody*. Some activists argue that the police protect and therefore symbolize the "enemy." Thus attacks on police officers reflect attacks on the CIA, the contras or whomever. Certainly, resistance to police brutality is understandable. But the "fight mode" that some activists switch into at demonstrations seems more like an itch for action than a thoughtful response to the situation. Let the counter-demonstrators seem belligerent. You know where you stand. If they raise good points, accept it and speak on those points in a reasonable manner. If they break into your picket line, move the picket line. Avoid direct confrontation. You are not trying to appeal to hard-line right-wingers; you are trying to appeal to those people milling about, watching the demonstration. Keep your focus on them and on the CIA recruitment inside the building. Your conviction in the rightness of where you stand will be the turning point for the unconverted.

Big Brother Has a Club: Police Brutality and Arrests

The scene is from a movie, you think. *This guy isn't really bleeding, is he? Shit, he is. He is.* Your cloth of accepted reality is tearing at the seams. *Jesus, stop that policeman and his club! What the hell is going on?* "Don't hit him, for godsake!" you yell, "Don't hit him!" *What is this, Korea? Chile? El Salvador? Stop. Stop. Please, stop.* You can't believe this is happening. It's unreal. *This is like a scene from a movie.*

Police brutality must be experienced to be believed. Suddenly, a demonstration turns into a bloody brawl. Time slows. Frantic, people are crying, screaming, running, fighting back. Then reality sets in: people are being hurt, people are in *pain.* What can you do against the updrawn baton? the attacking dog? the stinging in your eyes, nose and throat? The police are out of control and the situation is bleak.

The chances of a scene like this happening on your campus are becoming greater and greater.

As reported in *The Nation,* "The high stakes for the universities and the militancy of the opposition have led school after school to react to students' confrontations of CIA recruiters with confrontations of their own."[3] Responding to increasing dissent, university administrators, campus and city police across the country are resorting to physical repression. They have attacked, with surprising violence, even the most peaceful student demonstrations. At an Amherst rally, the University of Massachusetts administration called the state police on campus "for the first time in seventeen years." The police arrived in riot gear, leading attack dogs.[4]

In the 1980s, police have used mace, batons and dogs on students at the University of Colorado at Boulder, have used tear gas at the University of Minnesota at Minneapolis, have physically beaten students at the University of Illinois at Chicago, the University of Michigan at Ann Arbor, Northwestern University, the University of Texas at Austin—and this list is by no means complete. Remember Jackson and Kent State. In some ways, times haven't changed.

Philosophies differ regarding resisting arrest and police brutality. Most hold fast to pacifism and strict non-violence, seeing the attacking forces as victimized and innocent, accepting (though shielding them- selves from) the brutality in order to demonstrate the violent underpin- nings of the state. Pragmatically, strict non-violence may be used to keep all blame for violence on the state; non-violence helps to win sympathy and support.

Those who advocate violence either do so because they are just about ready to start fighting a revolution or they advocate its use on a limited scale, reluctant to give it up as a form of struggle. "Strategy and tactics cannot be confined to predetermined 'safe' guidelines,"[5] writes one *Guardian* reader in a tactical debate that spanned several issues of the paper in 1989. Certainly, an advanced degree of militancy causes more disruption to the state's plans than "'sit down and arrest me please' official tactics"[6] but there *is* the risk of alienation from a broader section of the North American population—as yet uneducated to the systematic abuses of the state. There is also the risk of playing into the hands of FBI and CIA smear campaigns and the mainstream media's sensation- alist angle hunting. Keep in mind that FBI infiltrators and disrupters have advocated extreme militancy or violence.

Judge by the times, the immediacy and disruptive potential of the situation, by your short- and long-term goals and by your philosophical or moral leaning. The debate in letters to the *Guardian* reflects a general disagreement within the the progressive movement as to where we are in the movement and how we want to get to where we are going. Resolving the issue requires our careful, strategic, principled thought— and a lot more discussion.

In the meantime, police brutality is an ugly reality—provoked or unprovoked. Non-violence training sessions are available through the Pledge of Resistance and War Resisters League chapters in your area (see Appendix B). Non-violence does not preclude militancy and achiev- ing the objectives of the demonstration. Training deals with how to best carry out those objectives without harm to yourself or other people. (See Appendix D for suggestions on how to be prepared for and deal with police brutality.)

Janine Hoft, a lawyer with the People's Law Office in Chicago and legal writer and consultant to the Chicago Religious Task Force's organizing manual, suggests the use of "legal observers" at demonstra- tions who have some knowledge of police behavior codes and can take notes when those codes are being broken. It is a good idea to videotape your rallies in an effort to pressure the police not to become violent or to record the violence if it should occur. Hoft also stresses the impor- tance of identifying and being witnesses to police brutality. "The person who is getting beaten up is not going to remember anything except the

club coming at them," she says. "It's important for people to be witnesses
to these actions and get the officer's badge number and name."[7]

If there are "impartial observers" in the vicinity, ask them for their
names and phone numbers so that you can contact them later for
testimony. Everyone present at the demonstration should share information and take notes about what happened as soon as they have the
opportunity so they don't forget important details.

"When someone is really getting beaten up, you should try to
intervene, though that may mean that you end up getting arrested
yourself," Hoft cautions. You can tell the officer that you see what they
are doing and that might stop them. But it might not.

When the going gets rough at a demonstration, it's good to have
a backup plan or two. According to Penn State activist Travis Parchman,
who faced expulsion after a demonstration, "the mistake we made…in
getting ourselves expelled is that a lot of people [started] spontaneous

Author's Story: Friends in Strange Places

The graduation processional into the basketball auditorium
was less formal than I expected. We jostled for seats next to our
closest friends and stood on our chairs scanning the multitudes of
proud family members, looking for our parents.

My neck was beginning to hurt from craning it to see in the
upper decks when someone called my name. I thought it was my
father. *How'd he get down so close?* Someone pointed in the direction
of the call and said, "That guy wants you." I looked down the aisle
and took a few futile seconds assessing the situation. He was one of
the campus police officers from the anti-CIA demonstration the
previous fall.

"What does he want you for?" asked one of my best friends
from the seat next to me.

"I don't know."

Reluctant as I was to do so, I'd have to go talk to him to find
out. I wiggled through the row of restless seniors and followed his
lead to an open area near the stage, thinking: *What does he want?
Am I going to graduate? Oh God, please, my grandmother's here and
everything.*

Given the hostile and violent confrontation protesters had
with police on the day of the rally and ensuing charges, counter-
charges and general, unfriendly relations, I didn't think the man
would have much good to say to me. So I was shocked to my shoes
when he started to talk.

actions and ran off doing [different] things because they were frustrated at the time."[8]

On the other hand, Minneapolis activist Jill Zemke notes that the controversial action that took place on that campus in response to police brutality "certainly was not planned."[9] Demonstrators, subjected to police clubbing, macing and tear gassing, responded by smashing in the glass doors of the recruiting office. As mentioned earlier, the action's ramifications were felt as far away as Nicaragua—and Minneapolis activists generally agree that their strong defense of their actions that day led to a deepening of the discussion around the issue.

This, of course, does not mean we should all start smashing in windows at demonstrations. It does mean that you will not always have total control of a situation, especially when the police are getting out of hand. Know that your carefully laid plans may disintegrate completely. Plan for the worst. If something does occur that is akin to the Minneap-

---

"I just wanted to say congratulations. I'm glad you made it." I squirmed in the unfamiliar territory. He *did* seem sincere.

"Well, thanks." *Anything else?*

"I saw you at the debate and I was very impressed. I think you really believe what you're doing is right..."

He went to the debate? I didn't remember seeing him.

"...and I know we went through a scuffle there at the demonstration, but I was only doing my job and you gotta do that. I know you have to fight for what you think is right and my people did that and it made things better." He is African-American. "So I just want to say, I'm glad you're graduating."

I absorbed all this, admittedly taken aback.

And then I felt real good.

"Thank you. Thank you. I'm glad you said that. Thanks a lot." I shook his hand and we wished each other good luck in the future.

Back at my seat, I smiled through the honors and the speeches.

I had opened his mind a little and, in return, he had opened mine. Never give up on people because they may initially conflict with you. Ultimately, we are all human and have the capacity for empathy. Our possibilities exist first in recognition. We need to recognize more possibilities.

olis or Boulder incidents, defend your actions and focus the discussion on the Central Intelligence Agency.

Ironically, students assaulted by police officers at demonstrations are often charged with assault and battery by police. Amherst activist Mark Caldiera recalls a rally in 1986 at which "one person assaulted a police officer's club with his face."[10] In most states, your chances of successfully charging the police with brutality are bleak at best. Rarely do these charges get time in court, much less a prosecution. Especially in a demonstration situation, where the chaos muddles fact and fiction, and your word is up against the word of an officer, it is very difficult to get anyone in the court system on your side. If you feel, however, that your case deserves a shot at being heard, don't be dissuaded. Talk to a lawyer about the viability of a police brutality charge.

Look Before You Leap: University Disciplinary Charges and Hearings

Students who have faced university disciplinary charges because of their actions at anti-CIA demonstrations generally urge caution in planning and carrying out demonstrations.

Activist Travis Parchman feels that anti-CIA demonstrators at Penn State could have saved themselves a lot of trouble if they had bothered to check out the university's disciplinary codes before going into the demonstration. According to him, Penn State had quietly changed its code during the preceding summer because of a public embarrassment to the university the year before in which the administration was forced to drop charges against a group of students demonstrating against racism on campus.

"So they changed the whole system in order to make sure that would never happen again," Parchman explains.[11] His group was not aware of the changes the following fall, and three people faced suspension and expulsion from the university as a consequence. "Understanding the legal precedents and the immediate history of how the university has handled different disciplinary cases…might keep a lot of people from getting into unnecessary disciplinary problems and still be able to come off with your point in a rather militant way without stepping over certain lines…Or [at least] know where [the lines] are."[12]

The Penn State disciplinary code—which "mirrors others" according to Penn's school newspaper, the *Collegian*—prohibits student defendants from having a lawyer or recording the proceedings at hearings, even when students face severe punishments. Administrators defend the code as legitimate within a private setting: "The hearing is within the university and it's not a...legal case," said Penn State's director of the Office of Conduct Standards.[13]

Similarly, Michigan State University disallows legal representation and recording at hearings. As MSU's vice president for student affairs (perhaps too aptly) put it: "There is no evidence that the criminal justice system in this country works, so why try to duplicate it?"[14]

There is a strong case to be made against the lack of due process at schools like Penn State and MSU. Hoft thinks it's "outrageous" that students are not allowed legal consultation at school hearings—especially in cases involving politically motivated actions where students face severe penalties like suspension, expulsion and fines. Furthermore, statements made at university hearings can be used later against activists who face court cases. Parchman and two other defendants threatened Penn State with a lawsuit, but backed down when the university eased the punishments against them. Their threat was, in terms of alleviating their charges, effective.

If you are faced with unfair disciplinary proceedings, raise a fuss, by all means. "Students should demand their right to a lawyer," Hoft advises, "Demanding your rights is the only way to get them, or at least, more of them." If you do go ahead with a suit against the university, you are in a better legal position "if you have asked first for a lawyer. Basically, that sets up the record for an appeal of your sanctions. If you did not ask for an attorney, they can call your appeal 'irrelevant,'" Hoft warns.

At other universities, legal representation is allowed, and transcripts of all hearings are available to the public. If your hearing is open to a public audience, use your time on the witness stand to defend your actions and explain why you were doing them. At a school hearing, twelve students at Northwestern University faced disciplinary charges for blocking doors to the CIA recruiting site. With reporters and almost 100 students and faculty watching the proceedings, activists were able to make strong public statements about the CIA and the complicity of the university and its police forces in abetting the Agency.

Although Northwestern students were allowed the consultation of an attorney, they were strongly discouraged from it by a nominally neutral university advisor. The university's case would be represented by a professional prosecutor, but the advisor assured the students not to worry. "He may look and sound intimidating," he said, "but just be yourselves. That's what's going to appeal to people." Fortunately for the activists, they decided to utilize the services of a lawyer anyway. She advised them during the hearing not to bring any witnesses to the stand because the prosecution had failed to identify even one of the demonstrators as being present at or blocking the placement center doors. The students' own witnesses may have been forced to identify the demonstrators during the university's cross-examination. No witnesses were called and all twelve student defendants walked out of the hearing room with unblemished records. If your university allows you to have an attorney present at proceedings, do so. Your educational career is not worth risking on the advice of impartial advisors. Get partial advisors.

Finally, use your hearing as an educational forum on the CIA, not just within the hearing room but in the pages of your school newspaper, in your own flyers and in letters to faculty and staff. If your hearing proceedings are essentially a vacuum of First Amendment due process rights, consider challenging the university in a higher court, or at least threatening the university with a challenge.

Most important, know your rights and your university's disciplinary codes *before* you act so that you are not unpleasantly surprised in the aftermath.

Selective Use of Student Conduct Codes

Universities have also been known to attack the student groups that carry out demonstrations against the CIA or against university policies in general. The University of Minnesota at Minneapolis administration waged a campaign against the Progressive Student Organization to revoke its student-group status. According to activist Jennifer Leazer, the campaign amounted to a kind of conspiracy that included the use of the Student Conduct Code (SCC), outdated postering rules and the singling out of specific leaders within the PSO.[15]

Research into the SCC and its "disruptive demonstrations" clause revealed that both were "subject to interpretation by university officials, and allow…for selective enforcement and prosecution…Similar codes, some with the identical disruptive demonstrations clause, were adopted in the early '70s by universities nationwide."

The implications of regulations that allow for their selective use against students and student groups is stated best by Leazer: "As the student movement grows and becomes a powerful force, we will face the internal structures which have been designed to kick activists off campus without rights to lawyers or due process."[16]

In response to UM's onslaught, the PSO filed suit against the university and upped the publicity around the administration's actions and the inherent bias of the SCC. Frightened by the strength of the

PSO's defense, the university eventually dropped charges against individuals within the PSO and eased up on the organization itself.

Student groups facing discriminatory use of disciplinary codes should research the codes and make their political enforcement an issue. The best defense is a good offense. (See Appendix B for resources and support organizations.)

The Criminal Justice System

All that applies to university hearings is doubly true for the court system. Know your rights. Know the laws. Know what you are getting into. The severity of penalties for the various "crimes" committed at demonstrations differs from state to state and city to city. There are also a variety of correctional regulations which can supersede the "rights" of arrestees. The advice of people who have been arrested recently in your jurisdiction, on similar charges, can be invaluable. Get a copy of your state's criminal code and consult with sympathetic lawyers before you enter into a confrontational situation—especially one in which you have planned to risk arrest by engaging in civil disobedience or by disrupting official business on your campus. Remember that it is especially unfair to those who do not wish to be arrested for any reason to be unaware of the possibility that city or state laws might be violated. Make sure everyone knows what might happen at your demonstration.

Arrests

Whether the arrests are planned or not, you should be prepared to face this eventuality in a demonstration situation. Take some basic precautions. Do not carry weapons, objects that might be considered weapons or contraband into a rally. Leave your address books and membership lists at home, unless you want the police to have this information. Bring some identification to speed up processing, unless you plan to use a false name or give no name as part of a planned non-cooperation strategy to extend your protest into the "justice" system. If you are on some kind of prescription medication, bring the medicine with you in its original container to verify yourself as the legitimate user of the drug and to facilitate obtaining the drug while at the police station. If possible, notify a friend who will not be at the demonstration that you may be arrested and give her or him all your statistical information and information about where to get bail money. If you will not be giving the police your real name, make sure your friend knows the name that you will use. Keep 25 cents to make a phone call from jail. It is also a good idea to deal with any parking or traffic tickets before you may be arrested.

Resisting arrest is considered a criminal activity. Even if you feel as though you are being arrested without cause or being arrested in a violent manner, the prevailing belief is that a police officer is always right regarding the law and that you should therefore obey whatever he or she tells you to do even if you emphatically disagree.

Resisting arrest means failure to cooperatively follow the police or let the police lead you to the police car or wagon. Going limp (and forcing officers to carry you) can be considered resisting arrest. Some people resist arrest as a matter of principle and will actually run from or struggle to get away from an arresting officer in order to further the objectives of the demonstration. Others withhold physical cooperation with the arrest by going limp but do not actively avoid police—in essence saying, "I know this is necessary and your job but I do not agree." Others fully comply and walk straight into the police wagon on their own accord. The choice is yours.

Usually, charges against demonstrators include numerous resisting arrest charges—sometimes compounded on top of other criminal charges. During arrests at a sit-in at a Senator's office in Chicago, seven people went willingly to police vans while two went limp and had to be carried. Charges against the seven who followed police orders of their own accord were dropped, while the two who resisted arrest were found guilty and given three months supervised probation. Be aware that resisting arrest has its consequences.

Jail

At the jail, police officers will ask for your name, address and social security number. Police may also confiscate your personal belongings and submit you to either a "pat down" or full body search. According to law, women cannot be searched by male officers. It is also against the law to strip search (body search) people arrested for minor infractions of the law. For instance, if you are charged with a misdemeanor, the police cannot ask you to take off your clothing or search your rectum. Activists who have been through illegal strip searches have used the restriction against police in court. However, the legality of strip searches may change as prisoners are transferred from police custody to a correctional facility for overnight or longer incarceration.

The police should allow you to make one phone call. According to Hoft, "this is supposed to be part of processing procedure. You can demand it as your right, but it all depends on the personality of the cop. As bad as it sounds, they don't really have to give you your rights. They may say, 'So, sue me,' and who has the money to do that? The phone call is really a right with a small 'r.' "

Pledge of Resistance member and seasoned arrestee Cinny Poppen warns against angering the police. "Sometimes the consequences can be pretty grim and unpleasant," she says.[17] As long as you are in the police station, the police are pretty much in charge.

You do have the right to legal consultation, if you desire it, before processing. If you feel that any of your rights are being denied or not met within a "reasonable" period of time, record the name and badge number of the officer refusing to grant your requests.

Sometimes the police will photograph and fingerprint each demonstrator. If they ask for any additional information beyond name, social security number and mother's maiden name, you are not required to give it. You have the right to remain silent. *Use it.* If the police are questioning you about specifics of the organization or the demonstration, they may be collecting information for the FBI or the CIA.

The police should set your bail within a reasonable amount of time—before you make your phone call—and may set you free "on your own recognizance" if they feel that the charges against you are relatively minor. On the other hand, it all depends on the political situation.

According to Verne Lyon, CIA projects "Resistance" and "Merrimac" involved close collaboration with local and campus police forces and the monitoring of student activists. The CIA may be the organization deciding how high to set your bail. Evidence suggests that there is close cooperation between the police and the CIA or FBI, especially in situations that involve anti-CIA activists. Even the decision to press or drop charges could be influenced by the Agency. "Certainly, the FBI has worked extensively with police, and the CIA has begun to hold hands with the FBI as well. The most important thing to remember is *not to talk to the police.* Don't make any statements to them. You don't have to tell them where you work or anything beyond vital statistics," Hoft says.

Bonds set should be reasonable and, at least in Chicago, cannot exceed $100 for misdemeanor cases. Cash bonds are not required for City Ordinance or Federal trespass violations, but police are allowed to use their discretion in whether or not to set them. They are usually more inclined to set a bond if they know that you have the cash available. Therefore, it's not a good idea to carry too much cash with you to a demonstration.

You may demand no cash bonds or equal bonds for all arrested during the demonstration. This is called "jail and bail solidarity" and is good for group support and morale, especially if there are repeat offenders present in the arrested group or varying charges among you. Hopefully, the police will find it too much of a hassle to keep all of you at the station and will allow you these concessions.

If you do not have the cash available to pay your bond, the police have the obligation to get you to a judge within a "reasonable" period of time (usually that night or the next morning) who will then decide to let you go on your own recognizance, lower your bond payment or let you languish in jail a while longer.

You should not have to spend more than 24 hours at the jail unless you are part of a very large group of arrestees (over 50) or if you choose to do so as a form of resistance to the justice system. If anything out of the ordinary occurs during your brief respite at the police station, make note of it and make sure to get officer names and badge numbers.

Court

At the police station you will receive a notice for your first court date which should include the time and location of the courtroom. At this point, says Hoft, "it is important for activists to sit down together and make decisions about how to best use their resources."

You may or may not wish the advice of a lawyer. Your constitutional right includes the option for a *pro se* defense in which you act as your own attorney. However, it is probably wise to get the consultation of a lawyer before you tell the judge that you are going to defend yourself. You should weigh the seriousness of the charges against you, the number of people arrested and charged with similar crimes, the attitude of the judge regarding *pro se* defendants and your own desires. Many defendants arrested as a group ask to be tried as a group, and this is usually granted in order to speed up the whole process. The judge that you end up with (which may vary with court dates until the actual trial) will determine much of what you will be allowed to do regarding your trial. Judges vary widely in terms of personality, open-mindedness, political leanings and leniency. Once you go through the trial experience, you will be astounded by the arbitrary power the judge has in a courtroom.

You may not even want to go to trial. Usually, the prosecution will be ready with some kind of deal on the first court date. You should be able to plead guilty to charges and accept the sanctions offered by the prosecution. Sometimes, people within a group of defendants arrested at the same demonstration would rather not go through the court procedures because of time, money, family responsibilities or other pressing commitments. No one should be pressured into staying on with the group if she or he has the inclination to plead guilty.

"The question you should ask is, 'Can we get any political mileage out of a trial? If so, how much?' Depending on the situation, it may be worthwhile to get back on the streets as soon as possible," Hoft says.

If you do choose trial, you can choose to defend yourself before a single judge in a bench trial which may last only a few minutes. "Bench trials can be convenient," Hoft maintains, "because you don't have to plead guilty and you do get a chance to say what's on your mind. On the other hand, you don't reach as many people and it's not as sexy for the media." She says that more and more activists are opting for a *pro se* defense at a bench trial to speed up the process. The People's Law Office offers *pro se* training for those interested in this course of action. (See Appendix B.)

If you decide to exercise your right to a jury trial (that is, if your state allows jury trials for the kind of crime(s) you are charged with), be prepared to expend a lot of time, energy and money, especially for lawyer's fees. A *pro se* defense is much more difficult in a full-scale jury trial, though sometimes activists within a group of defendants being represented by a lawyer choose to defend themselves. Many report it as a very empowering experience. *Also, the court will not allow you to be absent from your own trial because you have to work or go to school* (though sometimes in emergency situations, you can be tried *in absentia*, especially if you are being tried as part of a group). The court also will not allow you to miss court appearances, and you will have no input regarding the dates on which these appearances are set.

The Best Defense

Your defense can be based on the fact that you did not commit the crimes with which you are charged or that the crimes committed were done out of "necessity" in order to prevent a greater evil.

Activists and lawyers should be creative about developing a defense strategy. The goal is to provide the jury or judge with the reasons why you acted and to overcome the judge's inclination to prohibit you from telling your reasons because he or she decides they are not relevant. The necessity defense is one strategy, but other arguments may be made.

The crime(s) you are charged with may be described as "unreasonable" or "unlawful." International law and the history of the CIA can be used to show that the reasonableness or lawfulness of your actions may be protected by the First Amendment and similar provisions within state constitutions. Many activists have successfully asserted a First Amendment defense in protest cases. The necessity defense provides a framework within which to discuss the issues and type of evidence you want to present. The logic of necessity is illustrated in the example of an anxious father-to-be speeding his pregnant mate to the hospital in order to get her there before labor intensifies. Though he may be breaking traffic laws, he is doing so to prevent an even greater evil from happening: miscarriage or death of the mother. Therefore, the man should be acquitted, based on the immediate circumstances of his crime. "Conduct which would otherwise be an offense is justifiable by reason of 'necessity' if the accused was without blame in occasioning or developing the situation and reasonably believed such conduct was necessary to avoid a public or private injury greater than the injury which might reasonably result from his own conduct."[18] Your state laws may or may not include necessity, though they don't always have to in order for you to use it as a defense. Furthermore, your judge may or may not let you use it as a defense, even if your state permits its use at the judge's discretion.

Opinions regarding the use of the necessity defense differ greatly. It has been used successfully by activists who were arrested during demonstrations against the CIA and in other situations where U.S. foreign policy was the issue at hand. Obviously, using the necessity defense entails a lot of hard work. If you choose this defense, you and your lawyer will probably want to search through the canons of state law to support your claim to necessity, gather expert witnesses—perhaps pay for their transportation to and from the trial—and in other ways document and present CIA atrocities to jurors and prove that your action was intended to somehow stop or hinder those atrocities from occurring.

The most famous anti-CIA necessity defense included Amy Carter and Abbie Hoffman in Massachusetts in 1987. The defense included the testimony of notables like former Attorney General Ramsey Clark, *Pentagon Papers* leaker Daniel Ellsberg, ex-CIA agent Ralph McGehee, former contra Edgar Chamorro and people's historian Howard Zinn. Leonard Weinglass of Chicago Seven fame led the defense. Unsurprisingly, the case was covered extensively (if not substantively) by the mainstream media, including magazines like *Newsweek,* network news and large newspapers, as well as by smaller left-leaning publications.

Jill Zemke argues that the personalities involved in that trial were a significant factor in its success. "Only Amy Carter and Abbie Hoffman could really do that," she says, "A court is not the place to raise issues of political concern, unless you have the kind of personalities that can pull it off and attract attention." She believes that the court system can be a waste of good time for activists: "If you can do an action and not go through legal processes, so much the better."

On the other hand, political battles have been fought and won in the U.S. court system, where judge or jury decision making can be advantageous to political defendants. In fact, the jury system—though limited by prevailing attitudes and judicial power—is one of the more democratic forums in our society. International law expert Francis Anthony Boyle promotes the use of the necessity defense to defend civil resistance activities on a wide range of issues in *Defending Civil Resistance Under International Law,* a manual that no attorney or defendant using the necessity defense should be without. In his manual, Boyle contends that "it is the American criminal jury system that shall prove to be the last bastion of democracy and law" against U.S. foreign policy's assault on both. Furthermore, if and when necessity cases are increasingly won, they create legal precedents that other activists can rely on to support their actions:

> It is crucial for preserving the future of our democratic system of government...that we conscientiously and systematically pursue analogous trial strategies for the defense of...protesters under international law that will eventually result in a series of dismissed charges, acquittals or at least hung juries in these cases. If properly publicized, each dismissed charge, acquittal or hung jury will encourage other private citizens to engage in similar nonviolent civil resistance activities.[19]

Pleading necessity allows you to get a lot "off your chest" and really give the reasons for what you did. It is not as though activists block doors, invade recruiting offices, disrupt meetings and walk around chanting and holding signs for the fun of it. There is a reason for what we are doing and the necessity defense is the channel through which we can express our motivations in the courts and actually win. In the Massachusetts case, "a six-member district-court jury, whose members included a 77-year-old man and 64-year-old woman," a jury that even a local district attorney described as "representatives of 'conservative middle America,'" found the CIA "guilty as charged" of "arranging assassinations, torturing and generally terrorizing the population of Nicaragua and lying about its actions."[20]

The defendants were acquitted accordingly, based on Weinglass's persuasive arguments that students "had no alternative" but to occupy the placement building, given that the CIA was participating in rampant violations of U.S. treaty law and was uncontrollable either by Congress (in its limited attempts at control) or by U.S. citizens. All the expert witnesses testified on behalf of these arguments, and the jury essentially came to the same decision that the protesting students had come to months earlier: the CIA's gross violations of international and domestic law and of basic human morality must be stopped—even if it requires drastic measures that violate some lesser laws.

Hoft, who has used the necessity defense successfully in two trials and served as a consultant to other lawyers engaged in necessity trials, sees the defense as "a good political education tool." The relative fame of the defendants "doesn't really matter" she claims. "If you do the groundwork with the media and get them interested, you can get some publicity out of it."

What a lot of people ignore about necessity trials is the educational transformation of the jury itself. "Juries have been so moved at these trials," Hoft says. "It's important just to reach those 12 people...people who have never even thought about the CIA and really couldn't care less to begin with. You can grab those people and force them to think about it." When juries are forced to think about it, they have consistently sided with activists. "The jury system consists of common, everyday, ordinary citizens. Most Americans consider themselves to be law-abiding and peaceful, and strongly believe that their government should be law-abiding and peaceful as well."[21] Even in cases where judges have instructed juries to disregard testimony about CIA atrocities, the evidence has outweighed the instructions, and jurors have come up with acquittals again and again. Hoft recalls one such case after which one of the jurors told reporters that he voted in favor of the defendants because he felt the government should not be breaking international laws. "Of course, the judge had told him that information was totally irrelevant, and it was still what he based his decision on," Hoft points out.

Chip Berlet of the National Lawyers Guild's Civil Liberties Committee bemoans the fact that "while necessity is wonderful and it works, it's rare."

It may, in fact, be its effectiveness that is causing its decline. "Necessity is so profound—it goes straight to the heart of the policies of the CIA and the criminal justice system—that judges are reluctant to allow it as a defense. It hits the nail right on the head and, therefore, hits the underpinning of their system as well," Hoft claims. However, she advises activists not to be dissuaded by the necessity defense's track record in their state. "You should act on your political motivations. Law follows activism...The people create new laws by what they do."

One of the key components of a necessity defense is that the defendants' actions during the demonstration in question reflect attempts to stop the CIA from carrying out its activities. Weinglass presented the jury with evidence that campus recruiting was a vital lifeline to the CIA and that disruption of recruiting was therefore a disturbance of CIA activities in general. If you are arrested for assaulting an officer or resisting arrest, it may be somewhat more difficult to argue that you were interfering with the CIA.

Keep in mind that your judge has more than a lot to do with your decision. Contact a progressive lawyer who has some experience with the necessity defense and ask for his or her advice. Your plans may change as you work your way through the pre-trial process.

Just the threat of necessity at the Boulder trial caused the prosecution to drop charges against anti-CIA defendants in 1987. The judge in that trial was willing to subpoena Oliver North and Richard Secord for testimony on the CIA. At the 1989 Northwestern anti-CIA demonstrators' trial, however, the judge ruled out necessity almost immediately and threatened to hold defendants and their lawyers in contempt of court if they mentioned anything about the CIA's activities. Though ruling out motivational evidence seems akin to ignoring the motivations of a murder, for instance—something that few judges would do—it is certainly within each judge's jurisdiction, even if it shouldn't be.

If you cannot use necessity and are definitely guilty of crimes charged, you may want to work out a deal with the prosecution. If you feel that you have been unfairly charged, then it may be worth going through a trial. A lot depends on the charges against you—which may range from misdemeanors to felonies. Students recently found guilty of charges incurred during anti-CIA demonstrations have received sanctions as lenient as supervision (similar to the penalty for a traffic offense, which can be cleared from your record for a fee) and rehabilitative or community service programs, and as tough as probation and stiff fines (as high as $7,000) which tie up students' time with fundraising.

Be aware that there are quite a few activists sitting in prison for actions against the state on other issues and that imprisonment is always a possibility, though remote. As Berlet reminds us, "If you can't do the time, don't do the crime."[22]

Most importantly, find a lawyer you can trust that is sympathetic to the cause. This book cannot tell you what to do in your specific situation, but a good lawyer can.

Big Brother Is One of You:
Monitoring, Infiltration and Disruption
of Domestic Activists

The area of government monitoring, infiltration and disruption of dissenting domestic organizations is one that has been relatively unexplored by today's student movement. We are, in fact, blindly moving into a situation where the lessons of yesterday are left unlearned and our vulnerability to covert attacks by local police forces, the FBI, CIA, NSA and branches of the armed forces is increasing. We desperately need to analyze the varying forces that caused the decline of groups like Students for a Democratic Society (SDS) and the Black Panthers in the early 1970s so that we can build a student movement that is constantly alert to those forces.

Activist and lawyer Brian Glick has written a readable, inexpensive and indispensable book on covert action against U.S. activists entitled *War At Home.* Copies of the book have been circulating among student activists, but full-scale discussions of the implications of its contents have yet to take place. The state of our movement reflects a similar stage in the 1960s when "talk of CIA-style covert action against domestic dissidents was generally dismissed as 'paranoia,'"[23] though "FBI and police harassment was blatant during the 1960s, and surveillance and infiltration were suspected."

According to Glick, "full-scale covert operations are already underway to neutralize today's opposition movements before they can reach the massive level of the 1960s."[24] One way to guard ourselves against the divisive tactics of our government's "counterintelligence" organizations is to study those tactics so that we do not fall prey to them.

A Police State To Call Our Own: A Brief History of
Covert Operations Against U.S. Activists

The best known counterintelligence program against U.S. activists and dissenting domestic organizations was "COINTELPRO," initiated in the 1960s by the FBI. An FBI memorandum in 1967 succinctly outlined the goals of COINTELPRO: to "expose, disrupt, misdirect, discredit, or otherwise neutralize" what the FBI considered "subversive" organizations or individuals within the United States.

The program—which emphasized "close coordination with local police and prosecutors"[25]—specifically targeted, among other individuals and organizations, the Communist Party-U.S.A., Puerto Rican independence organizations, radical Chicano groups, the Socialist Workers Party, Martin Luther King, Jr., the Student Non-Violent Coordinating Committee, the Congress of Racial Equality, the Black Panther Party, the National Welfare Rights Organization, Black student unions, churches and community organizations, the American Indian Movement (AIM), Students for a Democratic Society (SDS), the Peace and Freedom Party, the Institute for Policy Studies, and "a broad range of anti-war, anti-racist, student, G.I., veteran, feminist, lesbian, gay, environmentalist, Marxist, and anarchist groups..."[26]

Not only was the scope of its attack all inclusive, so too were the methods of disruption used by the FBI and various cooperating organizations. Tactics included planting agents within groups to gather information for the FBI or actively disrupt activities. Forged personal letters to activists' spouses were written to foment domestic squabbles that would distract activists from their political work. The FBI even sent a tape to Martin Luther King, Jr., detailing his sexual activities. This was followed by a letter forged to look as though it came from another civil rights activist. The letter accused him of betraying the movement and urged him to commit suicide as penance for his sins.[27]

COINTELPRO at its most extreme included the use of violence against activists, either by instigating violence from right-wing extremist groups, street gangs and some factional leftist organizations or by directly attacking those organizations. In 1973, the FBI "led a paramilitary invasion of the Pine Ridge Reservation in South Dakota" where the American Indian Movement had taken up arms and fortressed itself. While the FBI waged a smear campaign against AIM, depicting it as violent, the Bureau and its local counterparts "killed 69 residents of the tiny Pine Ridge reservation"[28] in three years. To this day, AIM activist Leonard Peltier sits in maximum security prison for the alleged murder of two FBI agents in a gun fight initiated by the Bureau.

COINTELPRO attacks on the Black Panther Party in the late '60s and early '70s included the use of infiltrators who both provided inside information to the FBI and encouraged the Party to increase its weapons supplies and engage in illegal "fundraising" (burglary and armed robbery). FBI-paid infiltrator in the Chicago BPP William O'Neal obtained information needed for the Chicago police to break into Panther Chairman Fred Hampton's apartment and open fire on its sleeping (possibly drugged by O'Neal) inhabitants. Hampton was killed and five others were wounded in the gunfire. Survivors were dragged outside, beaten and then arrested for attempted murder and aggravated assault. Totaled, the BPP fired one round from a shotgun—the reflex of a Panther who was reeling from a pointblank shot in the chest—and the police fired well over 50 times during the attack. This outrageous crime was one of many in a vicious, shameless FBI program to destroy the Black Panther Party.[29]

The Central Intelligence Agency has also participated in domestic spying. Through its Operation CHAOS, the CIA collected files on over 300,000 individuals in the United States.[30] In 1969, CIA Director Richard Helms recommended that computer networks be used "to share information about American dissidents between the CIA, the FBI, the National Security Agency and military intelligence units."[31] Using a computer system called HYDRA, the CIA garnered information on individuals and groups from all of these intelligence organizations. Though CHAOS was officially terminated in 1974, "CHAOS information was preserved and continued to be used after [its] termination."[32]

The CIA has also infiltrated dissenting organizations and "in 1971 and 1972 the Agency secretly provided training to about 12 county and city police forces in the United States on the detection of wiretaps, the organization of intelligence files, and the handling of explosives."[33]

The National Security Agency is another organization with "frightening" surveillance capacities.[34] Using a computer system called HARVEST, the NSA can monitor thousands of phone conversations at a time, honing in on and recording specific conversations according to pre-programed desired information. For example, HARVEST may be triggered to record calls to a specific person or calls in which certain "buzzwords" are mentioned: "Cuba," "FMLN" or perhaps "ANC," "CIA" or "protest."

According to author Ford Rowan, the collaborative efforts of the various government intelligence organizations—enhanced by the use of sophisticated computer systems—have prepared the government for a domestic "emergency" in which "the president could order [dissenting Americans] labeled as subversives to be detained by police and military units."[35] It was revealed in the Iran-contra hearings that the government, through the Federal Emergency Management Agency (FEMA), has detention camps in place and ready for use if such an "emergency" situation should ever occur. Journalist Alfonso Chardy reported in the *Miami Herald* that FEMA had developed a secret contingency plan "written as part of an executive order...that Reagan would sign and hold within the NSC until a severe crisis arose. The plan called for suspension of the Constitution, appointment of military commanders to run state and local governments and declaration of martial law during a national crisis...including domestic opposition to a U.S. military invasion abroad."[36] If George Bush has acted to stop FEMA's efforts to institute a state of siege in this country, we have yet to hear of it.

As things stand today, we do, in fact, have our very own U.S. police state—operating on the subtlest levels during periods of relative quiet, but ready for a full oppressive onslaught should domestic dissent become too powerful.

The CIA and Student Groups: Footing the Bill for the National Student Association

The U.S. National Student Association (NSA) held its first convention in 1947. From that year, the Association grew both in size and influence—using its power to set a Cold War agenda in place at the International Student Conference attended by student organizations from around the world. The international branch of the NSA "was able to sponsor yearly international relations seminars, foreign student leadership training projects, scholarships for foreign students, and still maintain a large travel budget for its international commission staff and its overseas representatives."[37]

Though its domestic operations were decidedly liberal—the NSA, for instance, opposed the war in Vietnam, supported students against the draft and participated in the civil rights struggle—the NSA's international operations took on a more conservative hue, adamantly opposing any sort of communist or socialist movements in the Third World. This dichotomy may have confused some of its members, especially those who went on to work for SDS and more radical organizations at home.

However, in 1966, the confusion was cleared up. *Ramparts* magazine published the fact that the NSA was the recipient of large amounts of indirect funding from the Central Intelligence Agency. Through a student whistleblower inside the NSA, *Ramparts* reported that numerous front organizations had been passing CIA money on to the Association with the knowledge of many upper-ranking student officials. In fact, the CIA was the NSA's primary source of funding. NSA officials were required to sign "national security" secrecy oaths about the CIA relationship. Furthermore, the CIA had a significant say in NSA operations. Student agents were "enjoined against making...diplomatic overtures without first requesting the permission of the Agency."[38] In return for their cooperation, student agents received draft deferments arranged by the CIA.

Though some NSA officials were uncomfortable with the CIA's control over the organization, they were somewhat powerless to reveal it. The NSA prided itself on being an independent student organization, free from "government controls. It was this quality that was supposed to distinguish their organization from national unions of students in the communist world."[39] When the information was finally revealed, the NSA crumbled under the weight of its covert participation with the Agency.

Today's Threat: What Do Anti-CIA Activists Have to Fear?

The question, more aptly put, might be "What do all activists have to fear?" The answer is, unfortunately, a lot. Recent revelations of FBI spying and disruption of organizations like CISPES indicate that little has changed. According to Glick, COINTELPRO-like activity abounds. The FBI's investigation of CISPES has extended to organizations and individuals as "terrorist" and "illegal" as the Southern Christian Leadership Conference, United Auto Workers and U.S. Senator Christopher Dodd.[40] Sanctuary organizations, Physicians for Social Responsibility, anti-racist organizations, travelers to Cuba and Nicaragua, Palestinian self-determination advocates, Black activists, Puerto Rican activists and prominent Jesse Jackson supporters have all been targets of recent FBI disruption campaigns. Newly appointed FBI director William Sessions "seems either untroubled by the shadows of the past or incapable of taking steps to banish them decisively."[41] And although Attorney General Richard Thornburgh "issued new guidelines in early September [1989] that apply to investigations of U.S.-based groups suspected of participating in international terrorism," the guidelines are secret—boding ill for activists in the years to come.[42]

Covert operations against domestic dissidents "have persisted and become an integral part of government activity."[43] The government "can sustain its legitimacy, while effectively marginalizing or eliminating domestic dissent, if it makes the victims of official violence appear to be the aggressors and provokes dissident movements to tear themselves apart through factionalism and other modes of self-destruction."[44] Meanwhile, the government is able to claim no part in the political repression of its citizens.

Today, domestic covert activity has an even larger legitimate range of operations, thanks to the Reagan administration, which "endorsed such action, legalized it, sponsored it, and raised it to the level of patriotic virtue."[45]

"Much of what was done outside the law under COINTELPRO has since been legalized by Executive Order No. 12333 (December 4, 1981) and new Attorney General's 'Guidelines on General Crimes, Racketeering Enterprise and Domestic Security/Terrorism Investigations'

(March 7, 1983)."[46] Through the use of Executive Orders, Ronald Reagan gave the CIA extended license to carry out domestic operations and limited the public's access to information about those operations.

According to Reagan's 1981 Executive Order No. 12333, government infiltration "for the purpose of influencing the activity of " domestic political organizations has received official sanction.[47] Additionally, the FBI may now break into and search a person's private property without a search warrant if the Attorney General finds probable cause to believe the search is "directed against a foreign power or an agent of a foreign power."[48] Glick warns that "this signals open season on CISPES, sanctuary churches, anti-apartheid groups, and anyone else who maintains friendly relations with a country or movement opposed by the administration or who dares to organize protest against U.S. foreign policy."[49]

As students, we are faced with a network of professors, university officials and even students who work with the CIA providing the names of and information on student activists who are opposed to the Agency. The right-wing student organization Young Americans for Freedom (YAF) has admitted to keeping files on campus organizations and "submitting regular reports to the FBI."[50] It is safe to assume that our organizations are monitored and may be infiltrated.

What Can We Do?

Glick's book contains a detailed chapter on resisting the government's attempts at disruption "in a way that minimizes its interference with our work."[51] Caution can easily become paranoia, and the fear that spreads when activists suspect infiltration is one of covert action's most effective disruptive weapons. We should proceed, but with caution. Factionalism and feuds within the movement must be examined at their roots. The failure of today's progressive student movement to attain unity would be a great success for the secret police state and its masters.

Individually, activists should be more than aware that their actions may have serious consequences. Verne Lyon notes that there is a price to pay for social responsibility. "Once you become politically active you face certain ramifications," he says. You can be labeled "left-wing" or "radical" and lose your chance at jobs in corporations or in the government. The worst thing that might happen is the "massive roundup" of activists during a national state of emergency. Lyon doesn't doubt this possibility. "You saw what happened with the Japanese," he warns.

If you suspect that you are being monitored or you would like to see if there is a file on you at CIA or FBI headquarters, initiate an FOIA request for all documents indexed under your name or the name of your organization (see Appendix B).

There are a tremendous number of obstacles that activists in the United States must face. But there are also many ways around the obstacles. The sacrifices you make should be made with your goals and your reasons for pursuing those goals in mind. We have chosen David's path, for better or for worse, and—as all strugglers for peace and justice in the history of the world have proven—history will absolve us.

Claiming Victory: Turning the Tide of CIA Presence on Campus and Expanding the Issue

The student movement has been critical for raising the issue of CIA operations, especially in Central America...I hope that it increases, expands and becomes a mass movement.

Ex-agent Ralph McGehee[1]

We have to change our own society...before we can expect that these types of activities undertaken by the CIA will be stopped.

Philip Agee[2]

In February 1984, Matthew Rothschild wrote in *The Progressive:* "the CIA is enjoying a remarkable renaissance on American college campuses. Gone is the militant protest, gone is the stigma...the Agency now recruits openly on 300 campuses."

"At Princeton," he penned, "there hasn't been a protest in at least three years...the CIA is once again a legitimate institution." Rothschild concluded by mourning the acquiescence of 1984's college students to the Agency's show of respectability as both "frightening and strange."[3]

Despite the ominous predictions of the late '70s and early '80s and almost a decade of Reagan mania, today's college students are back on track. Although "the military's efforts to renew on-campus projects, such as ROTC and CIA activity, have met less resistance since the collapse of the student and faculty anti-war protests after the Vietnam War...in recent years, renewed campus activism has begun to change this, providing some obstacles to the expansion of universities' links to the military."[4]

The CIA, "badly in need of recruits" as it claims to "shift its mission" in the 1990s, has upped its college recruitment sites from approximately 250 to 450, according to CIA spokesperson Mark Mansfield.[5] Nevertheless, student activists have booted their butts off campus indefinitely at at least 13 universities—and that includes Princeton University.

In the late 1980s, Agency recruiters were met with increasingly larger demonstrations and plenty of stigma at almost a third of the universities they visited. The CIA's Officer in Residence program has already failed at the University of California at Santa Barbara and is encountering protest at the Rochester Institute of Technology, the University of Texas at Austin and even at George Washington and Georgetown Universities.

Because of student protests, the CIA has terminated at least its overt recruiting efforts at Brown, Columbia, Princeton, Rutgers, State University of New York at Albany, the University of Colorado at Boulder, the University of Iowa, the University of Massachusetts at Amherst, the University of Minnesota at Minneapolis, the University of New Mexico, the University of North Carolina at Chapel Hill and the University of Pennsylvania. At some universities, the respite has been brief—for a year or two. At others, the CIA has not been back since 1986. At Chapel Hill, the Agency was forced to meet furtively in motel rooms as it did at the height of its unpopularity in the 1960s and '70s.

The CIA has even been compelled to designate a "Coordinator for Academic Affairs" to try to smooth relations with increasingly hostile student bodies. "At some universities," says Philip Agee, "a policy has been established that before a recruiting session the CIA has got to come and explain what they do…Years ago, this wasn't necessary. They just went in there and did their recruiting…Now it's amazing that they have to go out and do a P.R. thing before the recruiting takes place."[6]

The CIA is on the run from the only places where it makes any kind of public appearance—which is as it should be.

"Everytime they come to a campus," Verne Lyon stresses, "there *must* be a demonstration against both the Agency and its policies. We have to keep up the vigil." Though the vigil may involve a lot of hard work, it is worth the effort—both in terms of the educational work that goes on and in terms of the measurable successes achieved.

"The CIA can be driven off campus," Minneapolis activist Mike Turner asserts. Demonstration and education "raise the publicity costs" for the CIA, he says. After a large, heated and well-publicized demon-

College Anti-CIA Actions[7]

A partial list of universities where anti-CIA actions occurred between 1987 and 1991:

Bates College
Bowling Green State University
Brandeis University
Brown University
California State University—Chico
California State Polytechnical
  University
Colby College
Colorado State University—
  Fort Collins
Columbia University
Dayton University
DePaul University
Detroit University
Duke University
Fort Lewis College
Georgetown University
George Washington University
Hastings College of the Law—
  San Francisco, CA
Humboldt State University—
  Arcata, CA
Hunter College
Iowa State University
Illinois State University—
  Bloomington
Johns Hopkins University
Kent State University
Louisiana State University
Louisville State University
Marquette University
Miami University—Dayton
Middlebury College
New York University
Northern Colorado University
Northwestern University
Ohio State University—Columbus
Ohio University—Athens
Pennsylvania State University
Princeton University
Regis College
Rensselaer Polytechnic Institute
Rutgers University

Saint Louis University
Stanford University
State University of New York
  (SUNY)—Albany
SUNY—Purchase
Union College
University of California (UC)—
  Berkeley
UC—Los Angeles
UC—San Diego
UC—Santa Barbara
UC—Southern California
University of Colorado (UC)—
  Boulder
UC—Denver
University of Connecticut
University of Illinois (UI)—
  Bloomington
UI—Champaign
UI—Chicago
University of Iowa—Iowa City
University of Louisville
University of Maine
University of Massachusetts—
  Amherst
University of Michigan—Ann Arbor
University of Minnesota—
  Minneapolis
University of New Hampshire—Dur-
  ham
University of New Mexico
University of North Carolina
University of Pennsylvania
University of Puget Sound
University of Oregon—Eugene
University of Rhode Island
University of Rochester
University of Texas—Austin
University of Vermont
University of Wisconsin—Madison
Wayne State University
Western Maryland University
Wooster College
Yale University
  (Total: 75)

stration at his school, the CIA stopped coming back, at least openly, to recruit. According to Turner, the Agency decides that the potential recruits at a university are not worth all the bad publicity they may get from dissenting students and community members.

In any event, the CIA can be demonstrated against even though it may not appear openly at your school. Northwestern University students, for instance, after booting the CIA off campus for two quarters, organized a demonstration in the Agency's absence—to celebrate their success and demand a total restriction on CIA-university cooperation.

By actually keeping the CIA from recruiting, we sever a vital lifeline to the Agency. According to Agee, "the CIA depends on the colleges and universities for their inflow of personnel—to work on the staff at the CIA's headquarters in Virginia and for their assignments overseas...That is why it is so important to turn off this faucet of...recruits."[8]

Mansfield claims that demonstrations have had little effect on the Agency's recruiting effort. "If we move off campus, it's by our own choice." He holds that moves from Minneapolis and Boulder campuses were made "in the interest of the safety of the students who come to interview and the safety of our own personnel. We just prefer to do it off campus."[9]

However, one Minnesota journalist observes that "there are indications that public opposition slows recruiting down"[10] At the University of Oregon at Eugene, consecutive demonstrations in 1989 and 1990—at which recruiting was effectively halted by activists—caused local Agency recruiter Thomas Culhane to consider cancelling interviews there in the future. These second thoughts were reported in the school newspaper. "We've been giving them grief for three years," says activist Phil Nebergall, "he doesn't want to come back."[11]

According to University of California Berkeley Law School dean Jesse Choper—who participated in one of the Agency's "Dean Program" seminars in October of 1990, one Agency official explained during the seminar that some of the schools chosen to participate in the program were chosen because they were schools where the CIA was "having trouble recruiting due to student protests."[12] So the CIA does seem to care if and when protests occur. Mansfield does not deny that the CIA has been forced to recruit elsewhere ("by their own choice"), and protests may eventually force the CIA underground for good.

Certainly, public opposition causes the local community to take a look at what the CIA is doing. According to Lyon, "the average person doesn't really know anything about the CIA. The university is really the only place where anti-CIA activism is taking place and it must be maintained." By showing the CIA that it is not wanted, we de-legitimize the Agency; we prevent it from gaining the "respectable" ground it desires by pulling the welcome mat out from under its feet.

If you do succeed in ridding your campus of the Agency, publicize your success. "It's a great victory when any group on any campus can keep the CIA from recruiting. We should be quick to claim victory," Jill Zemke advises. "Say that the CIA is not coming back. Victories are very important to continue the struggle, to sustain the movement nationally. And once you get the CIA off, you can move on to the general issue of intervention."

U.S. Foreign Policy

Jennifer Leazer, another Minneapolis activist, claims that when the CIA finally stopped coming to the university, "one of the things that helped to carry us over was the educational process that linked the CIA to other issues: a racist foreign policy, and domestic racism. [It] linked us to Latino groups. The places where the movement is the strongest is where those [affected] people are part of the struggle. We're trying to build a movement based on all these issues."[13]

The CIA is essentially "part of the larger 'National Security State,' which envelops military-industrial firms, the universities and the Pentagon."[14] Questioning the CIA's presence on campus is really questioning the complicity of the university in U.S. militarism and foreign policy. As Noam Chomsky argues, addressing only single issues and events is "a poor substitute for a challenge to the deeper causes...A strong peace movement would be challenging military-based state capitalism and the world system it dominates."[15] The CIA issue is important because of the educational processes that activists and the community go through while working on it. Even if we don't get the CIA off our campuses immediately, the campaign against it and the issue's implications for radicalizing the population are worthwhile in themselves.

At Minneapolis, activists have gone on to target the ROTC program and the university's broader cooperation with government foreign policy. At Amherst, students are organizing against university support of what author Jonathan Feldman calls the U.S. "warfare state" in his book *Universities in the Business of Repression.*

Each university or college is a community in itself that can either contribute to the progress of society or aid in society's destruction. Opposing the CIA, ROTC or militarism in general is an attempt to redirect the university's contributions to society and the world from harmful and greed-based to beneficial and humanitarian. We must recognize both the problem of university militarism *and* the need for "economic conversion"—that is, the need for universities to move from their dependency on military-type grant research and funding to civilian-based programs such as mass transportation, housing, community medicine and disease research.

There is also a necessity for curriculum changes and curriculum accountability, which reinforce the principles of a morally grounded university. Professors who teach a narrow or inaccurate view of U.S. policy must be held accountable. Economic motivation and its devastating consequences should be essential to any political science or history course. A course on U.S. imperialism and domestic racism should be mandatory for incoming freshmen. African-American, multicultural and women's studies departments should be instituted and get the funding and staff they need.

Finally, students should be learning that democracy means full participation in the nation's government. And that means full knowledge of the government's activities, as well as knowledge about how to change those activities. Education should be understanding and empowerment—and should be available to all.

Obviously, a tall order—but these are some of the many kinds of change that students can bring to the university and the nation. "The transformation of university curriculum and research can make universities part of an overall process of converting our war economy and ideology to a peaceful alternative." Universities are "central actors" in the warfare state. By educating others, students and other members of the university community can transform the university into a "support for an anti-interventionary ideology," and by targeting the school's institutional structures that are in collaboration with the government, we begin "weakening [the warfare state's] supporting pillars."[16]

Economic Conversion

Suggestions for conversion projects that involve planning for the peace-related employment of university faculties and staff currently at work for the military industry should be an integral part of a comprehensive attack on university militarism. Feldman writes: "Strategies which simply call for cutting defense budgets and throwing the military off campus are not an adequate response to the realities confronting military-dependent communities." Instead, we must create scenarios which are too reasonable to resist. Feldman notes that models developed at the University of California at Berkeley and in Japan can provide us with the successful examples we need to support our vision. "Alternative use" committees can be formed to do studies on the needs and capacities of the university. What do we want to do with all the money we've been spending on defense? Invest in alternative energy sources? Cross-cultural curriculum programs? Research a cure for AIDS or technologies to clean up non-biodegradable environmental poisons? Then, which buildings could we use? Who would work on it?

Ultimately, drastic changes in the power structure must be made before massive conversion will be an attainable reality, and "there are no magic answers, no miraculous methods"[17] to radically alter the power structure of the United States. But it shouldn't be too hard to convince those in our communities that the economy needs conversion immediately. Even some Congressional members are beginning to see the need for it. Granted, the struggle before us will be a long one: "The groundwork for great social movements of the past was laid through many years of searching, intellectual interchange, social experimentation and collective action, organization and struggle. The same will be true of the coming stages of social change."[18] In the meantime, it is our responsibility to take as many steps as we can within the university community to transform our campuses into centers for social change and well-being. The odds confronting us are awesome and, as with the CIA issue, we may not achieve our immediate goals. But suggesting alternatives at this time is also an educational tactic, a part of a stage, that reveals both the corruption of the government and the servile complicity of the university.

Matt Nicodemus, peace activist and instructor at Stanford and Humboldt State University, has developed a list of goals "for action on issues of military-industrial-intelligence community involvement with universities" that includes some immediately attainable targets for student activists:

- inform students and others on campuses about choices that they're facing in regard to military involvement with their fields of interest.
- inform students about the activities of companies and institutions that recruit them for jobs.
- provide support for those on campus who question and break away from military ties.
- defend and strengthen academic departments and disciplines which suffer due to military-related budgeting.

- increase [universities'] role and stature as centers of learning and productive, humane innovation.[19]

Nicodemus also offers a graduation pledge for social responsibility that he co-authored for Humboldt as a model for other schools. It reads: "I pledge to thoroughly investigate and take into account the social and environmental consequences of any job opportunity I consider." In the past several years, this voluntary declaration has been adopted by students throughout the country.[20]

Although most college students today may *seem* unconcerned about their role in a militarized society, recent surveys of technical studies graduates reveal that "respondents mention increasingly frequently that they are unhappy with the job prospects outside the defense sector: a typical comment is 'The reason I have had such trouble finding a job is that I do not want to do defense related work.'"[21]

A survey of undergraduate physics majors at the University of California at Berkeley elicited "some fairly heartening results...60 percent of the respondents [who had worked in military related jobs] stated that they were either 'disturbed' (45 percent) or 'very disturbed' (15 percent) by the experience. Of those who had held only non-military jobs, 41 percent stated that they would never accept military-related work."[22]

When we look to the high school graduates coming in to our universities—many of whom have already participated in some form of activism—we can only be encouraged.

Perhaps our peers are less content than they appear to be with the status quo. Perhaps they also recognize a rapidly changing world situation in which U.S. militarism and imperialism cannot sustain us.

The potential for significant change exists in our colleges and universities. Let us dedicate ourselves to tapping that potential and creating a nation that uses its vast resources and creativity to protect the planet and provide a better life for all of its inhabitants.

Appendix A

Bibliography on the CIA and Covert Action

Introductory Readings on the CIA and U.S. Foreign Policy

Philip Agee, *Inside the Company: CIA Diary,* London: Penguin Books, 1975.

— and Louis Wolf, eds., *Dirty Work: The CIA in Western Europe,* Secaucus: Lyle Stuart, 1978.

William Blum, *The CIA: A Forgotten History,* London: Zed Press, 1986.

Central Intelligence Agency, *Freedom Fighters Manual,* New York: Grove Press, 1985.

Darrell Garwood, *Under Cover: Thirty-Five Years of CIA Deception,* New York: Grove Press, 1985.

John Prados, *Presidents' Secret Wars: CIA and Pentagon Covert Operations Since World War II,* New York: Morrow, 1986.

John Stockwell, *Praetorian Guard: The U.S. Role in the New World Order,* Boston: South End Press, 1991.

—"The Secret Wars of the CIA," transcript of a two-part radio broadcast available from Other Americas Radio.

Howard Zinn, *A People's History of the United States,* New York: Harper and Row, 1980.

Selected references for CIA activities

Guatemala

Americas Watch Annual Reports, available from Americas Watch, 36 W. 44th Street, New York, NY 10036, (212) 972-8400.

Amnesty International Annual Reports, available for $10 from Amnesty International, 322 8th Ave., New York, NY 10001, (212) 807-8400.

Richard Immerman, *The Foreign Policy of Intervention: The CIA in Guatemala,* Dallas: University of Texas Press, 1983.

Stephen Kinzer, *Bitter Fruit,* New York: Doubleday, 1982.

Jean-Marie Simon, *Guatemala: Eternal Spring, Eternal Tyranny,* New York: W.W. Norton, 1987.

Indonesia

Amnesty International Annual Reports, see address listed above.

Noam Chomsky and Edward S. Herman, *The Washington Connection and Third World Fascism,* Boston: South End Press, 1979.

Ralph McGehee, *Deadly Deceits: My 25 Years in the CIA,* New York: Sheridan Square Publications, 1983.

Vietnam and the Phoenix Program

Victor Marchetti and John D. Marks, *The CIA and the Cult of Intelligence,* New York: Knopf Books, 1974. (Updated paperback edition, Dell Publishing, 1989.)

Ralph McGehee, *Deadly Deceits: My 25 Years in the CIA,* New York: Sheridan Square Publications, 1983.

Chile and the Mapuche Indians

"The Case of the Mapuche in Chile," a pamphlet issued by the Letelier-Moffitt Memorial Fund for Human Rights at the Institute for Policy Studies, 1601 Connecticut Ave., N.W., Washington, D.C. 20009, (202) 234-9382.

Samuel Chavkin, *Storm Over Chile: The Junta Under Siege,* Chicago: Lawrence Hill Books, 1989.

"Covert Action in Chile: 1963-1973," *Staff Report of the Select Committee to Study Governmental Operations with Respect to Intelligence Activities,* United States Senate, Washington, D.C.: Government

Printing Office (GPO), 1975. Available from the Superintendent of Documents, Government Printing Office, Washington, D.C. 20402.

Saul Landau and John Dinges, *Assassination on Embassy Row,* New York: Pantheon Books, 1980.

Orlando Letelier, "Chile: Economic 'Freedom' and Political Repression," pamphlet issued by the Institute for Policy Studies, 1601 Connecticut Ave. NW, Washington, D.C. 20009, (202) 234-9382.

Robinson Rojas Sandford, *The Murder of Allende and the End of the Chilean Way to Socialism,* New York: Harper and Row, 1975.

Angola and Africa

Ellen Ray, William Schaap, Karl Van Meter and Louis Wolf, eds., *Dirty Work II: The CIA in Africa,* Secaucus: Lyle Stuart, 1980.

John Stockwell, *In Search of Enemies: A CIA Story,* New York: W.W. Norton, 1978.

East Timor

Amnesty International Annual Reports, see address listed above.

Noam Chomsky and Edward S. Herman, *The Washington Connection and Third World Fascism,* Boston: South End Press, 1979.

Nicaragua and the CIA-contra war

Americas Watch Annual Reports, see address listed above.

Amnesty International Annual Reports, see address listed above.

Edgar Chamorro, *Packaging the Contras: A Case of CIA Disinformation,* available for $5 from the Institute for Media Analysis, 145 West 4th Street, New York, NY 10012.

Noam Chomsky, *Turning the Tide: U.S. Intervention in Central America and the Struggle for Peace,* Boston: South End Press, 1985.

Leslie Cockburn, *Out of Control: The Story of the Reagan Administration's Secret War in Nicaragua, the Illegal Arms Pipeline, and the Contra Drug Connection,* New York: Atlantic Monthly Press, 1987.

Walter Lafeber, *Inevitable Revolutions,* New York: W.W. Norton, 1985.

Holly Sklar, *Washington's War on Nicaragua,* Boston: South End Press, 1988.

CIA torture training

A.J. Langguth, *Hidden Terrors,* New York: Pantheon, 1978.

CIA and FBI domestic surveillance

Ward Churchill and Jim Vander Wall, *Agents of Repression: The FBI's Secret Wars Against the Black Panther Party and the American Indian Movement,* Boston: South End Press, 1988.

—*The COINTELPRO Papers: Documents from the FBI's Secret Wars Against Dissent in the United States,* Boston: South End Press, 1990.

"CIA Domestic Spying More Extensive," report by the Center for National Security Studies, Washington, D.C., Sept. 10, 1979.

Richard Criley, *The FBI v. The First Amendment,* Los Angeles: The First Amendment Foundation, 1990. Copies available from The First Amendment Foundation, 1313 West 8th Street, Suite 313, Los Angeles, CA 90017, (213) 484-6661.

"Electronic Surveillance within the United States for Foreign Intelligence Purposes," *Senate Select Committee to Study Governmental Operations with Respect to Intelligence Activities,* Washington, D.C.: GPO, 1976.

Ross Gelbspan, *Break-ins, Death Threats and the FBI: The Covert War Against the Central America Movement,* Boston: South End Press, 1991.

Brian Glick, *War at Home: Covert Action Against U.S. Activists and What We Can Do About It,* Boston: South End Press, 1989.

Christy Macy and Susan Kaplan, *Documents,* New York: Penguin Books, 1980.

Ford Rowan, *Technospies,* New York: G.P. Putnam's Sons, 1978.

Drug experiments and MKULTRA

Martin Lee and Bruce Shlain, *Acid Dreams: The CIA, LSD and the Sixties Rebellion,* New York: Grove Press, 1985.

John D. Marks, *The Search for the Manchurian Candidate: The CIA and Mind Control,* New York: Times Books, 1979.

The CIA and drug running

Leslie Cockburn, *Out of Control: The Story of the Reagan Administration's Secret War in Nicaragua, the Illegal Arms Pipeline, and the Contra Drug Connection,* New York: Atlantic Monthly Press, 1987.

Henrik Kruger, *The Great Heroin Coup: Drugs, Intelligence and International Fascism,* Boston: South End Press, 1980.

Jonathan Kwitny, *The Crimes of Patriots: A True Tale of Dope, Dirty Money and the CIA,* New York: W.W. Norton, 1987.

Clarence Lusane, *Pipe Dream Blues: Racism and the War on Drugs,* Boston: South End Press, 1991.

Alfred McCoy and Leonard Adams, *The Politics of Heroin in Southeast Asia,* New York: Harper and Row, 1972.

Additional readings

Ben H. Bagdikian, *The Media Monopoly,* Boston: Beacon Press, 1987.

Francis Anthony Boyle, *Defending Civil Resistance Under International Law,* Dobbs Ferry, NY: Transnational Publishers, 1987. Special edition for *pro se* protesters available from the Center for Energy Research, 333 State Street, Salem, OR 97301, (503) 371-8002.

"Covert Operations and Covert War: Statement of the Church of the Brethren, 1988 Annual Conference," 12-page pamphlet, Elgin, IL: Brethren Press, 1988. See Appendix C for information on how to order.

Richard O. Curry, *Freedom At Risk,* Philadelphia: Temple University Press, 1988.

Jonathan Feldman, *Universities in the Business of Repression,* Boston: South End Press, 1989.

Edward S. Herman, *The Real Terror Network: Terrorism in Fact and Propaganda,* Boston: South End Press, 1982.

Loch K. Johnson, *America's Secret Power: The CIA in a Democratic Society,* New York: Oxford University Press, 1989.

Penny Lernoux, *Cry of the People,* New York: Penguin Books, 1980.

Prexy Nesbitt, *Apartheid in Our Living Room,* Cambridge: Political Research Associates, 1986.

Warner Poelchau, ed., *White Paper? White Wash!: Philip Agee on the CIA and El Salvador,* New York: Sheridan Square Publications, 1981.

Appendix B

Support Organizations and Resources

- The Africa Fund and
  The American Committee on Africa
  198 Broadway, Suite 402
  New York, NY 10038
  (212) 962-1210

- The American Friends Service Committee
  1501 Cherry Street
  Philadelphia, PA 19012
  (215) 241-7165

- Anti-Repression Resource Team
  P.O. Box 3568
  Jackson, MS 39207
  (601) 969-2269

- Association of National Security Alumni
  c/o Verne Lyon
  921 Pleasant Street
  Des Moines, IA 50309
  (515) 283-2115

- Association of National Security Alumni
  Washington Liaison Office
  c/o David MacMichael
  2001 S Street, N.W.
  Washington, D.C. 20009
  (202) 483-9325 or 483-9322

- The Campus Sanctuary Committee
  1110 Library South
  University of California
  Riverside, CA 92521
  (714) 787-3740

- The CIA Off Campus National Clearinghouse
  523 South Plymouth Court, Suite 800
  Chicago, IL 60605
  (312) 939-0675
  Twenty-four-hour hotline: (312) 427-4559

- The Committee in Solidarity with the People of El Salvador
  (CISPES)
  P.O. Box 12056
  Washington, D.C. 20005
  (202) 265-0890
- The Movement Support Network
  c/o Center for Constitutional Rights
  666 Broadway
  New York, NY 10012
  (212) 614-6464
- National Commission for Economic Conversion and
  Disarmament (ECD)
  1621 Connecticut Ave., N.W.
  Washington, D.C. 20009
  (202) 462-0091
- National Committee Against Repressive Legislation
  (NCARL), National Office
  1313 West 8th Street, Suite 313
  Los Angeles, CA 90017
  (213) 484-6661
- NCARL Washington, D.C. Office
  236 Massachusetts Ave., N.E., Suite 406
  Washington, D.C. 20002
  (202) 543-7659
- The Pledge of Resistance National Resource Center
  4228 Telegraph Ave.
  Oakland, CA 94609
  (415) 655-1181
  Twenty-four-hour hotline: (415) 655-1201
- Political Research Associates
  678 Massachusetts Ave., Suite 205
  Cambridge, MA 02139
  (617) 661-9313
- RESIST
  One Summer Street
  Somerville, MA 02143
  (617) 623-5110
- SANE/Freeze
  711 G Street, S.E.
  Washington, D.C. 20003
  (202) 544-3868

- U.S. Public Interest Research Group (PIRG)
  215 Pennsylvania Ave., S.E.
  Washington, D.C. 20003
  (202) 546-9707

Non-Violence Training

- Pledge of Resistance, see address above.
- War Resisters League
  339 Lafayette Street
  New York, NY 10012
  (212) 228-0450
  Write for their "Handbook on Non-Violent Action" and the "National Directory of Non-Violence Trainers," available for $3 each.

Legal Assistance

- American Civil Liberties Union
  132 West 43rd Street
  New York, NY 10036
  (212) 944-9800
- Center for Constitutional Rights
  666 Broadway
  New York, NY 10012
  (212) 614-6464
- Law Students in Action
  c/o The National Lawyers Guild
  55 Avenue of the Americas
  New York, NY 10013
  (212) 966-5000
- Meiklejohn Civil Liberties Institute
  P.O. Box 673
  Berkeley, CA 94701
  (415) 848-0599
  A series of legal defense packets including necessity and First Amendment defenses is available at duplication cost.
- The National Lawyers Guild
  55 Avenue of the Americas
  New York, NY 10013
  (212) 966-5000

- The People's Law Office
  1180 North Milwaukee Avenue
  Chicago, IL 60622
  (312) 235-0070

Information on How to File a Freedom of Information Act (FOIA) Request

- "A Citizen's Guide on Using the Freedom of Information Act and the Privacy Act of 1974 to Request Government Records," Committee on Government Operations, U.S. House of Representatives, 1987, available for $1.75 from the U.S. Government Printing Office, Washington, D.C.
- "Fill in the Blank" FBI and CIA FOIA forms, send self-addressed, stamped envelope to: The National Lawyers Guild Civil Liberties Committee, 14 Beacon Street, Suite 407, Boston, MA 02108.
- "Using the FOIA—A Step by Step Guide," available for $2 from the Center for National Security Studies, 122 Maryland Ave., N.E., Washington, D.C. 20002.

Student Networks

- Black Student Communication Organizing Network
  P.O. Box 3164
  Jamaica, NY 11431
  (718) 526-7056
- D.C. Student Coalition Against Apartheid and Racism
  (D.C.-SCAR)
  P.O. Box 18291
  Washington, D.C. 20036
  (202) 483-4593
- East Coast Asian Student Union
  27 Beach Street, Suite 3A
  Boston, MA 02111
  (617) 426-5313
- Ella Baker-Nelson Mandela Center for Anti-Racist Education
  200 West Engineering Building
  Ann Arbor, MI 48109
  (313) 936-1809

- General Union of Palestinian Students
  P.O. Box 22181
  Alexandria, VA 22304
- Graduation Pledge Alliance
  P.O. Box 4439
  Arcata, CA 95521
- Movimiento Estudiante Chicano de Aztlan (MECHA)
  c/o Chicano Studies
  18111 Nordhoff Street
  Northridge, CA 91330
  (818) 885-2734
- National Collegiate Black Caucus
  P.O. Box 5042
  Central City Station
  Atlanta, GA 30302
  (404) 577-0928
- National Gay and Lesbian Task Force Campus Project
  1517 U Street, N.W.
  Washington, D.C. 20009
  (202) 332-6483
- Northeast Student Action Network
  P.O. Box 1050
  Cambridge, MA 02142
- The Progressive Student Network (PSN)
  3411 West Diversey, Room 16
  Chicago, IL 60647
  (312) 227-4708
- The Student Action Union (SAU)
  P.O. Box 456
  New Brunswick, NJ 08903
  East: (201) 745-5885
  Central: (313) 483-6098
  West: (415) 841-3706
- The United States Student Association
  1012 14th Street, N.W., Suite 207
  Washington, D2WatchC 20005
  (202) 347-USSA

Appendix C

Educational Resources

Periodicals

- *Campus Watch*
  Subscriptions:
  Bill of Rights Foundation
  523 S. Plymouth Ct., Suite 800
  Chicago, IL 60605
  (312) 939-0675
  Other correspondence:
  P.O. Box 9623
  Warwick, RI 02889
  Published twice during the academic year. Individual subscriptions are $6; institutions $10.
- *CovertAction Information Bulletin*
  P.O. Box 34583
  Washington, D.C. 20043
  (202) 331-9763
  Published quarterly. Individual subscriptions are $17; institutions $22.
- *First Principles: National Security and Civil Liberties*
  Center for National Security Studies
  122 Maryland Avenue, N.E.
  Washington, D.C. 20002
  (202) 544-1681
  Published quarterly. One-year subscriptions are $15; students $10.
- *The Guardian*
  33 West 17th Street
  New York, NY 10011
  (212) 691-0404
  Published weekly. Annual subscriptions are $33.50; six-month student subscriptions are $12.50.
- *In These Times*
  Institute for Public Affairs
  2040 N. Milwaukee Avenue
  Chicago, IL 60647
  (312) 772-0100

Published weekly. Individual subscriptions are $34.95; institutions
are $59.

- *Lies of Our Times (LOOT)*
  Institute for Media Analysis
  145 West 4th Street
  New York, NY 10012
  (212) 254-1061
  Published eleven times a year. One-year subscriptions are $24.
- *Propaganda Review*
  Media Alliance
  Fort Mason Building D
  San Francisco, CA 94123
  Published quarterly. One-year subscriptions are $20.
- *Unclassified*
  Association of National Security Alumni
  921 Pleasant Street
  Des Moines, IA 50309
  (515) 283-2115
  Published bi-monthly. One-year subscriptions are $20.
- *Z Magazine*
  Institute for Social and Cultural Communications
  150 West Canton Street
  Boston, MA 02118
  (617) 236-5878
  Published eleven times a year. One-year subscriptions are $25.

Speakers

- Philip Agee
  Ex-CIA agent, author of *Inside the Company* and *On the Run.*
  c/o Speak Out!
  Jean Caiani
  2215-R Market Street
  San Francisco, CA 94114
  (415) 864-4561
  Speak Out! is a political speaker's bureau founded by South End
  Press and *Z Magazine.* Over 100 speakers are available, including
  author/linguist Noam Chomsky, Pentagon Papers leaker Daniel
  Ellsburg, author and lecturer Holly Sklar, feminist author and oral
  historian Margaret Randall, human rights lecturer and author Rita
  Maran, South African feminist poet and activist Rozena Maart,
  Dave Dellinger, Philip Agee, and Michael Parenti. Twenty percent

of all proceeds from Speak Out! engagements are used to help
fund progressive causes. Write or call for a free brochure.

- Chip Berlet
  Target of CIA surveillance and covert operation against anti-war activists. Available to debate CIA Off Campus issue.
  c/o Political Research Associates
  678 Massachusetts Avenue, Suite 205
  Cambridge, MA 02139
  (617) 661-9313

- Gordon Chapman
  Ex-CIA agent, lecturer on international affairs, civil liberties and
  movements for social change.
  710 Boundary Avenue
  Silver Spring, MD 20910
  (301) 587-6796

- Jonathan Feldman
  Author of *Universities in the Business of Repression* and former Program Director for the National Commission on Economic
  Conversion and Disarmament.
  1801 Clydesdale Place, N.W.
  Washington, D.C. 20009
  (202) 462-1261

- Mary Fleischer
  Ex-CIA employee and formerly married to a CIA operative; cur-
  rently a writer, lecturer and anti-nuclear activist.
  P.O. Box 1124
  Frazier Park, CA 93225
  (805) 245-1883

- Ken Lawrence
  Journalist and expert on CIA-campus issues.
  c/o The Anti-Repression Resource Team
  P.O. Box 3568
  Jackson, MS 39207
  (601) 969-2269

- Ralph McGehee
  Ex-agent and author of *Deadly Deceits: My 25 Years in the CIA.*
  c/o Lucretia Miller
  P.O. Box 1404
  Fond du Lac, WI 54936-1404
  (414) 923-5715

- Barry Romo
  Former First Lieutenant in the U.S. Army during the Vietnam War;
  member of the Vietnam Veterans Against the War for 20 years.
  P.O. Box 408594
  Chicago, IL 60640
  (312) 327-5756

- Jack Ryan
  FBI agent fired for refusing to spy on peace activists.
  c/o Catholic Worker House
  225 South Saratoga
  Peoria, IL 61605
  (309) 674-5455

- John Stockwell
  Ex-agent and author of *In Search of Enemies*.
  c/o K&S Speakers
  875 Main Street
  Cambridge, MA 02139
  (617) 876-8090

- Louis Wolf
  Co-founder and co-editor of the *CovertAction Information Bulletin*,
  co-editor of *Dirty Work: The CIA in Western Europe* and *Dirty Work
  II: The CIA in Africa.* Has lived in Laos and the Philippines.
  C.A.I.B.
  P.O. Box 34583
  Washington, D.C. 20043
  (202) 331-9753

- Howard Zinn
  Historian and author of *A People's History of the United States*.
  29 Fern Street
  Auburndale, MA 02166

Films, Audio and Video Tapes

- *CoverUp,* an in-depth video documentary about the Iran-contra
  scam, including contra-cocaine trafficking and a brief history of
  CIA covert operations. Available from:
  The Video Project
  5332 College Ave., Suite 101
  Oakland, CA 94618
  (415) 655-9050
  Other videos available from The Video Project: *The Secret World of*

the CIA, MacMichael on Nicaragua and videos on Latin America, the arms race, war and peace and the environment. Ask for a complete catalog.

- Bill Moyers' *The Secret Government: The Constitution in Crisis,* a thorough and well researched series on U.S. covert operations from the inception of the CIA. Available for $49.95 from:
Public Affairs Television
356 West 58th St.
New York, NY 10019

- *Salvador,* a film about U.S. involvement in El Salvador directed by Oliver Stone. Available from:
Cinecom Films
1205 Broadway
New York, NY 10001
(212) 239-8360
This film may also be available at video rental outlets.
Also available from Cinecom: *Romero* and *Latino.* Call or write for more information.

- *Missing,* a film about the 1973 coup in Chile.
Available from:
Swank Motion Pictures
910 Riverside Drive
Elmhurst, IL 60126
(800)-876-3330
This film may also be available at video rental outlets.

- *The Houses Are Full of Smoke,* a three-part series on the CIA in Central America. Available from:
Circle Films
2445 M Street, N.W., Suite 225
Washington, D.C. 20037
(202) 331-3838.

- For assistance in finding films and videos not listed here contact:
Kevin Duggan
The Media Network
121 Fulton St., Fifth Floor
New York, NY 10038
(212) 619-3455
Using a database, The Media Network can locate films, videos and works in other media on a wide range of social issues. Send for a series of evaluative media guides to issues including covert action, Central America, the environment, AIDS, peace and disarmament, reproductive health and rights and hundreds of other topics.

- Audio cassette tapes and transcripts of radio programs on Central and South America are available from:
Other Americas Radio
P.O. Box 85
Santa Barbara, CA 93102
(805) 569-5381
Ask for a free catalog.

Other Resources

- For CIA brochures and publications write:
Public Affairs
Central Intelligence Agency
Washington, D.C. 20505
- For a $49 intelligence database which cross-references intelligence-related names and countries for IBM PC compatibles contact:
NameBASE
Public Information Research
P.O. Box 5199
Arlington, VA 22205
(703) 241-5437
- For a $99 computer database on the CIA, write:
CIABASE
P.O. Box 5022
Herndon, VA 22070
- PeaceNet, an extensive national network receiving echoes from as far away as Managua and Santiago. For information on how to join, write or call
PeaceNet
3228 Sacramento Street
San Francisco, CA 94115
(415) 923-0900
- NoWar, Chicago-based with a focus on draft resistance and military issues, (312) 939-4411
- Beyond War, New York-based, focus on peace and nuclear disarmament, (718) 442-1056
- Amnet II, based in Cambridge, MA, focus on civil liberties and anti-covert-action issues, (617) 221-5815
- NYONLINE, New-York based, a clearinghouse for text files on peace issues, anti-war, anti-covert action, Central America, South Africa and others, (718) 852-2662

Pamphlets and Flyers

- "At War With Peace: U.S. Covert Operations," a 12-page pamphlet available for $2.50 from NCARL, 1313 West 8th Street, Suite 313, Los Angeles, CA 90017, (213) 484-6661.
- "Goals for Action on Issues of Military-Industrial-Intelligence Community Involvement with Universities," a flyer available from Matt Nicodemus, 619 G Street, Arcata, CA 95521, (707) 826-7033.
- "Organizing for Resistance: Historical and Theological Reflections on Organizing," a handbook by the Chicago Religious Task Force on Central America. Copies are available from the Task Force for $3 plus $1 postage and handling. Order from CRTFCA, 59 East Van Buren Street, Room 1400, Chicago, IL 60605, (312) 663-4398.
- "Covert Operations and Covert War: Statement of the Church of the Brethren, 1988 Annual Conference," a 12-page pamphlet available from the Church of the Brethren, Brethren Press, 1451 Dundee Ave., Elgin, IL 60120, (800) 323-8039.

Appendix D

Avoiding Police Violence

The following is an excerpt from the Chicago Religious Task Force's "Organizing for Resistance" manual:

We can do things to minimize the actions of the police and maximize the effectiveness of our actions:

- Stay calm. Shouting, running and angry words create tension. Panic increases the possibility of injury.
- Be determined. If it appears difficult to block the door chosen by the...group because the police are treating people very roughly, the group needs to have a quick consultation. Do we go to another door? Do we do what we planned even though some of us might get bruised? Do we try to divert their attention before blockading? The possibilities are infinite.
- Be prepared. Wear clothing that is appropriate for the situation (e.g., are you going to be sitting on the ground?). Don't wear clothing with hoods. The police can drag you by the hood and hurt your

neck. Jewelry is also a problem. Glasses might be broken. You might consider not wearing them.

- Be alert. If the police seem to be hurting someone, urge them to stop hurting them or to loosen the handcuffs, etc. It is important for all of us to be advocates for each other.

- People should be prepared for a variety of police responses at an action. These may be intended to intimidate, divide and immobilize demonstrators.

  (a.) Intimidate: Police may appear in large numbers, or on horseback, or dressed in full riot gear: helmets, clubs and guns. They may issue threatening commands beyond even their legal prerogatives.

  (b.) Divide: Police may try to befriend demonstrators and appeal to their "good sense" to be more obliging and thus sacrifice some objectives of the demonstration...Generally, individuals are assigned to communicate with the police and demonstrators should refer police to these contacts...Whatever is said to [the police] can be used against you or others later on...Be aware that sometimes cameras that are filming are really police, not press. When press people are asked to show their credentials they are supposed to do that.

  (c.) Immobilize: In addition to the usual police responses, eg. arrests, physical removal and dispersal, there are more drastic methods used at times. Remember, these are worst case scenarios, not what usually happens at nonviolent demonstrations...

- Police striking with clubs—The important thing to do in this case is to protect your head and vital organs. Clasp your hands over your head, elbows drawn in over your ears, drawing the knees up with legs tucked underneath. This forms a ball, face down, stomach, breasts and genitals covered. If you are sitting for a blockade and the police have clubs, protect your neck by putting your chin to your chest.

- Use of dogs—Dogs are trained to respond to fast motion and to individuals attempting to run away. Do not run, stay perfectly still until the dog is called off...

- Use of tear gas or mace—Their use affects everyone present (e.g. media, workers, passers-by) and is therefore not a very likely response at this time...[Author's note: tear gas and mace have been used on students demonstrating against the CIA within the last two years.] They cause intense tearing and irritation to the eyes, nose, mouth and lungs. If gas is used, cover your nose and mouth with a wet cloth and leave the immediate area to regroup else-

where. Do not pick up tear gas canisters unless hands are protected! If someone is gassed, remove them to clean air immediately, wash the face and eyes with plain water (mace should be
treated with a 5% Boric Acid solution, if possible.)

Notes

Chapter 1

1. From the introduction to "Alleged Assassination Plots: An Interim Report of the Senate Select Committee to Study Governmental Operations with Respect to Intelligence Activities," New York: W.W. Norton, 1975, p. XIX.

2. Technically, a CIA "agent" is not a full-time employee of the Agency, but a contracted individual who furnishes services (information, infiltration, etc.) to CIA operatives or officers. However, common jargon has relegated the word "agent" to designate both temporary and permanent employees of an intelligence-gathering organization. For brevity's sake, I use the popular definition.

3. There are more than enough well-researched works on U.S. "intelligence" and its impact abroad and at home. Please see the Bibliography for a partial list of works arranged by subject matter.

4. Francis Anthony Boyle, *Defending Civil Resistance Under International Law,* Dobbs Ferry, N.Y.: Transnational Publishers, 1987, p. 5.

5. For an in-depth legal analysis of the CIA's breaches of international law, especially in relation to civil disobedience, see "Defendants Trial Memorandum," in *Commonwealth v. Amy Carter, et. al.,* District Court for the Commonwealth of Massachusetts, April 5, 1987. See also Boyle.

6. William M. Leary, ed., *The Central Intelligence Agency: History and Documents,* Alabama: University of Alabama, 1984, p. 129. Restrictions on domestic activity are found in Section 102 (d), Paragraph (3) of the National Security Act of 1947, Public Law 253.

7. Ralph McGehee, *Deadly Deceits: My 25 Years in the CIA,* New York: Sheridan Square Publications, 1983, p. 62, and Ford Rowan, *Technospies,* New York: G.P. Putnam's Sons, 1978, p. 67.

8. Leary, p. 7.

9. "CIA Used Satellites for Spying on Anti-War Demonstrators," *New York Times,* July 17, 1979, p. A10.

10. "Rightwing Youth Group Reveals Dirty Tricks on College Campuses," *Our Right to Know,* a newsletter published by the Fund for Open Information and Accountability (FOIA), spring 1989, p. 19.

11. Howard Witt, "Canadians test CIA over brainwashing," *Chicago Tribune,* October 3, 1988, p. 3.

12. John Marks, *The Search for the Manchurian Candidate,* New York: Times Books, 1979, p. 57.

13. Ibid., p. 217.

14. Jacob V. Lamar, Jr., "The Misadventures of El Patron," *Time,* November 16, 1987, p. 31.

15. Ibid.

16. Brian Barger, "The Contras and Cocaine," *Penthouse,* December 1987, pp. 78-165.

17. Alfred W. McCoy, *The Politics of Heroin in Southeast Asia,* New York: Harper and Row, 1972, p. 14.

18. Ibid., p. 16.

19. Ibid., pp. 145 and 278.

20. Ibid., pp. 85, 135, 144 and 301.

21. Ibid., pp. 247-9 and 289.

22. Ibid., p. 126.

23. Ibid., p. 350.

24. Ibid., pp. 222 and 353.

25. Amos J. Peaslee, *International Government Organizations,* 2nd ed., Vol. 2, The Hague, Netherlands: Martinus Nijhoff, 1961, p. 1777.

26. McGehee, pp. 131-41.

27. Kim Willenson, *The Bad War: An Oral History of Vietnam,* New York: New American Library, 1987, p. 216.

28. Ibid., pp. 152-3.

29. Neil Sheehan, *Bright, Shining Lie: John Paul Vann and America in Vietnam,* New York: Random House, 1988, p. 18.

30. Victor Marchetti and John Marks, *The CIA and the Cult of Intelligence,* New York: Knopf Books, 1974, p. 245.

31. Sheehan, p. 18.

32. John Stockwell, *In Search of Enemies: A CIA Story,* New York: W.W. Norton & Company, 1978, pp. 115-16.

33. John Stockwell, "The Secret Wars of the CIA," transcript of a two-part radio broadcast, Santa Barbara: Other Americas Radio, p. 9.

34. Robin Knight, "Angola: Trapped in the cross fire," *U.S. News and World Report,* February 16, 1987, p. 30.

35. Stockwell, "Secret," p. 7.

36. Peaslee, p. 1646.

37. Ibid., p. 1647.

38. "Covert Action in Chile: 1963-1973," *Staff Report of the Select Committee to Study Governmental Operations with Respect to Intelligence Activities,* United States Senate, Washington, D.C.: GPO, 1975, pp. 6-39. Available from the Superintendent of Documents, GPO, Washington, D.C. 20402.

39. Robinson Rojas Sandford, *The Murder of Allende,* New York: Harper and Row, 1975, p. viii.

40. Ariel Dorfman, "Cultural Survival," *Case of the Mapuche in Chile,* Washington, D.C.: Institute for Policy Studies, 1980, p. 7.

41. Boyle, p. 170.

42. James LeMoyne, "Can the Contras Go On?" *New York Times Magazine,* October 4, 1987, p. 65.

43. "Defendants," p. 12.

44. LeMoyne, p. 65.

45. Michael Duffy, "Escalating the contra battle: Reagan wins a vote on military aid but loses in the World Court," *Time,* July 7, 1986, p. 26.

46. Noam Chomsky, *Turning the Tide: U.S. Invervention in Central America and the Struggle for Peace,* Boston: South End Press, 1985, pp. 10-13.

47. Boyle, p. 171.

48. *Amnesty International Report: 1985,* London: Amnesty International Publications, 1985, p. 175.

49. Boyle, pp. 188-9.

50. LeMoyne, p. 66.

51. Clyde H. Farnsworth, "Lenders Say Managua Has a Long Road Back," *New York Times,* February 28, 1990, p. A16.

52. Mark A. Uhlig, "Nicaraguan Opposition Routs Sandinistas," *New York Times,* February 27, 1990, p. A12, and LeMoyne, p. 65.

53. Alan J. Day, ed., *Treaties and Alliances of the World,* 4th ed., London: Longman Group, 1986, p. 18.

54. Ibid., p. 54.

55. Stockwell, "Secret," p. 28.

56. A.J. Langguth, *Hidden Terrors: The Truth About U.S. Police Operations in Latin America,* New York: Pantheon Books, 1978, p. 251, and Stockwell, "Secret," p. 29.

57. See human rights records in Amnesty International and Americas Watch reports for countries with CIA-trained police forces: Argentina, Brazil, The Congo, the Dominican Republic, etc.

58. LeMoyne, p. 34.

59. Langguth, p. 236.

60. Ibid., p. 265.

61. Ibid., p. 286.

62. Ibid., p. 139.

63. Ibid., pp. 125 and 138.

64. Ibid., p. 162.

65. Ibid., p. 216.

66. Ibid., p. 225.

67. Allen Nairn, "Behind the Death Squads," and "Confessions of a Death Squad Officer," *Progressive,* May 1984, pp. 27-8.

68. Stockwell, "Secret," p. 14.

69. Steven V. Roberts, "Reagan Signs Bill Ratifying U.N. Genocide Pact," *New York Times,* November 5, 1988, p. 28.

70. Day, p. 47.

71. Jean-Marie Simon, *Guatemala: Eternal Spring, Eternal Tyranny,* New York: W.W. Norton, 1987, p. 14.

72. Arturo Arias, "Culture, Genocide and Ethnocide in Guatemala," in *Guatemala: Tyranny on Trial,* Susanne Jonas, ed., San Francisco: Synthesis Publications, 1984, p. 108.

73. Ricardo Falla, "We Charge Genocide," in ibid., p. 114.

74. Simon, p. 15.

75. McGehee, p. 57, and Noam Chomsky and Edward S. Herman, *The Washington Connection and Third World Fascism,* Boston: South End Press, 1979, p. 208.

76. Kathy Kadane, "Ex-agents say CIA compiled death lists for Indonesians," *San Francisco Examiner,* May 20, 1990, p. A-1.

77. Ibid.

78. Ibid., p. A-22.

79. Chomsky and Herman, p. 208.

80. McGehee, p. 58.

81. *Official Records: Resolutions Adopted by the General Assembly, Part One, First Session, 10 January to 14 February, 1946,* London: Church House, 1946, p. 188.

82. Robert K. Woetzel, *The Nuremberg Trials in International Law,* New York: Frederick A. Praeger, Inc., 1960, p. 239.

83. *Charter of the International Tribunal,* August 8, 1945, October 6, 1945, 59 Stat. 1544 E.A.S. 472, "London Agreement." See the *Temple Law Quarterly,* January 1946, p. 163. Emphasis added.

84. Boyle, p. 237.

85. Woetzel, p. 238. Emphasis added.

86. "Defendants," p. 15.

87. Ibid., p. 16.

88. Johnny E. Killian, ed., *The Constitution of the United States: Analysis and Interpretation,* Washington, D.C.: GPO, 1987, p. 918.

89. Boyle, p. 32.

90. Killian, p. 919.

91. "Defendants," p. 1.

92. Jimmy Breslin, "A Son Follows Suit in the Matter of Oil," *New York Newsday,* September 9, 1990, p. 3.

93. Ibid.

94. Philip Agee, "The Gulf Crisis and the Cold War," a letter to the *Covert-Action Information Bulletin,* January 1991, p. 3, and Michael Emery, "How the U.S. Avoided Peace," *Village Voice,* March 5, 1991, p. 22.

95. Noam Chomsky, *Towards a New Cold War: Essays on the Current Crisis and How We Got There,* New York: Pantheon Books, 1982 p. 98.

96. Emery, p. 22.

97. Robert Hennelly, "Toxic Ambition: How the West Peddles Chemical Weapons," *Village Voice,* March 5, 1991, p. 28, and Jonathan Vankin, "The HP Connection," *Metro,* San Jose, CA, January 24, 1991, p. 15.

98. Emery, p. 22.

99. Letter to the Kuwaiti Minister of the Interior released to Reuters Press service by Iraq after the invasion of Kuwait, pp. 1-2.

100. Emery, p. 23.

101. Ibid., p. 22.

102. Ibid.

103. Murray Waas, "How America Lost Kuwait," *Metro,* San Jose, CA, January 24, 1991, p. 9, also under the title "Who Lost Kuwait?" in the *Village Voice,* January 22, 1991.

104. Ibid., p. 10.

105. Ibid., p. 11.

106. Agee, "Gulf," p. 4.

107. "Another Hussein: Hafez al-Assad," broadcast on *Sixty Minutes,* CBS, March 10, 1991.

Chapter 2

1. Boston: South End Press, 1989, p. 5.

2. Quoted in a *Campus Watch* interview, February 1989, p. 8.

3. Peter Cary, "Where Spies Really Matter," *U.S. News and World Report,* August 28, 1989, p. 24.

4. Steve Bennish and Frank Mullen, "007 Hitt Street," *Columbia Daily Tribune,* June 17, 1988, p. 39.

5. Loch Johnson, *America's Secret Power: The CIA in a Democratic Society,* New York: Oxford University Press, 1989, pp. 160-2.

6. David Wise, "Campus Recruiting and the C.I.A.," *New York Times Magazine,* June 8, 1986, p. 20.

7. John Quirk, *CIA Entrance Examination,* New York: ARCO, 1988, p. 39.

8. Robin Winks, *Cloak and Gown: Scholars in the Secret War, 1939-61,* New York: Morrow, 1987, p. 54.

9. Robert Witanek, "The CIA on Campus," *CovertAction Information Bulletin,* no. 31, winter, 1988, p. 27. Of course, it is very likely that if the CIA is keeping files on students that it is interested in hiring, it is also keeping files on students that it would like to get off its back. CIA surveillance of student dissenters is examined more fully in Chapter Six.

10. Charles Betz, "CIA recruiting continues though not as visibly," *Minnesota Daily,* January 20, 1989, p. 8.

11. Interview with the author, July 21, 1989.

12. Jeff McConnell, "East bloc's changes bring a CIA struggle," *Boston Globe,* November 15, 1990, p. 3.

13. William Corson, *The Armies of Ignorance,* New York: Dial Press, 1977, p. 310.

14. Ibid., p. 311.

15. Ken Lawrence, "Testimony to the University of Wisconsin at Madison Faculty Committee on CIA Campus Activity," September 9, 1985, p. 2.

16. *New Times,* January 23, 1976, pp. 37-39.

17. "How the CIA turns foreign students into traitors," by the editors, *Ramparts,* April 1967, p. 23.

18. Jeff McConnell, "Libyan Witch-Hunt: The War at Home," *Counterspy,* April 1982, p. 31.

19. McConnell, "East bloc's," p. 3.

20. Corson, p. 311.

21. Ibid., p. 313.

22. "How I got in and why I came out of the Cold," as told to the editors, *Ramparts,* April 1967, p. 17.

23. Quirk, p. 103. Original emphasis.

24. Interview with the author, November 12, 1989.

25. Wise, p. 30.

26. "How I got in," p. 20.

27. Quirk, p. 49-67.

28. McGehee, p. 7.

29. Quirk, pp. 69.

30. Timothy S. Robinson, "Academics Still Secretly Inform CIA," *Washington Post,* June 12, 1978, p. A21.

31. Vernon Elliott, "CIA Continues to Expand Officer-in-Residence Program," *Campus Watch,* February 1989, p. 1.

32. Vernon Elliott, "Inquiry Over CIA Officer-in-Residence Program at RIT Stirs Controversy," *Campus Watch,* spring, 1990, p. 3, and Elliott, "CIA Continues to Expand," p. 1. This list is incomplete. Some of these officers may have left their posts at the universities, given the temporary and controversial nature of the program.

33. Louis Wolf, "News Notes," *CovertAction Information Bulletin,* no. 30, summer, 1988, p. 68.

34. Ken Lawrence, "Academics: An Overview," in *Dirty Work II: The CIA in Africa,* Ellen Ray, et al., eds., Secaucus, NJ: Lyle Stuart, 1980, p. 80.

35. Witanek, p. 26.

36. John Trumpbour, "Harvard, the Cold War and the National Security State," in *How Harvard Rules: Reason in the Service of Empire,* John Trumpbour, ed., Boston: South End Press, 1989, p. 70.

37. Lawrence, "Academics," p. 81. See also John Marks, "The CIA at Home," in *Uncloaking the CIA,* Howard Frazier, ed., New York: The Free Press, 1978, p. 161.

38. Witanek, p. 25.

39. Jeff McConnell, "CIA's college program questioned," *Boston Globe,* December 17, 1987, p. A21.

40. Susan B. Glasser, "CIA Analyst to Interview Agency Officials," *Harvard Crimson,* February 24, 1988, p. 1.

41. Lawrence, "Academics," p. 80.

42. "African Studies in America—The Extended Family—A Tribal Analysis of U.S. Africanists: Who They Are; Why to Fight Them," New York: Africa Research Group, 1970, and other reports released by the Africa Research Group contain valuable information on the little-known workings of the CIA in a variety of areas. Copies are available from the Anti-Repression Resource Team. See Appendix B.

43. Interview with the author, November 12, 1989.

44. Witanek, p. 28.

45. Ibid.

46. John Trumpbour, "Living with the Bomb," in Trumpbour, p. 130.

47. Lawrence, "Academics," p. 80.

48. Christopher Simpson, *Blowback: America's Recruitment of Nazis and Its Effects on the Cold War,* New York: Weidenfeld and Nicolson, 1988, p. 117.

49. Lawrence, "Academics," pp. 83-4.

50. Witanek, p. 26.

51. Lawrence, "Academics," p. 83.

52. Ibid., p. 87.

53. Ibid., p. 90.

54. Ibid., p. 92.

55. Marks, *Search,* p. 157.

56. Phil Agee, Jr., and Vernon Elliott, "Professor Recalls CIA Opening Mail," *Campus Watch,* Spring 1990, p. 1.

57. Bill Schapp, "Deceit and Secrecy: Cornerstones of U.S. Policy," *Covert-Action Information Bulletin,* no. 16, March, 1982, p. 31.

58. Eugene Walsh, "The CIA at Georgetown: A Secret Tradition," *The Georgetown Voice,* April 20, 1989, p. 6.

59. Jerrold L. Walden, "Proselytes for Espionage: The CIA and Domestic Fronts," *Journal of Public Law,* v. 19, no. 2, 1970, p. 193.

60. Ibid., p. 184.

61. Jon Wiener, "School for Spooks," *The Nation,* September 5, 1987, pp. 204-6.

62. Amit Joshi, "Coalition protesting CIA funded research," *Daily Illini,* March 14, 1990, p. 1.

63. Steven Thomas Seitz, "Hypocrites, McCarthyites, Left-Wing Radicals and the CIA," an open letter to the University of Illinois, Urbana-Champaign [n.d.], and "Leftist protest of CIA funding manipulative, misguided," *Daily Illini,* April 12, 1990, p. 10.

64. Corson, p. 312.

65. Representative Louis Stokes, *Congressional Record—House,* October 12, 1989, H7010, 1420.

66. Lawrence, "Academics," p. 93.

67. Bennish and Mullen, p. 39.

68. Louis Wolf, letter to the author, October 24, 1989. Original emphasis.

69. Bennish and Mullen, p. 39.

70. Witanek, p. 25, and Warren Hinckle, "The University on the Make," *Ramparts,* April 1966, pp. 11-22.

71. Witanek, p. 26.

72. John Kelly, "The CIA in America," *Counterspy,* spring, 1980, pp. 44-5.

73. Marks, *Search,* p. 217.

74. Ibid., pp. 60 and 118.

75. Lawrence, "Testimony," p. 3.

76. "NU drops controversial anti-terrorism program," *Daily Northwestern,* September 19, 1986, p. 3.

77. Jonathan Feldman, *Universities in the BUsiness of Represssion,* Boston: South End Press, 1989, p. 23.

78. Allen Nairn, "Behind the Death Squads," and "Confessions of a Death Squad Officer," *Progressive,* May 1984, pp. 27-8.

79. Stansfield Turner, *Secrecy and Democracy,* Boston: Houghton MIfflin Co., 1985, p. 106.

80. Ibid., p. 107.

81. Ibid., p. 109.

82. Corson, p. 312.

83. Philip Agee, "Commentary," *Campus Watch,* February 1988, p. 9.

84. Feldman, pp. 216-8.

85. Earl Bolton, "Agency-Academic Relations," in *Documents,* Christy Macy and Susan Kaplan, eds., New York: Penguin Books, 1980, pp. 69-70.

86. Witanek, p. 25.

87. Evan Hendricks, *Former Secrets,* Washington, D.C.: Campaign for Political Rights, 1982, p. 179.

Chapter 3

1. Quoted in "Abbie Hoffman: An American Dissident," *Business Today,* Fall 1988, p. 35.

2. Interview with the author, December 17, 1990.

3. Tony Vellela, *New Voices: Student Political Activism in the '80s and '90s,* Boston: South End Press, 1988, p. 5.

4. "Abbie Hoffman," p. 35.

5. The Africa Fund, "Annual Report, 1988," New York: The Africa Fund, 1988. See Appendix B for address.

6. Vellela, p. 22.

7. Ibid., p. 21.

8. Interview with the author, July 17, 1989.

9. Vellela, pp. 42-3.

10. Ibid., p. 149.

11. Ibid.

12. Ibid., p. 7.

13. Ibid., p. 168.

14. Mark Gevisser, "Lesbian and Gay Students Choose," *The Nation,* March 26, 1988, p. 413.

15. Vellela, p. 166.

16. John Zeh, "MIT provost raps ROTC for ousting gays," *Guardian,* May 10, 1990, p. 7.

17. Vellela, pp. 167-8.

18. Christopher Johnson, "Demo Models," *The Nation,* June 11, 1990, p. 809.

19. Premilla Nadasen, "Fighting Institutional Racism at the Institute," *Resist,* October 1990, p. 1.

20. Vellela, p. 88.

21. "Coalition of Student Groups Called a Two-Day Strike for Diversity," *Guardian,* May 2, 1990, p. 7.

22. Ellen Morris, "Outfront," *Mother Jones,* September 1989, p. 11.

23. Barbara Ransby, "Black Students Fight Back," *The Nation,* March 26, 1988, p. 412.

24. Nadasen, p. 1.

25. Ibid., p. 7.

26. Vellela, p. 89.

27. Ibid.

28. Rabab Hadi, "N.Y. school adopts West Bank university," *Guardian,* May 9, 1990, p. 7.

29. Nora Cody, "Student strike shuts down CUNY," *Unity,* April 30, 1989, p. 5.

30. Glen Bessemer, "Rutgers students seize administration building," *Guardian,* May 9, 1990, p. 6, and Johnson, p. 808.

31. Vellela, p. 202.

32. Chomsky, *Turning,* pp. 250-1.

33. Though the subtitles in this book distinguish education from organization and organization from action, all forms of struggle bleed into each other. Organization is built on both education and action. Action is itself educational. Keep in mind that everything you choose to do will encompass all three elements.

34. "Organizing for Resistance," a handbook by the Chicago Religious Task Force on Central America, p. 1.

35. Eric Joselyn, "Closing the Company Store," *The Nation,* March 26, 1988, p. 418.

36. Interview with the author, August 7, 1989.

37. Vellela, p. 86.

38. Interview with the author, January 9, 1991.

39. Matthew Countryman, "Lessons of the Divestment Drive," *The Nation,* March 26, 1988, pp. 408-9.

40. Vellela, p. 86.

41. Ibid.

42. Ibid.

43. Nadasen, p. 1.

44. Ibid., p. 6.

45. See Appendix B for a list of sympathetic national organizations.

46. Charley MacMartin, "Black woman leads coalition to U. Texas win," *Guardian,* May 2, 1990, p. 7.

47. Interview with the author, August 7, 1989.

48. Speech at a Chicago Committee to Defend the Bill of Rights meeting, Winnetka, IL, August 13, 1989.

49. Interview with the author, July 21, 1989.

50. Ibid., August 10, 1989.

51. Vernon Elliott, letter to the author, October 23, 1989.

52. Elizabeth Greene, "Buoyed by Divestment Victories, Activists Protest CIA Recruiting," *Chronicle of Higher Education,* April 15, 1987, p. 38.

53. Interview with the author, September 23, 1989.

54. Interview with the author, November 13, 1989.

55. Vladimir Escalante, "A History of University Labor Struggles," in Trumpbour, p. 215.

56. "Coalition," p. 7.

57. Bessemer, p. 6.

58. Escalante, pp. 204-5.

59. John Trumpbour, "Introducing Harvard: A Social, Philosophical, and Political Profile," in Trumpbour, p. 24.

60. Erica Lepp and Joseph Hart, "Progressive Student Organization Work Report," University of Wisconsin, Madison 1986-87 school year, p. 1.

61. Melita Marie Garza, "After long years of calm, student protests are back," *Chicago Tribune,* May 6, 1990, p. 6. Emphasis added.

62. Ibid., p. 1.

63. See Appendix C, "Other Resources," for the CIA's address.

64. Trumpbour, "Introducing," p. 25.

65. Lepp, p. 1.

66. Appendix A includes a bibliography on covert action and the CIA. Appendix C lists films, videotapes and speakers available to activists for their own and for the general population's education.

67. Agee, "Commentary," p. 7.

68. Max Harvey, "CIA Off Campus," *Forward Motion,* December 1986, p. 39.

69. Ibid.

Chapter 4

1. As quoted in Chomsky, *Turning,* p. 48.

2. George Lardner, Jr., "CIA Struggles to Define Its Post-Cold War Role," *Washington Post,* November 13, 1990, p. A1.

3. "Covert Action in Chile: 1963-1973," *Staff Report of the Select Committee to Study Governmental Operations with Respect to Intelligence Activities,* United States Senate, Washington, D.C.: GPO, 1975, p. 48. Available from the Superintendent of Documents, GPO, Washington, D.C. 20402. Emphasis added.

4. Ibid., p. 27.

5. Penny Lernoux, *Cry of the People,* New York: Penguin Books, 1980, pp. 204-5.

6. "William Webster and the Cold Peace," *Unclassified: Newsletter of the Association of National Security Alumni,* February 1990, p. 1.

7. Paul Lewis, "Contras Said to Sell Arms to Salvador Rebels," *New York Times,* October 15, 1988, p. 22.

8. Chomsky, *Towards a New Cold War,* p. 98.

9. Stockwell, "Secret," p. 28.

10. Ibid., p. 16.

11. Interview with the author, November 12, 1989.

12. Alan Riding, "Latins Want Bush to Help on Debts," *New York Times,* November 29, 1988, p. 8.

13. "Notes and Comments," *The New Yorker,* December 4, 1989, p. 41.

14. Michael Massing, "Haiti: The New Violence," *New York Review of Books,* December 3, 1987, p. 49.

15. Ibid., p. 47.

16. Jeanne Woods, "Panel Discussion on Covert Action Legislation," NCARL annual meeting, Washington, D.C., October 21, 1989.

17. Chomsky, *Turning,* p. 48.

18. Interview with the author, November 12, 1989.

19. David Barsamian, "Interviewing John Stockwell," *Zeta Magazine,* September 1989, p. 57.

20. Stockwell, "Secret," p. 12.

21. "Organizing for Resistance: Historical and Theological Reflections on Organizing," a handbook by the Chicago Religious Task Force on Central America, 1987, p. 4.

22. Hortensia Bussa De Allende, "Chile: Made in U.S.A.," speech at "The CIA and World Peace" conference, Yale University, April 5, 1975.

23. Interview, with the author, November 12, 1989.

24. Marchetti and Marks, p. 68.

25. John Prados, *Presidents' Secret Wars: CIA and Pentagon Covert Operations Since World War II,* New York: Morrow, 1986, p. 81.

26. Ralph McGehee, testimony in *The People of the State of Illinois v. Ann Jarka, et al.,* Circuit Court of the 19th Judiciary Circuit, Lake County, Il., April 15, 1985, p. 9.

27. McGehee, *Deceits,* p. 140.

28. Stockwell, "Secret," p. 8.

29. Quirk, p. 111.

30. Ibid., p. 24.

31. Ibid.

32. Simon, p. 14.

33. Stephen Kinzer and Stephen Schlesinger, Bitter Fruit, New York: Double-day, 1982, p. 30.

34. Interview with the author, September 17, 1989.

35. Stockwell, "Secret," p. 23.

36. Sandford, p. viii. Sources vary on Chilean death tolls. See also Samuel Chavkin, *Storm Over Chile: The Junta Under Siege,* Boston: Lawrence Hill, 1989.

Chapter 5

1. Vellela, p. 205.

2. Boyle, p. 6.

3. Vellela, p. 207.

4. For more on media organizing strategies see Charlotte Ryan's *Prime Time Activism: Media Strategies for Organizing,* Boston: South End Press, July 1991.

5. Interview with the author, August 30, 1989.

6. Interview with the author, August 7, 1989.

7. Vernon Elliott, letter to the author, October 23, 1989.

8. For a list of college intelligence-related courses see the National Intelligence Study Center's (NISC) handbook, "Teaching Intelligence in the Mid-1980s," soon to be updated for the 1990s. Send orders to NISC, Suite 1102, 1800 K Street, N.W., Washington, D.C. 20006.

9. Elliott, "Inquiry," p. 4.

10. Interview with the author, November 13, 1989.

11. Konrad Ege, "Rutgers University Goes to College," *CounterSpy,* June-August 1984, p. 43.

12. Ibid.

13. Ibid., p. 44.

14. John Roosa, "Tufts University: Students Counter Spies," *National Reporter,* Winter 1985, p. 34.

15. Ibid., pp. 31-35.

16. "Panel Discussion of CIA Off Campus Activities," transcript from the Socialist Scholars Conference, New York, March 2, 1989, p. 4.

17. Roosa, p. 32.

18. Ibid., p. 34.

19. Anonymous source.

20. Chomsky, *Turning* , p. 251.

21. Trumpbour, "Introducing," p. 25.

22. Chomsky, *Turning,* p. 252.

23. Interview with the author, October 10, 1990.

24. Letter to the author, October 23, 1989.

25. "Panel," p. 12.

26. Ibid., p. 15.

27. Ibid., p. 12.

28. Ibid.

29. "Inquiry into the Elimination of Recruitment by the Central Intelligence Agency at the University of Wisconsin," presented to the executive committee of the Faculty Senate by the Madison Citizens Coalition Against the CIA, April 17, 1985, p. 2.

30. Ibid., p. 1.

31. Ibid., p. 2.

32. "Panel," p. 6.

33. Ibid., p. 5.

34. Mark Heimbach, "Military Funding Threatens UW Neutrality," in *Teaching Assistant Association Newsletter,* University of Wisconsin, Madison, November 18, 1987, p. 1.

35. Interview with the author, July 21, 1989.

36. Ege, p. 44.

37. Elliott, "CIA Continues," p. 1.

38. Interview with the author, November 15, 1989.

39. Interview with the author, November 16, 1989.

40. Greg Miller, "Students Prepare for CIA Recruiters," *Orion,* California State University, Chico, November 15, 1989, p. 1.

41. Erica Lepp and Joseph Hart, "Progressive Student Organization Work Report," Univ. of Wisconsin, Madison 1986-87 school year, p. 2.

42. Jerry Sena, "CIA Recruiters Told to Go Home," *Lumberjack,* Humboldt State University, April 25, 1990, p. 1.

43. "Report of the Ad Hoc Committee on the CIA and University Recruiting Policy," University of Maine Faculty Senate, February 28, 1990, p. 3.

44. Ibid., p. 1.

45. "Unanimous Resolution of the Colby Trustees," Colby College, April 9, 1988, p. 1.

46. Phil Handler, "Group protests CIA recruiting," *Daily Illini,* April 12, 1990, p. 1.

47. Kathleen Casey, "Nine arrested following anti-CIA rally at Rutgers," *The Star-Ledger,* Newark, April 6, 1988, p. 9.

48. Interview with the author, August 10, 1989.

49. Roosa, p. 35.

50. Miller, p. 6.

51. "The Straight Shit on NU's Board of Trustees," a report by the Anti-Apartheid Alliance at Northwestern University, 1984.

52. Feldman, p. 177.

53. *Oxford American Dictionary.*

54. Interview with the author, October 15, 1989.

55. Interview with the author, November 14, 1989.

56. Interview with the author, September 9, 1989.

Chapter 6

1. George Hackett, "The Amy and Abbie Brigade," *Newsweek,* December 8, 1986, p. 55.

2. Max Harvey, "CIA Off Campus," *Forward Motion,* December 1986, p. 38.

3. Eric Joselyn, "Closing the Company Store," *The Nation,* March 26, 1988, p. 17.

4. Ibid.

5. Rich Richardson, "Opinion and Analysis," *Guardian,* February 15, 1989, p. 19.

6. T.S. [no name], "Letters," *Guardian,* November 23, 1989, p. 2.

7. Interview with the author, November 7, 1989.

8. "Panel," p. 6.

9. Interview with the author, September 9, 1989.

10. "Panel," p. 6.

11. Interview with the author, August 7, 1989.

12. "Panel," p. 16.

13. Colin Barr, "PSU Disciplinary System Mirrors Others," *Collegian,* February 16, 1989, p. 1.

14. Ibid.

15. Jennifer Leazer, "Administration Attacks Minnesota PSN," *Progressive Student News,* January- February 1988, p. 3.

16. Ibid.

17. Interview with the author, November 15, 1989.

18. Boyle, p. 9.

19. Boyle, p. 11.

20. Chandler Rosenberger, "The Case Against the CIA," *Boston Phoenix,* April 24, 1987, pp. 8-18.

21. Boyle, p. 7.

22. There may be people in jail as a result of recent anti-CIA demonstrations, but not to my knowledge.

23. Brian Glick, *War at Home: Covert Action Against U.S. Activists and What We Can Do About It,* Boston: South End Press, 1989, p. 7.

24. Ibid., p. 33.

25. Ibid., p. 9.

26. Ibid., p. 12.

27. Christy Macy and Susan Kaplan, eds., *Documents,* New York: Penguin Books, 1980, p. 179.

28. Glick, p. 22.

29. Ward Churchill and Jim Vander Wall, *Agents of Repression: The FBI's Secret War Against the Black Panther Party and the American Indian Movement,* Boston: South End Press, 1988, pp. 63-73.

30. Ford Rowan, *Technospies,* New York: G.P. Putnam's Sons, 1978, p. 67.

31. Ibid., p. 66.

32. "CIA Domestic Spying More Extensive," report by the Center for National Security Studies, Washington, D.C., September 10, 1979.

33. McGehee, p. 63.

34. Rowan, p. 140.

35. Ibid., p. 19.

36. Holly Sklar, *Washington's War on Nicaragua,* Boston: South End Press, 1988, p. 358.

37. Sol Stern, "NSA-CIA: A Short Account of International Student Politics and the Cold War," *Ramparts,* March 1967, p. 30.

38. Ibid., p. 35.

39. Ibid., p. 38.

40. Glick, p. 1.

41. Diana Gordon, "Can Sessions Tame the Bureau?" *The Nation,* October 30, 1989, p. 489.

42. Ibid., p. 488.

43. Glick, p. 5.

44. Ibid., p. 38.

45. Ibid., p. 30.

46. Ibid., p. 31.

47. E.O. 12333, 2.9.

48. Ibid., 2.4, 2.5.

49. Glick, p. 31.

50. "Rightwing Youth Group Reveals Dirty Tricks on College Campuses," *Our Right to Know,* a newsletter published by the Fund for Open Information and Accountability (FOIA), spring 1989, p. 19.

51. Glick, p. 39.

Chapter 7

1. Interview with the author, November 12, 1989.

2. Agee, "Commentary," p. 7.

3. Matthew Rothschild, "Central Employment Agency: Students Respond to the CIA Rush," *The Progressive,* February 1984, pp. 18-21.

4. Feldman, p. 223.

5. McConnell, "East bloc's changes," p. 3.

6. "Panel," p. 11.

7. Compiled from *The Nation,* March 29, 1988, pp. 416-19; *Progressive Student News,* October-December 1987, pp. 1-2; *Campus Watch,* February 1989 and Fall, 1990 (various pages); "Panel;" and the CIA Off Campus National Clearinghouse, Chicago.

8. Agee, "Commentary," p. 6.

9. Interview with the author, November 16, 1989.

10. Betz, p. 1.

11. Interview with the author, January 3, 1991.

12. Linda Tadic, "Choper, Boalt, and the CIA," *The Boalt Hall Cross Examiner,* December 1990, p. 1

13. Interview with the author, September 1989.

14. Feldman, p. 164.

15. Chomsky, *Turning,* p. 250.

16. Feldman, p. 147.

17. Chomsky, *Turning,* p. 253.

18. Ibid.

19. Matt Nicodemus, "Goals for Action on Issues of Military-Industrial-Intelligence Community Involvement with Universities" [undated flyer]. See Appendix C for information on how to order.

20. For an organizing packet on how to incorporate the pledge in commencement ceremonies, see Graduation Pledge Alliance under "Student Networks" in Appendix B. To obtain a complete list of action goals, see "Pamphlets and Flyers" in Appendix C.

21. Charles Schwartz, "The Challenge to Campus Activists," *United Campuses to Prevent Nuclear War Newsletter,* September 1987, p. 4.

22. "Newsnotes," *United Campuses,* p. 6.

Index

1984, 66

Afghanistan, 75
Africa, 32-33
Africa Research Group, 30-31
African National Congress
    (ANC), 98, 132
African Studies Association, 37
African-Americans, 84
African-American Institute, 30
African-American students and
    students of color, 48-49,
    54-56, 58
Agee, Philip, 16, 19, 21, 40, 57, 66,
    71, 98, 137-138, 140
AIDS, 35, 143
Air America, 4
al-Assad, Hafez, 17
al-Fahd, Fahd Ahmad, 15-16
Allegheny Foundation, 91
Allende, Hortensia Bussi De, 78
Allende, Salvador, 6, 74, 78, 102
American Civil Liberties Union
    (ACLU), 57
American Council of Education,
    63
American Indian Movement
    (AIM), 131
American Metal Climax
    Corporation, 30
Americas Watch, 7

Amherst, 61, 114, 118, 141
Amnesty International, 7
An-Najah University, 50
Anaconda corporation, 102
anarchists, 106, 131
Angola, 5-6, 25, 32, 80
    -FNLA, 5, 32
    -liberation movement, 5
    -MPLA, 5
    -UNITA, 5, 32
anti-war movement, 1960s, 3, 44,
    137
Arab students, 48-49
Arabs, 49-50
Arbenz, Jacobo, 80
Argentina, 9
Armas, Castillo, 10, 80
Armies of Ignorance, 24
Arthur Anderson and Company,
    102
Association of Arab-American
    University Graduates
    (AAUG), 49
Association of Asian Studies, 37
Atlanta Student Coalition Against
    Apartheid and Racism
    (A-SCAR), 51
Atwater, Lee, 49
Australian journalists, 11

Baltimore, 45

Baraka, Amiri, 50
Barricada, 108
Bates College, 139
Bay of Pigs, 80
Bean, Harold, 30
Bedlington, Stanley S., 30
Berkeley Mafia, 37
Berlet, Chip, 128-129
Bethlehem University, 50
Bir Zeit University, 50
Black activists, 54-56, 58, 134
Black Panther Party (BPP), 107,
    130-132
Black student unions, 131
Bloustein, Edward, 101-102
Bok, Derek, 39
Boland Amendment, 27
Bolivia, 8, 37, 74
Bolton, Earl, 41
Boston Psychopathic Hospital, 38
Boston University, 30, 97
Boston University, African
    Studies, 31
Boulder, 85, 92, 99, 104-106,
    108-109, 118, 129, 140
Bowling Green State University,
    139
Boyle, Francis Anthony, 2, 7, 127
Brandeis University, 139
Brazil, 8-9, 74
Britain, 12
Brown University, 57, 60, 138-139
Brown, William O., 31
Buddhists, 78
Burma, 4
Burundi, 33
Bush, George, 3, 16, 20, 70, 74,
    89, 112, 132

Caldiera, Mark, 95, 118

California State Polytechnical
    University, 139
California State University,
    Chico, 139
Calvin, Doug, 46
Cambodia, 62
Campus Sanctuary Network, 46
Campus Watch, 21, 30, 60, 88-89,
    97
Capen, Steve, 71
Carter administration, 29
Carter, Amy, 13, 126
Carter, Jimmy, 102
Casey, William, 8, 20, 79
Catholics, 78
"Censored History of Relations
    Between the University of
    California and the Central
    Intelligence Agency," 96
Center for Constitutional Rights
    (CCR), 58-59
Center for International Studies
    (CENIS), 31, 37
Central America, 68, 80, 137
Central Intelligence Agency (CIA)
    -and freedom of speech, 81-82,
        100, 105, 112-113
    -and homosexuality, 27, 29, 94
    -assassination lists, 11
    -assassination manual, 7
    -budget, 20, 79
    -Charter, 17
    -Clandestine Services, 28
    -cooperation with local police,
        123, 130, 132
    -Coordinator for Academic Af-
        fairs, 30, 64, 97, 138
    -covert operations, 75, 77, 79, 98,
        102, 130, 134-135
    -Deans Program/Seminar, 23,
        140
    -economic pressure, 6

-Entrance Examination Booklet, 21, 26
-European Non-State Actors Project, 33
-Graduate Studies Program, 22-23
-military coups, 6, 14, 74, 80
-Minority Undergraduate Studies Program, 22
-MKULTRA program, 3, 38
-Office of Equal Opportunity Employment, 36
-Office of National Estimates, 31
-Officer in Residence Program, 30, 61, 69, 89, 96-99, 138
-"old boy" network, 19, 29
-Operation CHAOS, 132
-Operation Phoenix, 5, 11
-operations in Angola, 79
-operations in Europe, 4
-operations in Vietnam, 4
-police training, 9-10, 15, 132
-police training camps, 9
-"Policy on Certain Sexual Conduct," 94
-Project MERRIMAC, 123
-Project RESISTANCE, 123
-propaganda, 5, 6, 79
-recruiting centers, 21
-recruitment sites, 138
-report on Indonesian operation, 11
-spotters, 21, 24
-Student Scholars, 22
-Student Trainee Program, 22-23
-Summer Fellowship Program, 36
-trained police forces, 9, 15
-Undergraduate Scholar Program, 22
-use of mercenaries, 7
-White Paper on Vietnam, 79
Cessna Aircraft company, 102
Chamorro, Edgar, 126
Chapel Hill, 138

Chardy, Alfonso, 132
Cheney, Richard, 47
Chicago, 58, 69, 123, 131
Chicago Committee to Defend the Bill of Rights (CCDBR), 59, 64
Chicago police, 131
Chicago Religious Task Force on Central America (CRTFCA), 78, 115
Chicago Seven, 126
Chicano groups, 131
Chico State University, 98
Chile, 6, 65, 74, 83, 102, 114
China, 4-5
Chinese, 11, 37
Chomsky, Noam, 68, 141
Choper, Jesse, 140
Christiansen, Greg, 94
Chritton, George, 61-62, 89-90, 97-99
Chronicle of Higher Education, 61
Church, Senator Frank, 1, 74
Church Committee, 39
Church Committee Report, 40, 74
City University of New York (CUNY), 50
civil disobedience, 84, 104-106, 108-109
civil libertarians, 112
civil resistance, 2, 127
Clark, Ramsey, 61, 126
Cline, William, 31
cocaine, 3
"Code of Offenses Against the Peace and Security of Mankind," 13
COINTELPRO (Counter-intelligence program), 130-131, 134
Cointreau, 38
Colby College, 60, 100-101, 139

Colby, William, 5-6, 11, 21
Cold War, 4, 74, 133
College Republicans, 112
Collegian, 118
Colombia, 3
Colorado, 105
Colorado State University, Fort
    Collins, 139
Columbia College, 50
Columbia University, 35, 49, 94,
    138-139
Committee in Solidarity with the
    People of El Salvador
    (CISPES), 45-46, 57,
    104-105, 134-135
*Commonwealth v. Amy Carter, et
    al.,* 13, 127
communism, 4, 27-29, 73
Communist Party, Indonesian, 11
Communist Party, U.S.A., 131
communists, 11, 33, 70, 76, 78
Congo, 8, 78
Congress of Racial Equality, 131
Congressional oversight, 6
Consortium for the Study of
    Intelligence, 90
contra atrocities, 106
contra war, 7-8, 68, 75
contras, 3, 7, 9, 68-70, 74, 80, 106
  -and drugs, 3, 68
Convention Against Torture, 2, 8,
    10
Cornell University, 35, 37
  -School of Industrial and Labor
    Relations, 35
corporate interest, 17
Corsican underworld, 4
Corson, William, 24
Costa Rica, 3
counterintelligence, 130
Counterspy, 37
Countryman, Matthew, 55

*CovertAction Information
    Bulletin,* 21, 37, 41
CoverUp, 68
Crawford, Deborah, 61
Crawford, Jerry, 22
crimes against humanity, 13-14
Cuba, 5, 75, 102, 132, 134
Cubans, 74
Culhane, Thomas, 140
Cuomo, Mario, 50
curriculum accountability, 142

D.C. Student Coalition Against
    Apartheid and Racism (DC-
    SCAR), 51
Dauer, Manning, 33
Dayton University, 139
death squads, 9-10, 78
*Defending Civil Resistance Under
    International Law,* 127
Defense Supply Service, 91
democratic centralists, 106
DePaul University, 139
Desert Storm, 14
Detroit University, 139
Deutch, John, 47
Diem regime, 37
Dodd, Senator Christopher, 134
domestic law, 2, 13, 17, 95-96,
    98-99, 101, 105, 109,
    121-123, 126, 128
domestic surveillance, 3, 97, 130,
    132, 134-135
Dominican Republic, 9
drug epidemic, 67
drugs, 3-4, 68, 81
  -and contras, 3, 68
  -dealing, 81
  -international traffic, 4
  -running, 3
Duke University, 139
Dulles, Allen, 80

Duvalier, Jean Claude, 76

Eastern Europe, 73
economic conversion, 142-143
Ecuador, 1, 8
Eisenhower, President, 80
El Salvador, 9-10, 28, 45-46, 51,
    65, 70, 76, 78, 103, 114
  -death squads, 38, 69
  -FDN, 92
  -FMLN, 74, 92, 98, 132
  -*Mano Blanca,* 38
  -military, 38, 102-103
  -ORDEN, 38
  -Treasury Police, 38
Ella Baker-Nelson Mandela
    Center for Anti-Racist
    Education, 55
Ellerson, Mark, 24-25
Elliott, Vernon, 60, 88-89, 93
Ellsberg, Daniel, 126
Ethiopia, 25
Evanston, 64
Executive Office, 67
Executive Order No. 12333,
    134-135
Executive Orders, 89, 132,
    134-135

Fagan, Edward, 24
Fairfield College, 51
Far East, 77
Federal Bureau of Investigation
    (FBI), 3, 19, 31, 59, 101,
    115, 130-132, 134-135
Federal Emergency
    Management Agency
    (FEMA), 132
Feldman, Jonathan, 19, 40,
    141-142
Ferguson, Ann, 61

Filipino Communist Party, New
    People's Army, 90
Firestone Tire and Rubber, 102
First Amendment, 66, 100, 120,
    126
First National Bank of Chicago,
    102
Firth, Noel, 30
Ford administration, 29
Fort Bragg, 9
Fort Lewis College, 139
Foster, Sharon, 37
Fourth Estate, 86
France, 12
Freedom of Information Act
    (FOIA), 41, 88-89, 135
Fund for International Social and
    Economic Education, 35

G.D. Searle Inc., 102
G.I.s, 4
Gates, Robert, 20
gay and lesbian students, 47-48,
    53-56, 58, 94-95
Gay Awareness Week, 48
Gaza Strip, 50
Geneva Convention, 2, 7, 83
genocide, 10, 14
Genocide Convention, 2, 10
George Washington University,
    30, 89, 138-139
Georgetown University, 30, 35,
    47, 53, 138-139
  -American Language Institute, 35
  -Ethics and Public Policy Center,
    90
  -Hospital, 38
  -Labor Studies Program, 90
Germany, 12
Geschickter, Charles, 38
Geschickter Fund for Medical
    Research, 38

Glasnost, 73
Glaspie, April, 16
Glick, Brian, 130, 134-135
Godson, Roy, 90
Golden Triangle, 3
Good Morning America, 85
graduation pledge for social
    responsibility, 144
Green, Justin, 90
Guardian, 115
Guatemala, 8, 10, 65, 78, 80, 83
Guayasamin, Oswaldo, 1-2
guerrilla theater, 69
Guevera, Che, 37
"Guidelines on General Crimes,
    Racketeering Enterprise
    and Domestic
    Security/Terrorism
    Investigations," 134
Gulf Oil company, 14
Gulf War, 17
Guyana, 8

Haiti, 76
Hampton, Fred, 131
Harris, Kevin, 108
Harris Trust and Savings Bank,
    102
Harvard, 31-32, 35, 38-40, 48, 53,
    62-63
  -Center For International Affairs
    (CFIA), 32
HARVEST, 132
Hastings College of the Law, 139
Heimbach, Mark, 23, 59, 63, 96
Helms, Richard, 132
heroin, 4
high school students, 22, 63, 64
Hilger, Gustav, 32
Hill, Kate, 94

Historically Black Colleges and
    Universities (HBCU), 36
Hoffman, Abbie, 43, 126,
Hoft, Janine, 115-116, 119,
    122-125, 128
Hooker, James, 32, 35
Hoover, J. Edgar, 59
House Un-American Activities
    Committee (HUAC), 59
Howard University, 33, 36, 49
Hull, John, 3
Hulnick, Arthur, 30, 97-98
Human Ecology Fund, 38
Humboldt State University,
    Arcata, 99, 139, 143-144
Hunter College, 139
Huntington, Samuel P., 32
Hussein, King, 16
Hussein, Saddam, 15-17
HYDRA, 132

IBM, 70
Illinois, 64
Illinois State University,
    Bloomington, 46, 139
Indonesia, 11, 37, 65, 78, 98
Inland Steel, 102
Inman, Bobby, 102
Institute for Policy Studies (IPS),
    131
Institute for Social Research, 35
International Control
    Commission, 79
International Court of Justice, see
    also World Court, 7, 99, 101
international law, 2, 4-17, 83,
    95-96, 98-99, 101, 125,
    127-128
  -and individual responsibility, 13-
    14
  -as activist tool, 2, 95, 98-99

-as binding on all citizens, 13, 96
-as guide toward peace and stability, 17
-as supreme according to U.S. Constitution, 14, 83, 96
-as trial defense element, 125, 127-128
International Military Tribunal (IMT), see also Nuremberg Tribunal, 13
International Monetary Fund (IMF), 76
International Police Academy, 35
International Socialist Organization, 57
International Student Conference, 133
International Telephone and Telegraph (ITT), 102
Iowa State University, 139
Iran, 8, 14-15, 25
Iran-contra scandal, 68, 132
Iran-Iraq War, 15
Iranian government, 24
Iranian students, 24
Iraq, 14-16
Islam, 32
Israel, 49-50
Italian Communist Party, 4
Ivy League, 19, 39

Jabbari, Ahmad, 24-25
Jackson State University, 114
Jackson, Jesse, 51, 70, 114, 134
Jacksonville University, 30
jail and bail solidarity, 124
Janney, F.W.M., 29
Japan, 143
Japanese, 135
Java, Indonesia, 11
Jesus Christ, 47

Johns Hopkins University, 32, 45, 90, 139
Johnson, Alexis, 102
Johnson, President, 79
Jordan, 16

K-Mart, 106
Karoly, David, 61, 90
Kelly, Christine, 60, 102
Kelly, John, 16
Kennan, George, 73, 76
Kennecott corporation, 102
Kent State, 113-114, 139
Khomeini, Ayatollah, 15, 75, 80
King, Martin Luther, 107, 131
Kline, Michael, 30
Kopkind, Andrew, 32
Korea, 114
Kraft, Inc., 102
Kraft, Michael, 38
KROCK, 71
Ku Klux Klan, 54, 83
Kuomintang, 4
Kurds, 15
Kurtzweg, Laurie, 30, 89
Kuwait, 14-16

Langley, 23
Laos, 4
Latin America, 1, 9, 35, 45-46, 73-74, 78, 98
Latin American Studies, 37
Latino groups, 141
Lawrence, Ken, 30, 32-33, 38
Leazer, Jennifer, 120, 141
Lemarchand, Rene, 33
Lernoux, Penny, 74
Libya, 25
Libyan students, 25
Lockard, Durwood, 31
Lodge, Henry Cabot, 102

Lone Star Steel, 102
Louisiana State University, 139
LSD, 3, 38
Luckett, Toni, 58
Lumumba, Patrice, 54
Lyon, Verne, 59, 71, 81, 88-89,
   123, 135, 138, 140

MacMichael, David, 71, 74
MacNeil-Lehrer Report, 66
Madison, 54, 59, 83, 96, 100-101
Mafia, Sicilian-American, 4
Maher, Sean, 43
Maine, 99
Maish, Kemba, 33-34, 36
Mandela, Nelson, 54
Mann, Dean, 89-90
Mansbach, Richard, 33
Mansfield, Mark, 138, 140
Mapuche Indians, 6
Marchetti, Victor, 79
marijuana, 3
Marks, John, 34
Marquette University, 139
Marten, Robert, 11
martial law, 132
Marx, Karl, 76
Marxist-Leninist, 27
Maryland National Bank, 45
Massachusetts, 127
Massachusetts Institute of
   Technology (MIT), 31, 37,
   47, 90-91
Massachusetts Mental Health
   Center, 38
Matthews, David, 30
Matthews, Tracye, 55-56
Mayan Indians, 10-11
McDonald, Ronald, 70
McGehee, Ralph, 28, 31, 71, 75,
   77, 79, 126, 137

McInnis, James, 30, 69
Menand, Louis, 100
Meo tribe, 4
Merisko, Robert, 30
Miami, 3, 33
Miami Herald, 132
Miami University, Dayton, 139
Michigan State University, 37, 49,
   55, 119
   -African Studies Center, 32
   -Asia Foundation, 31
Middlebury College, 139
Millikan, Max, 31
mind control, 3, 67
Minneapolis, 71, 85, 103, 108-109,
   113, 117, 138, 140-141
Minnesota, 140
"Mobilization for Justice and
      Peace in Central America
      and Southern Africa", 45
Monroe, Haskell, 36
Morgan Guaranty Trust, 102
Mossadegh, Prime Minister
      Mohammed, 14, 80
Movement for the Emancipation
      of Women in Chile
      (MEMCHA), 46
Movimiento Estudiantil Chicano
      de Aztlan (MECHA), 48
Moynihan, Senator Daniel
      Patrick, 102
Mtumba mountains, 78

Nabisco, 70
Nablus, 50
Nation, 53, 114
National Airlines, Iran, 24
National Commission for
      Economic Conversion and
      Disarmament (NCECD), 40

National Committee Against
    Repressive Legislation
    (NCARL), 57, 59
National Iranian Oil Company, 24
National Lawyers Guild, Civil
    Liberties Committee, 128
National Organization for
    Women (NOW), 47
National Security Act of 1947, 2
National Security State, 141
National Strategy Information
    Center, 90
National Welfare Rights
    Organization, 131
Native Americans, 48
Nazi Foreign Office, 32
Nazi Party, 83
Nazis, 9, 12, 84
Nebergall, Phil, 140
necessity defense, 125-129
New England, 38
New Times, 24
*New Voices: Student Political
    Activism in the '80s and
    '90s*, 55
New York, 50, 58, 71
New York Review of Books, 76
New York Times, 7, 20, 38, 98
New York Times Magazine, 28
New York University, 57, 139
Newsweek, 126
Nicaragua, 3, 7-8, 45-46, 69, 75,
    78, 117, 127, 134
    -National Guard, 7
    -Sandinistas, 7, 69, 74-75, 80
Nicodemus, Matt, 143-144
Nitze, Paul H., 74
North Carolina, 9
North, Oliver, 3, 40, 129
North Vietnam, 79
Northeast Student Action
    Network (NSAN), 51, 53

Northern Colorado University,
    139
Northwestern University, 38-39,
    43, 46-48, 53-54, 57, 59-61,
    68, 85-86, 94, 102, 112-114,
    119, 129, 139-140
    -Law School, 94
    -Traffic Institute, 38-39
November 29th Committee for
    Palestine (N29), 49
Nuremberg, 12
Nuremberg Tribunal, see also
    International Military
    Tribunal, 2, 12-13, 17, 83
    -Charter, 13
    -Principles, 2, 12, 17, 83

O'Neal, William, 131
O'Sullivan, Gerry, 90, 96
Oberlin, 48
objectivists, 112
Occupied Territories, 49-50
Office of Strategic Services,
    (OSS), 19, 24, 39
Ohio State University, Columbus,
    139
Ohio University, Athens, 85, 139
Olson, Frank, 38
OPEC, 16
opium, 4
Organization of American States
    (OAS), 2, 6, 83
    OAS charter, 2, 6
Orwell, 66
Orwellianisms, 41

Palestine, 49
Palestinians, 49, 134
Palmer, General Bruce, 5
Pan Am, 102
Panama, 8

Parchman, Travis, 54, 58-59, 88, 116, 118, 119
Peace and Freedom Party, 131
Peltier, Leonard, 131
Pennsylvania, 90
Pennsylvania State University, 53-54, 57-59, 62, 90, 116, 118-119, 139
Pentagon, 40, 45, 90, 141
Pentagon Papers, 126
People's Law Office, 115
Persian Gulf, 14-17
Peru, 8
Philadelphia, 95
Philippines, 31, 90
Physicians for Social Responsibility, 134
Pine Ridge Reservation, 131
Pinochet Ugarte, Augusto, 6
plausible deniability, 27
Pledge of Resistance, 45, 115, 123
Poppen, Cinny, 123
Portugal, 25
Princeton University, 25, 35, 53, 77, 94, 109, 137-139
  -Institute for Advanced Studies, 77
pro se defense, 124-125
Progressive, 38, 137
Progressive Student Network (PSN), 51, 53-54, 92
psychedelic explosion, 3
Puerto Rican activists, 134
Puerto Rican independence organizations, 131

Quirk, John, 80

Rambo, 46
Ramos, Arnoldo, 92
Ramparts, 25, 28, 88, 133

Rawick, George, 32
Reagan, Nancy, 4
Reagan, Ronald, 3, 10, 46, 48, 70, 79, 89, 132, 135, 137
Reagan administration, 15, 48, 89, 134
Reagan-Bush era, 112
Regis College, 139
RENAMO, 69
Rensselaer Polytechnic Institute, 139
Riot Act, 71
Rivkin, Arnold, 31
Roberto, Holden, 5
Roberts, Oral, 70
Robinson, Cedric, 90, 97-98
Rochester Institute of Technology, 30, 89, 138
Rogers, Carl, 38
Rold, Cindy, 94
Roosevelt, Franklin, 7, 80
Roosevelt, Kim, 14
ROTC, 47, 137, 141
Rothschild, Matthew, 137
Rowan, Ford, 132
Russian, 26
Russians, 5, 74
Rutgers University, 33, 47, 50-51, 60, 62, 71, 101-102, 138-139

Sabeh, Sheikh, 16
Safran, Nadav, 32
Saint Louis University, 139
San Francisco Examiner, 11
Sandinistas, 7, 69, 74-75, 80
Santa Barbara, 85
Saudi Arabia, 15, 32
SAVAK, 14-15, 75
Scaife Family Charitable Trusts, 91
Scaife Foundation, 91

Schutzstaffel (S.S.), 1
Schwarzkopf, Jr., Norman, 14
Schwarzkopf, Sr., Norman, 14
Search for the Manchurian Candidate, 34
Secord, Richard, 129
Seitz, Steven Thomas, 35
Sessions, William, 134
Shah of Iran, 14-15, 75, 80
Shan States, 4
Shapiro, Harold, 102
Shatt al Arab, 15
Sheehan, Neil, 5
Smith-Richardson Foundation, 91
Socialist Workers Party, 131
Somoza, Anastasio, 7
Sortwell, Caryl, 92
South Africa, 5-6, 45, 62-63, 65, 67, 78, 102
South African government, 54
South Dakota, 131
South Vietnam, 4, 9, 37
South Vietnamese government, 5, 37
Southeast Asia, 4, 37, 67, 78
Southern Christian Leadership Conference, 134
Soviet Union, 5, 12, 27
St. John's University School of Law, 24
Standard Oil Company, 14
Stanford University, 35, 139, 143
-engineering department, 35
State University of New York, Albany, 138-139
State University of New York, Purchase, 139
Stavis, Morton, 58
Stennis, Senator John C., 40
Steps to Freedom, 45
Stockwell, John, 1, 6, 61, 71, 75, 78-79, 92, 98

Stolz, Richard F., 23
Student Action Union (SAU), 51, 53-54, 60
Student Non-Violent Coordinating Committee, 131
Student to Student International Solidarity, 45
Students for a Democratic Society (SDS), 130-131, 133
Students for America, 112
Suharto, General, 11, 37
Sukarno, President, 11
Sumatra, Indonesia, 11
Supremacy Clause, U.S. Constitution, 12-13
Supreme Court, 14
Syria, 17

Take Back the Night, 46, 48
Texaco Oil Company, 14, 102
Texas, 9
Texas A & M University, 37
Texas Rainbow Coalition, 58
Third World, 34, 62, 76, 78, 84, 133
Thornburgh, Richard, 134
torture, 8-9, 15
Tufts University, 90, 102
-Fletcher School of Law and Diplomacy, 90
-Murrow Center for Public Diplomacy, 90
Turner, Michael, 64, 71, 103, 138, 140
Turner, Stansfield, 29, 39-40, 102

Union College, 139
Union of Clerical and Technical Workers, 62
United Auto Workers, 134

United Coalition Against Racism
(UCAR), 51
United Nations (UN), 2, 4, 8, 12,
78, 83
-Charter, 2, 4, 83
-General Assembly, 8, 12
-International Law Commission,
13
United States
-advisors, 9
-Agency for International Devel-
opment (AID), 4, 9
-Army Intelligence, 5
-as guilty of Geneva Convention
violations, 7
-as signatory to international
laws, 2, 7, 12, 78, 83, 96
-Attorney General, 134-135
-Bill of Rights, 81
-Bureau of Narcotics and Danger-
ous Drugs, 3-4
-companies, 14-15, 74-75, 143
-Congress, 16, 36, 77-78, 81, 128
-Constitution, 13, 17, 81-83, 98,
132
-Defense Department, 19, 20, 25,
31-32, 41, 103
-Embassy, Indonesia, 11
-Immigration and Naturalization
Service (INS), 25
-intelligence agencies, 79
-Inter-American Police Academy,
9
-militarism, 141, 144
-military, 9, 132, 137-138, 142-144
-military intelligence, 79
-National Security Agency
(NSA), 19, 31, 79, 132
-National Security Council, 75, 77
-National Student Association
(NSA), 133-134
-Senate, 14
-sponsored trade embargoes, 8

-State Department, 4, 11, 16, 20,
31, 66, 73, 76, 90, 101
-Anti-Terrorism Assistance
Program, 38, 39
-Office of Intelligence, 31
-Office of Public Diplomacy,
45
-warfare state, 141, 142
United States Student
Association, (SA), 50, 108
United States v. Belmont, 14
United States v. Pink, 14
Universal Code of Human Rights, 83
Universal Declaration of Human
Rights, 2, 8
*Universities in the Business of
Repression,* 19, 141
university militarism, 142
University of Arkansas, 47
University of California (UC), 45
-at Berkeley, 35, 41, 50, 139-140,
143-144
-Academic Senate, 49
-Center for South and Southeast
Asian Studies, 37
-United Front Coalition, 49,
62
-at Los Angeles, 139
-Higher Education Research
Institute, 63
-at San Diego, 139
-at Santa Barbara, 30, 48, 61, 89,
97-99, 138-139
-at Southern California, 139
-Student Cooperative Union, 96
University of Chicago, 58
University of Colorado (UC),
-at Boulder, 64, 92, 104-106, 109,
114, 138-139
-at Denver, 46, 139
University of Connecticut, 139
-at Storrs, 26
University of Denver, 35

University of Florida, 33, 38
University of Illinois (UI), 101
  -at Bloomington, 139
  -at Champaign-Urbana, 35, 62, 139
  -at Chicago, 61, 70, 90, 92, 102, 111, 114, 139
University of Iowa, 68, 138
  -at Ames, 33
  -at Iowa City, 139
University of Louisville, 139
University of Maine, 92, 99, 139
University of Maryland, 34
University of Massachusetts administration, 114
University of Massachusetts, Amherst, 95, 138-139
University of Miami, 30
University of Michigan, 37, 49-50, 60
  -at Ann Arbor, 114, 139
  -Student Assembly, 50
University of Minnesota, Minneapolis, 63, 65, 68, 99, 108, 114, 120, 138-139
University of Missouri, Columbia, 36
University of New Hampshire, Durham, 139
University of New Mexico, 48, 138-139
University of North Carolina, 60, 139
  -at Chapel Hill, 138
University of Oregon, Eugene, 139-140
University of Pennsylvania, 95, 138-139
  -Foreign Policy Research Institute, 90
University of Puget Sound, 139

University of Rhode Island, 23, 139
University of Rochester, 139
University of Texas, Austin, 30, 58, 69, 114, 138-139
University of Texas, El Paso, 37
University of Vermont, 139
University of Wisconsin, Madison, 21, 23, 38, 46, 48, 50, 59-60, 95, 139
Uruguay, 8, 9

Vang Pao, 4
Vellela, Tony, 55
Vengroff, Richard, 26
Viet Cong, 5, 79
Vietnam, 67, 75, 78, 80, 98, 133
Vietnam veterans, 71
Vietnam War, 3-5, 32, 44, 137
Vietnamese, 5
Vietnamese conflict, 79
Viets, Hermann, 23
Vijayan, Suju, 94
Villanova University, 90
Virginia, 140

Walker, Jimmy, 105-108
Walz, "Skip," 21
War At Home, 130
war crimes, 12
war criminals, 7
War on Drugs, 4
War Resisters League, 115
Washington, D.C., 8, 28, 45-47, 51, 76
Washington University, St. Louis, 24
Wayne, John, 70
Wayne State University, 49, 139
Webster, William H., 15-16, 23, 74
Weinglass, Leonard, 126, 128-129

Wesleyan, 46
West Bank, 50
Western Maryland University,
    139
White House, 16
Wilkinson, Frank, 59
Wisconsin, 95
Wise, David, 20, 28
Witanek, Bob, 87-88
Wolf, Louis, 37
women's movement and
    feminism, 46-48, 54-56
Wooster College, 139
World Court, see also
    International Court of
    Justice, 78, 84, 139
World War II, 4, 12, 19, 27

Yale University, 21, 29, 35, 78, 139
Young Americans for Freedom
    (YAF), 112, 135

Zahedi, General Fazzolah, 14
Zemke, Jill, 108, 117, 126, 141
Zenith Radio corporation, 102
Zinn, Howard, 63, 126
Zionist groups, 50

About the Author

Ami Chen Mills is a recent graduate of Northwestern University where she majored in journalism and creative writing. She has served as a summer research associate on the U.S./Cuba Dialogue Project at the Institute for Policy Studies and participated in IPS delegations to Chile and Cuba. She is currently a student representative for the National Committee Against Repressive Legislation and a freelance writer based in California. Ami is available as a consultant for developing CIA Off Campus campaigns and as a speaker for workshops, panels and/or lectures on the CIA and the university.

Contact:
> Jean Caiani
> Speak Out!
> 2215-R Market Street
> San Francisco, CA 94114
> (415) 864-4561

Has this book helped?

We welcome your comments and suggestions regarding the information presented in this book. If you have found the contents have helped in developing a CIA Off Campus campaign, or if you have criticisms about suggestions offered here, please contact us. And, of course, we want to hear about your successes as well!

Write to:
> CIA Off Campus National Clearinghouse
> c/o the Bill of Rights Foundation
> 523 South Plymouth Court, Suite 800
> Chicago, IL 60605
> (312) 939-0675

About South End Press

South End Press is a nonprofit, collectively-run book publisher with over 150 titles in print. Since our founding in 1977, we have tried to meet the needs of readers who are exploring, or are already committed to, the politics of radical social change.

Our goal is to publish books that encourage critical thinking and constructive action on the key political, cultural, social, economic and ecological issues shaping life in the United States and in the world. In this way, we hope to give expression to a wide diversity of democratic social movements and to provide an alternative to the products of corporate publishing.

If you would like a free catalog of South End Press books or information about our membership program—which offers two free books and a 40% discount on all titles—please write us at South End Press, 116 Saint Botolph Street, Boston, MA 02115.

Other titles of interest from South End Press:

New Voices: Student Political Activism in the '80s and '90s
Tony Vellela

Universities in the Business of Repression: The Academic-Military-Industrial Complex and Central America
Jonathan Feldman

How Harvard Rules: Reason in Service of Empire
John Trumpbour

Praetorian Guard: The U.S. Role in the New World Order
John Stockwell

Break-ins, Death Threats and the FBI: The Covert War Against the Central America Movement
Ross Gelbspan

COINTELPRO Papers: Documents from the FBI's Secret Wars Against Dissent in the United States
Ward Churchill and Jim Vander Wall

Freedom Under Fire: U.S. Civil Liberties in Times of War
Michael Linfield